VILLAGE
The New Tourist Destination of Nepal

Nepal's Village Tourism

VILLAGE
The New Tourist Destination of Nepal

Nepal's Village Tourism

SURENDRA BHAKTA PRADHANANG

ADROIT

Published by
ADROIT PUBLISHERS
4675/21, Ganpati Bhawan, Ansari Road,
Daryaganj, New Delhi-110 002
Phones : 011-23266030

Distributors
AKHIL BOOK DISTRIBUTORS
e-mail: akhilbooks@yahoo.com
akhilbooks@hotmail.com

ISBN - 10 81-87392-87-8
ISBN - 13 978-81-87392-87-3

Printed in India on behalf of M/s Adroit Publishers
by Arpit Printographers • E-mail: arpitprinto@yahoo.com

VILLAGE TOURISM CONCEPT

IS

DEDICATED

TO

MY NATION

AND

THE WELFARE OF THE PEOPLE

IN NEPAL

AND

ABROAD

Contents

ACKNOWLEDGEMENTS

Writing textbook on Village: The New Tourist Destination of Nepal is not easy when the concept has newly developed and when it is hard to collect relevant information. Village: The New Tourist Destination of Nepal is a style in tourism, it has its own originality and speciality. It explores villages and villages' peculiarities creating curiousity for tourists. It is interesting to see sector such as adventure, nature and culture luring tourists in Nepal. Village tourism could be a great satisfying factor in tourism. Today the international tourism market is based on products which are linked with those sectors.

Gone are the days when some affluent groups of tourism entrepreneurs kept tourism-bridle in their hands taking tourism as a race-horse in the Nepalese tourism market. Nepal's tourism industry is traditionally limited to certain areas like Kathmandu, Chitwan, Pokhara, Sagarmatha and Annapurna regions. Basically, tourism in Nepal is concentrated on Kathmandu by 90 per cent. These tourism entrepreneurs who are being involved in tourism sector are not positive in developing village tourism in Nepal. In such circumstances, village tourism has to cope with much harship for its development. In fact, the concept of village tourism propounded is the blessing and virtue of God.

Apart from this, village tourism creates tourism democracy in the industry for people's participation at grassroot village level. A simple villager can start tourism industry from village level and generate income and employment opportunities. This book intends to help the process of economic revolution through village tourism in Nepal and abroad. Every Nepali can build up his capability for developing village tourism by reading the book.

The author has designed the village tourism course of study and written a textbook for the Graduate student of Hotel Management and Tourism for Silver Mountain School of Hotel Management affiliated to Preston University of USA. Besides, it is equally relevant to the Graduate student of Tribhuvan University, Purbanchal University , Department of Tourism and Hospitality Management of George Washington University and Sustainable Travel International of USA.

In particular, I would like to thank Mr Ram Krishna Regmee for his valuable feedback to write the book. I am also indebted to my family and family associated members who provided me the precious time and golden opportunity for writing. Thanks are due to Dr. Rohit Saiju, Mrs. Reetu Shrestha, Mrs Bemy Pradhan, Mr Bibhas Amatya, Mr Abhas Saiju, Aika Saiju and Mrs. Tara Kayasth for their valuable support and assistance to prepare my manuscript. I would express my sincere thank to Mr Suraj Rana and Mr Shiv G.C. for their valuable assistance for computer typing. I would also like to express my sincere appreciation to Mr. Rajendra Bantawa, former president of TAAN, who continuously encouraged me to put forward the concept of village tourism in Nepal and abroad. I would also thank Mr Brain T. Mullis, the president of Sustainable Travel International of USA for his support and promotion of Nepal's village tourism in USA and abroad.

A special thank goes to Kathmandu Research Centre (KRC) that provided the valuable information, data and suggestions to produce the book.

Dr. Surendra Bhakta Pradhanang

FOREWORD

Village tourism concept propounded by Dr Surendra Bhakta Pradhanang of Nepal is dedicated to the welfare of people and country, which is an appropriate strategy for the developing countries like Nepal. Indeed, it is fascinating people and tourists day by day. On the ground of people's economic benefit and tourism demand, the concept is being developed.

Dr Pradhanang's theory of village tourism sketches the road map for village development to make village and village people more economically active, so that village people easily get 'job with bread and butter'.

Kathmandu Research Centre (KRC) has gladly explored Dr Pradhanang's concept in favour of national development as best guidelines for national planning and strategy. Very soon, Nepal can be a rich country, if village tourism is properly implicated in the national development agenda. KRC feels the urge to explore villages of Nepal is today's challenge to the spokeman of national development and social justice. The textbook, Village: The New Tourist Destination of Nepal penned by Dr Pradhanang is praise worthy and outstanding contribution to Nepal and Nepalese. His contribution to the nation and people ought to be evaluated as noble deed.

The book states how village tourism is a determinant factor for the prosperity of a nation. Since village tourism is a highly people's concern, various disciplines are involved in its setting.

Dr Pradhanang who is the propounder of village tourism in Nepal was awarded with the 'title of father of village tourism and discoverer of scientific tourism in Nepal' in 1999 and 2001. He has been dedicated to village tourism since 28 years. Normally, he is a Man of village literary talent. The recognition which he got at home is amply reflected to the world. His outlook for village and villager is always positive. Due to his high advocacy and strong determination to villages, people from villages came to see him how he is. KRC appreciates his devotion and noble work in support of village Nepal's peace, prosperity and progress. Finally, it is hoped that his book written for graduate students will be highly successful and beneficial to the people and country as a whole.

Kathmandu Research Centre
Kathmandu, Nepal
krcentre@hotmail.com

ACRONYMS

ACAP	Annapurna Conservation Area Project
DFID	Department for International Development
DNPWC	Department of National Parks and Wildlife Conservation
GDP	Gross Domestic Product
HMG	His Majesty's Government (Nepal government after 2063 B.S. change/Federal Democratic Republic of Nepal in 2065 B.S.)
STI	**Sustainable Travel International**
JITCO	Japanese International Technical Cooperation Organisation
KRC	Kathmandu Research Centre
LNP	Langtang National Park
MBNP	Makalu Barun National Park
MOTCA	Ministry of Tourism and Civil Aviation
NMA	Nepal Mountaineering Association
NPC	National Planning Commission
NTO	National Tourism Organisation
NTS	Nepal Tourism Statistics
NP	National Park
NTB	Nepal Tourism Board
NY	**New York**
NRS	Nepalese Rupees
RNAC	Royal Nepal Airline Corporation (Nepal Airlines after 2063 B.S. change)
RCNP	Royal Chitwan National Park

RNP	Rara National Park
SNP	Sagarmatha National Park
SPNP	Shey Phoksundo National Park
SNV	Netherlands Development Organization
SAARC	South Asia Association For Regional Cooperation
SASEC	South Asia Regional Economic Cooperation
STN	**Sustainable Tourism Network**
UNESCO	United Nations Educational, Scientific and Cultural Organization
UNDP	United Nations Development Programme
VDC	Village Development Committee
VALS	Values, Attitudes and Lifestyles
VT	Village Tourism
VTDC	Village Tourism Development Committee
WTO	World Tourism Organization
WCED	World Commission on Environment and Development

Part I : The Context of Village the New Tourist Destination of Nepal

Chapter 1

Tourism in Nepal

Introduction

We know, to our great satisfaction, that Nepal, has over the years come into the limelight of the world as an important tourist spot. Above all, the conquest of Mt. Everest by Tenzing and Hillary in 1953 stands as a remarkable landmark that testifies to the indomitable spirit of man. In fact, international tourists look upon the country with interest and glory to know Nepal has always been a non-colonial country having a long history of bravery and patriotism. Of course, we talk a great deal about the best service and satisfaction we can offer to our customers. And in this aspect it is the novelty of tourism that fits the bill optimally. The peculiar and still primitive life styles of the indigenous communities living in the outlandish pockets of villages in Nepal are invariably subjects of attention for every curious eye. The picturesque landscape of the countryside adorned by brilliantly blooming rhododendrons amidst brooks and bushes and brambles with colourful pheasants dotted here and there is a sight for Gods to see. Tourism in Nepal is largely looked upon as income elastic. Its importance is valued as the economic backbone to the Nepalese economy. Nepal is highly wedded to tourism industry, which has been today's concern in the process of the country's industrialisation policy. The economic activity which is importantly related with tourism is extended to the volume of business to a larger extent. Nepal is popularly known Shangrila and a home to eight of the world's ten highest peaks in the world and it is known for its pollution-free villages and warm hospitality extended by the local villages. Flooded rivers rushing out from the Himalayas provide world class rafting adventure. The biotic diversity of Nepal in terms of fauna and flora is also beautifully manifested through the peculiar ways of living among the diverse people whose rich heritage and culture along with their numerous festivals, rituals, folk dances and folk songs. The basic thing in Nepal is unique life of people peacefully living in their own way of satisfaction and socio-economic pattern, which is a fit subject for satisfaction and socio-economic pattern, which is a fit subject for exploration and tourism development in Nepal. Nepal is a dreamland for potential trekkers and mountaineers, which is often regarded as a haven for adventure and adrenalin and for paying visits to living ethnographic museum.

Sandwiched between India and Tibet (Autonomous Region of Tibet, P.R. China), Nepal has fantastic attraction to tourists. Mainly, as Nepal is the sanctuary for mountain climbers who get gravited towards Mt. Everest, it lends enchantment to many visitors who go back with an unforgettable experience. Nepal is a small hilly country cosmopolitan in nature with a variety of ethnic groups of people. In addition, the diversity of flora and fauna of Nepal conjures up various imaginations. Nepal is rich in natural vegetation ranging from tropical to alpine and

Map of Nepal

it has more than eight hundred bird species, some endangered animals and so on. Travel and tourism schedules are safely arranged by people from luxury and high standard hotels to trekking, ranging from roadside trekking in village walk. Nepal's best treasures are its natural village scenery, biodiversity of nature and diversified culture.

Mountain is the source of inspiration and fascination to man. Spiritually, the mountain is looked upon to heaven and the traditional belief that Kailash, the home of God Shiva gives the self-explanatory note of values of the mountain/ Himalaya.There are hundreds of ancestral beliefs and mythological stories seeking spiritual solace in the Himalayas. We know the story of Pandavas. After the victory of Pandavas in the battle of Mahabharata, Yudhishthir accompanied by his brave brothers and their consort, Draupadi, exiled himself to the Himalayas.

One can enjoy natural beauty of Himalayas and cultural riches through gentle walk. Every one looking busy in the fields is a farmer and the herders grazing animals on the steep hills of Nepal are young villagers. Yak drivers transporting goods over the high mountain are the Himalayan people. Visitors can see the Nepali style tea house in the trekking routes of Himalayan kingdom of Nepal. Besides camping, one can see well organised trek-eating and staying lodges/tea houses as one treks along dotted at different points and village destinations. Trekking tourism is most popular in Nepal where the best seasons are chosen as February-May (spring seasons) and September-November (autumn seasons). Nepal is a paradise for visitors as well as trekkers. Adventure based tourism is a magnet to tourists coming to Nepal. Tourists are welcomed by the people in Nepal to enjoy and experience the joys of the Himalayan kingdom in their holiday trips.

Historical Background of Travel and Tourism

The mobility of people is as old as human history and civilisation. For several centuries such mobility was confined to the privileged and adventure-loving people. Prior to the

Industrial Revolution (1730-1850) the people who were engaged in agriculture, worked and played on land as mask of their greatfulness to Nature for the harvest. There was no clear vision for work and leisure in those days of business life of people. By nature, work started early in the morning and confined till late in the evening. There was no respite from work in practice. Later on, work and leisure became more regulated and systematised with the working day beginning and ending at scheduled times. Similarly, non-work days were clearly mentioned. Initially, the working people used to enjoy excursions in the countryside to the places of pilgrimage, etc. by and large, due to increase in holiday entitlements and disposal incomes, people started visiting destinations for one or two week vacations.

The post industrial society of various countries brought a significant change in the concept of holiday and relaxation. As holiday entitlements continued, people became more conscious to take annual holiday or vacation and went for spending vacation in a long distance outside the country.

For several centuries, travelling was very difficult, uncomfortable, slow, time consuming and risky. Generally, in early days travellers made journeys on foot and went on horseback or by boat in some circumstances.

The early accounts of travelling relate to the ancient civilisations of Greece and Rome. Historically, Greece witnessed travel to the Olympic Games and festivals. In the fourth century B.C., an ardent advocate of tourism was recorded, it was xerophan, who refered to the benefit of travellers to Athens by recommending the construction of visitor accommodation at public expenditure.

Since travel has a long history in connection with trade, commerce and pilgrimage, travellers need overnight accommodation at the destinations where they would stay overnight during their journeys. The discovery of money by the Sumerians (Babglonia) and the development of trade and commerce in 4000 B.C. opened the special and modern travel era. Trade and commerce, a strong force for travelling at third century A.D., the first exploration was started by Alexander the Great or only about 700 years ago Morco Polo started exploration in several lands. The land migrations were taking place on foot, on horseback or by elephant, camel and boats in Europe, Asia and Africa. Chronologically the mobile activity of the people picked up under these considerations:

(*i*) Travel period or travel without tourism period
(*ii*) Travel with tourism period or travel and tourism period and
(*iii*) Travel and tourism with village tourism period or travel and sustainable tourism period.

Tourism is relatively a young industry which is growing fast in the world. The history of tourism is not more than 167 years old. Tourism expansion is a result of development that has come about in the form of various means of transportation generally the motor car and aeroplane. The value of tourism is very high for the world's political economy. Tourism, on the ground of global holiday making, is relatively concerned with world peace and prosperity.

In the other words, the world growth of tourism can be categorised into three stages:

1. Primary Stage (1841-1892)
2. Developing Stage (1893-1945)
3. Advanced Stage (1946-2005) or over.

1. Primary Stage

The concept of tourism as developed in 1841 is the effort of Thomas Cook who is the pioneer as well as programme framer of tourism of that period. At first, he managed a tour programme and sold a tourism business package to 570 passengers. Booking and selling system of the railway seats was started as service that is a product. He organised circular tour of Scotland carrying 5,000 tourists from 1841-1863. Thomas Cook, being most successful in his tourism business, started chartered trains and several excursion trips on a commercial basis. In 1955, Thomas Cook extended his field of tourism business in other countries of the world. He also published guide books, travel periodicals and so on. Similarly, he developed hotel coupon in

1887 and banking and foreign currency exchange business in 1889.

The American Express developed by Henry Wells in 1841 as a Carrier agency was merged into tourism business. Later on, the American Express issued its own moneyorder and Traveller's cheque for tourist's convenience in 1891. In 1870, an American entrepreneur, G.M. Pullman developed first class railway travel. In 1869, the opening of the Suez Canal brought about a revolutionary change in shortening the distance for transportation between the West and the East.

2. Developing Stage

The development of tourism followed the values of culture, economic and political power of the world. The conscious tourists respected learning and social refinements of the ancient world. People were attracted more in travel and tourism activity and their keen interest resulted in the increase in demand for tourism. That is why the eighteenth century considered as 'the golden age of travel and tourism' had boosted up tourism industry especially during the 30 years period (1763-1793). Several world class poets, authors and intellectuals visited foreign lands as tourists to broaden their knowledge and knowhow about ancient arts and crafts. The grand success of tourism led to develop further tourism to the nineteenth and twentieth centuries.

The provision of annual holiday in Europe was value-based landmark which initiated the people to travel more and widely. The provision was importantly established in terms of paid holiday programme of each individual in the world. The paid holiday has been today's free days from the routine of daily work-a time for leisure, recreation and amusement. Actually, the concept of annual paid holiday is the result of the Industrial Revolution in the world. The Revolution was the cause for the changes in economy and society. Tourism development turned into the mass tourism with the growth of 'holiday with pay'. Regarding paid holiday concept, some of eleven million people benefited by the Holidays With Pay Act of 1938 in UK. This paid holiday led to great mobility of the people from place to place and establishment of new industries wonderfully broadened mass tourism in the world. The concept of paid holidays extensively boosted tourism industry. Gradually, paid holiday has been worldwide. A minimum duration of one to three weeks is recognised by law and employment clause. 'The right to pay holiday' has been today's concern in support of universal travel recognition. The employees believe that the paid holiday provision affects nothing in the industrial output.

3. Advanced Stage

The concept of modern tourism flourished in the second half of the ninteenth century due to the development of the industrialised society in Western Europe and North America. By the twentieth century tourism was characterised by modern tourism changes in attitudes of people, viz.; pleasure seeking, travel for education, increase in disposal income, advancement in transport and social prestige have brought a significant development in travel and tourism. Once acquired the habit of tourist travel is not lightly given up. This has been made as a ground for tourism development in the world.

The massive development of road and air transport brought a wonderful change in modern tourism. The motor car brought a revolutionary change in holiday trends in pursuit of leasure and tourism. The development of jet travel in 1958 was the greatest achievement in tourism which brought a new dimension with the wonderful mode of airtransport. Charter flights at cheaper rate is the comfort and time saving to modern tourists. In airtransport development, the Boeing 747, the Mc-Donnell Douglas Dc10, the Air Bus A 300 and the Lockhed Tristar L-1011, and above all, Concorde and Tupolev 144 are wonderful landmarks in the Civil aviation history of the world. Airlines boosted up the international tourism at the fastest rate.

Historical Background of Travel and Tourism in The Context of Nepal

The earliest travel history of Nepal depicts the earliest inhabitants who were Tibeto-Burman ethnicity inhabited in small settlements and small kingdoms and tribal confederations of the Terai region in the Southern Nepal. Among several groups, the Sakya clan was renowned one, which is concerned with Gautam Siddhartha. He was Shakyamuni enlightened as Buddha who was born in Lumbini in 563 B.C. For the spread of Buddhism and knowledge about the truth of life, Buddha traveled to India, Burma, Tibet and so on. Lord Buddha who is believed to be an incarnation of God Vishnu, according to Vedic sources, traveled from place to place for the welfare of human beings. He explained about the rights and duties of mankind along with the mystery of life. Historically, Kathmandu valley's first rulers were known as Gopals or Abhras followed by the Kiratas who reigned until around 400 A.D.[1] The Lichhavis ruled from the late fifth century to approximately 750 A.D. During that period Emperor Ashoka visited Nepal and traveled to Lumbini and Kathmandu Valley for pilgrimage tour and also built some stupas and monuments for the promotion of Buddhism. The Lichhavis are believed to have migrated and traveled from north India to Nepal in 250 A.D. Manadev was the first king in the Lichhavi dynasty. After that Anshuvarma

Ranipokhari of Kathmandu

who opened travel and trade routes to Tibet is important for travel episode in Nepal. His daughter Bhrikuti, who was married to the Tibetan ruler Tsrong-tsong Gompa, is the cause of development of travel and trade in Nepal along with the balance of politics and diplomacy. The famous Chinese traveler Huen Tsang toured India and Nepal in the seventh century. From the travel standpoint Tsang's visit is considered as a good beginning to explore Nepal in the foreign land.

Narendradeva is also believed to have promoted travel and trade between Nepal and India and Nepal and China through matrimonial relationship with Indian royal families.

Malla Period

After the downfall of Lichhavis started the Malla period during which the travel foundation was sketched in Kathmandu by developing new travel and trade policy with Tibet and China. Ari Malla was the first ruler in the Twelfth century. The

Watching Pigeon in front of Kathmandu Durbar Square

Unique Durbar Square

historians say it is the period of Medieval Nepal (750 A.D.–1750 A.D.)[2] Due to the growth and development of travel and trade in the Malla period, a great empire for over the next two centuries was formed. Jayasthiti Malla ruled over Kathmandu valley at the end of fourteenth century and started 'sanskritiation' which has had a significant weightage in the valuation of unique culture, tradition and rite and custom for travel agenda. Yaksha Malla who ruled from 1428 to 1482 divided the Malla kingdom among his descendents into three fractional kingdoms Bhadgaon, Kathmandu and Patan. After the separation of what was known as the United Kingdom, the three separate kings of Kathmandu valley developed culture, art and architecture, temple, palace complex, custom, rite etc at the high degree in the fullest extent on the competitive basis .Those culture and art and architecture have been today's genuine assets for travel and tourism in Nepal.

Meanwhile, many tiny states of Nepal went to British India in support of its political power and cooperation to them. Thus the Englishmen took interest in Nepal and started traveling with a view of regional politics. Jaya Prakash Malla was also conscious of the rising power politics of Prithivi Narayan Shah on the one hand and on the other that of British India. That is

Mall Period Durbur Square

why he sent his messenger to visit British India to defeat Gurkha. In 1741 A.D. Prithivi Narayan Shah visited Bhaktapur and Banaras in 1743/44 and traveled those areas with curious eyes.

Shah Period

Prithivi Narayan Shah is the great warrior and traveler of Nepal. His travel in Bhaktapur was the outcome of his victory over Kathmandu valley. Prithivi Narayan (1769-1775) with whom we enter into the modern period of Nepal's history, was the first Shah ruler in the Kathmandu valley. During his period travel and trade was largely expanded in a regular basis within and outside the country Tibet, China and India. In 1763 A.D. an Englishman, Mirkashim visited Nepal and fought with Prithivi Narayan Shah. During the war period of 1788-1789, Nepal fought with Tibet and China. In the meantime, another Englishman traveled in Nepal. Col. Kirkpatric was the first foreigner who visited Nepal for pleasure and sight seeing from the western world in 1792. After 1801 A.D. some foreign experts on different subjects came to Nepal. Mr Everest, the British Surveyor, measured the height of the highest mountain of the world in 1843 A.D.

Patan Durbar Square

Rana Period

Among royal competitors, fighting continued until 1846 A.D. when Jang Bahadur Kunwar, a military commander established a dynasty of prime ministers that would rule until 1951. The Rana dynasty essentially became a parallel monarchy in which preeminent authority was the prime minister, a hereditary position with unclear rules of succession.

During his regime Jang Bahadur Rana visited Great Britain across Suez Canal and enroute countries Egypt, Cairo, Malta and so on.[3] His travel to visit Queen in England was the high level travel of Nepalese national. In 1847 A.D. a team of Nepalese Diplomatic Mission went to China with gift from the Government of Nepal to Emperor of China. Basically, around this time, the Government of Great Britain started to admit Nepalese in the military force. Since then, the common Nepalese also began to go to the western world.

The gradual relationship between Rana and British put forward travel agenda. The high British authorities were invited by the Rana for hunting in Nepal as a pleasure visit.

Later Bir Shamsher granted permission for entrance to the European people as a liberal and softened foreign policy in

Attraction of Durbar Square in Lalitpur

travel and trade sector. The trade facility provided to Great Britain in Nepal could be taken as the opening of the road to British. In 1893 A.D. the Prime Minister Bir Shamsher went to India on a royal visit. Chandra Shamsher also visited India in 1903 A.D. and Great Britain in 1908 A.D. respectively. The royal visit of Nepal in different countries had culturally begun as tradition. By and large, Nepal was recognised as a Himalayan Kingdom in the world. In 1921 A.D. British Reconnaissance team came to Nepal for mountaineering expedition in the Mount Everest region of Nepal where village and mountain wonderfully attracted visitors. Until 1944 A.D. there were regular visits of high ranked government authority between Nepal and Great Britain from time to time.[4]

Travel and Tourism from 1950-2006

After the end of Rana regime and the restoration of democracy, Nepal opened its entry gate of Annapurna and the Everest to international tourists for travel and tourism development in 1950 and 1953 respectively. Regarding tourism development infrastructure in 1950 A.D. Nepal built the airport on the ground of Gaucharan of Kathmandu. At first , Dakota Airplane landed on the grass land. Nepal was then popularised as a pleasing tourist destination in the world. In 1952, Nara Shamsher opened a hotel named Nepal Hotel in Jawalakhel to captivate tourists. To support it, Mandis was invited for hotel management. Later on, he also opened the hotel named Snow View Hotel at Lazimpat. Mr Boorish Lissanerich founded the tourist standard hotel, Royal Hotel at Bahadur Bhavan in Kantipur, Kathmandu. He organised banquet for 160 Royal invitees for coronation of His Majesty's Mahendra Bir Bikram Shah Dev. In 1953, Edmund Hillary and Tenzing Sherpa reached the top of the world, Mt. Everest. Since then, Nepal and Nepalese became famous in the world. Meanwhile, Thomas Cook & Sons organised a special tour for 60 tourists in the Kathmandu valley in 1955. Due to opening of the Tribhuvan Raj Path in 1956, travel and tourism grew in a new motion of speed of development. As per the Tourism Development Act 2014, Tourism Board was formed under the Ministry of Industry and Commerce in 1957. In 1959 Nepal participated in the meeting of International Union of Official Travel Organisation held in Manila. In the mean time, UNO discussed about the tourism industry and its benefits to the national economy.[5] Two tourism advisors George Lebree from France and Dr A. Ith from Switzerland came to Nepal in 1959 for consultation of tourism development in Nepal. In 1962, the Board was turned into full-fledged Tourism Department under the Ministry of Public Works, Transport and Communication. Similarly, Tourism Information Centers were formed in the Tribhuvan Airport, Pokhara Airport, Basantapur, Daman and so on. Taragaon Development Committee was established in order to enhance tourism related activities in both private and public sectors.

In 1972, Nepal's Tourism Master Plan was developed under the chairmanship of Royal Highness Himalaya Bir Bikram Shah. The plan addressed various aspects like the economics of tourism, regional planning, and action plan. Under the establishment of Nepal Tourism Development Committee, the development plan was set up and Hotel Management and Tourism Development Centre (HMTC) was also established. Presently, it is known as Nepal Academy of Tourism and Hotel

Management (NATHM). In 1978, tourism of Nepal was completely managed and authorised by the Ministry of Tourism. The first travel agency in Nepal was Shah and Rai. On behalf of government, once Tourism Department started tourism activities by establishing the Rhino Tour. In 1979, Tourist Police was established under the Ministry of Culture, Tourism and Civil Aviation. The main function and responsibility of Tourist Police is to look after the welfare of tourist and to assure them a pleasant and a memorable stay in Nepal. The function of tourist police is to advise and assist tourist in safety and security during traveling, trekking, rafting and hotel stay in any part of Nepal.

The Eighth Plan (1992-1997) set five major tourism strategies. Out of these three major points were most important from the standpoint of productivity in tourism sector. These are given below:

- To expand the tourism industry and tourism activities which would help to ease poverty and raise the living standard of the people.
- To promote environmental, historical and cultural heritage and raise the quality of services and facilities related to tourism.
- To make efforts for the creation of stable development within the tourism industry and link it to other economic sectors in a coordinated manner.

The prime objectives of the Ninth Plan (1997-2002) show that tourism has been taken as the basic lead factor of the country. A more liberal tourism policy would be taken to encourage domestic and foreign investors. Emphasis was given to attract a lot of tourists and to encourage them to spend more in the country by increasing their average length of stay. Tourism Policy 1995 seeks to encourage more foreign exchange earnings, develop regional balance and emphasise the promotion of village tourism. Furthermore, tourist activities would be extended in the villages on the basis of potential of tourism. In Ninth Plan 14 tourism model villages would be set up from each geographical region, i.e. Terai, Hill and Mountain. The

Tenth Plan (2002-2007) also continued to alleviate poverty through tourism and it emerged as a valuable part of the national economy. It stressed to develop tourism villages in Nepal.

Tourism contributes to the development of industry, trade, employment and other sectors of the national economy. It patronises, in fact, the macro level productivity in tourism sector. From 1985 onwards, tourist arrivals in Nepal from various parts of the world grew steadily except in 1989. In 1997 tourist arrivals went up to 4,21,857 and they spent an average of 10.49 days in Nepal. Analyzing 16 years (1982-1997) tourist arrival data, one finds the rate of increase is 6.8 per cent on an average. Simultaneously, the tourist expenditure pattern in 1982 was Rs 439.65 million and Rs 6698.70 million in 1997 (excluding Indian tourist expenditure).[6]

The tourist arrivals by purpose of visit in 1997 exhibit that tourists who visited for pleasure were the highest in number that is 2,49,360. Almost 59 per cent of tourists fell in this category. The second major reason for visiting was trekking and the third, official business. According to the sources, the number of tourists from Japan was the highest followed by USA and UK. Tourist from Asia was 52.8 per cent. Arrivals from Spain, France, Netherlands, North America, Eastern Europe, Central and South America, Australia and the Pacific region also increased phenomenally. Tourists from India alone increased by 32.3 per cent. Air service plays a vital role in tourism. In 1995, 89.4 per cent of the tourists arrived by air. Of the 4,21,857 arrivals, 1,22,401 were brought in by Indian Airlines 39,691 by the Thai Airways and 1,47,723 by the Royal Nepal Airlines. The rest used various other air services while 50,712 arrived by land. Out of the arrivals by land, 62.1 per cent came through Bhairahawa, 20.1 per cent through Kodari, 11.1 per cent through Kakarbhitta and 3.6 per cent through Birgunj.

The government of Nepal has undertaken a number of promotional and productive measures for tourism development, which are given below:

* Establishment of new tourist information centers,
* Development of tourism in Pokhara area,

* Expansion of additional physical facilities,
* Creation of additional facilities,
* Participation in the national and international fairs, exhibitions and conferences,
* Provision of monetary and financial incentives for tourism development
* Adoption of a liberal sky policy.

Besides, several tourism related industries, institutes and associations have been established like Hotel Association of Nepal (HAN), Nepal Association of Travel Agents (NATA), Trekking Association of Agents of Nepal (TAAN), Nepal Association of Rafting Agents (NARA), Everest Summiteers Association, Himalayan Rescue Association of Nepal (HRAN), Airlines Operators Associations of Nepal (AOAN), Board of Airlines Representative in Nepal (BARN), Federation of Nepalese Chamber of Commerce, Freight Forwarders Association of Nepal (FFAN), Handicraft Association of Nepal (HAN), Nepal Association of Tour Operators (NATO), Nepal Entrepreneurs Association of Tourism (NEAT), Nepal Incentive and Convention Association (NICA), Nepal Mountaineering Association (NMA), Non-star Hotel Association of Nepal (NSHAN), Restaurant & Bar Association of Nepal (REBAN), Thamel Tourism Development Committee (TTDC), Tourist Guide Association of Nepal, PATA Nepal Chapter, Kathmandu Research Centre (KRC), Tourism Concern Forum, Kathmandu Academy of Tourism and Hospitality, Silver Mountain School of Hotel Management, Nepal Tourism Board, Sustainable Tourism Network, Nepal Tourism & Hotel Management College, Nepal College of Travel and Tourism Management, Kathmandu Institute of Hospitality Management and so on . On the initiation of Dr Pradhanang Village Tourism Promotion Forum Nepal was established. The development of National Parks has also been instrumental in promoting productivity in the tourism sector. Among the eight National Parks, Royal Chitwan National Park and Sagarmatha National Park are the most popular destinations.

KATHMANDU RESEARCH CENTRE

Kathmandu Research Centre (KRC) involved in research study on tourism and economics in the tourism sector and national development is most important institution in the history of tourism in Nepal. It is the first tourism related institution established in 1980 and registered in the government of Nepal in 1984. It always thinks of the welfare of the nation and people through research study in tourism economics of Nepal. KRC is a pioneering institution in introducing and developing Nepal's Village Tourism Concept. It is mainly concerned with tourism development with special reference to village based tourism. It was involved in preparing the Nepal Tourism Policy 1995 and Tourism Sectoral Plan in the Ninth Plan with 14 model tourism villages such as Himalayan village, Hilly village and Terai village. Basically, it has a long term plan and policy with perspective economic development vision to develop unique tourism villages in 75 districts and 14 zones. It is committed to make Nepal a rich country and economically developed nation through the proper implication of village tourism concept. It gives valuable suggestions and guidelines for the development and promotion of village tourism and also encourages people and country to develop village tourism in village Nepal and abroad.[7] Apart from this, KRC worked for national interest. For example, survey on consumer awareness resulted 5 per cent alert in Kathmandu (1995), loss calculated to Nrs 130 million for an hour on electricity load shedding in Nepal (1997), survey and forecasting on midterm polls in Nepal (1999) and so on.

Human resource development for productivity improvement in tourism sector is presented below:

TABLE 1: Sectoral Manpower Development During 1972-1997

Sector	*Manpower Development in Number*		*Total*	*Percentage*
	Male	*Female*		
Hotel	3137	698	3835	31.81
Tour and Travel	1839	348	2187	18.14
Trekking	2174	16	2190	18.16
Other				
Courses/Workshop	721	134	855	7.09
Mobile Training	2136	854	2990	24.80
Grand Total/Percentage	10007	2050	12057	

Source : Nepal Tourism Statistics, 1997.

By 1997, 706 star (one star to five star) and tourist standard hotels were set up to provide 14,214 rooms and 27,612 beds. Also more than 549 travel agencies were established. Similarly, more than 10 airlines agencies and 100 transportation agencies, 369 trekking agencies and 259 rafting agencies, 69 registered and 90 unregistered were organised to facilitate tourists. Several other tourism related businesses like curio shops, cargo agencies, shopping centres, handicrafts, food and beverage products, cable car, tourist bus service, etc. were promoted. Other tourists activities like ballooning, rafting, hand gliding, rock climbing, golfing, and elephant polo had also been promoted. The Mountain Museum in Pokhara was established. The international and internal airports were also renovated and improved.

Nepal also organised various tourism promotional activities as part of 'Visit Nepal 1998', Trans Himalaya 2000, 'Destination Nepal 2002' renamed as Destination Nepal Campaign 2002-2003 (DNC). DNC was officially announced by the government of Nepal on January 9, 2002 and Nepal's Tourism Brand Development as 'Naturally Nepal'. Once is not Enough developed by Nepal Tourism Board at ITB Berlin, Germany on March 11, 2006 amidst a grand function, Celebration of Nepal's village tourism day in New York and Nepal by KRC. The major programmes incorporated with DNC were the 'International

Year of Mountains 2002'and 'Mt. Everest Golden Jubilee Celebrations 2002-2003'. The first tourism brand programme was conducted successfully at home country, Nepal on March 5, 2006. NTB selected ITB the best venue, realising its capacity to bring together the world's important stakeholders, tourism leaders and journalists. It is believed that the Brand image would be instrumental in increasing the number of tourists to Nepal.

Much emphasis has been laid on the economic aspect of tourism because of its contribution to the foreign exchange earnings, employment generation, national income and so on. The tourist expenditure on the national income is great. Thus, the greater the amount of tourist expenditure, the greater the beneficial impact on the Gross National Product and the National Accounts and vice versa.

Some achievements made by Nepal in the tourism sector could be presented as follows:

TABLE 2 : Sectoral Tourism Productivity

Particulars	*Fiscal Year*		
	1994/95	1995/96	1996/97
GDP contribution, by tourism sector (Rs Million)	2,939	2,892	3,034
No. of People employed in tourism sector	1, 00,000	2,00,000	3,00,000
Tourism Labour Productivity Level in (Rs)	29,390	14,460	10,113

Notes :

Direct employment 35,000 and indirect employment 65,000 = 1, 00,000 in 1994/95

Direct employment 50,000 and indirect employment 1,50,000 = 2,00,000 in 1995/96

Direct employment 90,000 and indirect employment 2, 10,000 = 3,00,000 in 1996/97

Source : Sample Survey/Kathmandu Research Centre.

The Asian Development Bank, World Bank and Nepal Industrial Development Corporation (NIDC) assisted for promotion and development of tourism in Nepal. Nepal became the member of International Union of Official Travel

Organisation, World Association of Travel Agents (WATA) and Pacific Asia Travel Association and participated in various international conferences.

The capital city Kathmandu is linked by international air services with direct flights from London, Paris, Frankfurt, Vienna, Amsterdan, Shanghai, Osaka, Hong Kong, Bangkok, Singapore, Bombay, Moscow, Lhasa, Paro, Dubai, Dhaka, Karachi and Doha. Travelers may also enter the country by surface (land) through six major entry points to Nepal– Kakarbhitta, Biratnagar, Birgunj, Bhairahawa, Mahendranagar from India and Kodari from Tibet/China.

Due to the Maoist people war (1996-2006) and frequent political parties' Nepal Band tourism in Nepal has gone down to worse position. After 1999 Nepal's tourism industry has undesirably reversed its gear from 20 per cent to 45 per cent in comparative analysis. In other words, it has had negative growth in tourist arrivals and tourism revenue. International tourists discarded Nepal as 'an unsafe and unsecured destination in the international tourism market'.

The latest tourism statistics shows the international visitors' arrival registered a decline of 4.4 per cent for the month of October 2006 as compared to the same duration of period of 2005. Analytically, 36,851 visitors came to Nepal during the period stated by Ministry of Culture, Tourism and Civil Aviation. A positive growth displayed in the countries like Malaysia (+8.9 per cent), Japan (+12.7 per cent) and South Korea (+57.1 per cent). Similarly, European countries like France (+16.6 per cent), Norway (+17.5 per cent), Spain (+7.9 per cent) and USA (+4.8 per cent) indicated the significant growth in October. However, tourist arrivals decreased in SAARC (–15.9 per cent), Europe (–2.6 per cent), China (–34.7per cent), Singapore (–52.7 per cent) and Thailand (–29.9 per cent) respectfully. The operating airlines namely GMG Bangladesh, Korean Air, Air Arabia, Etihad, Orient Thai and Sri Lankan Airlines may explore Nepal's tourism in a new horizon for development and promotion. If the peace and political stability are regularly secured, the history of tourism in Nepal once again can gain a new and prosperous mode.

TABLE 3 : Hotel Industry till 2006

Star	*No. of Hotel*	*No. of Rooms*	*No. of Bed*
5 Star	8	1641	3101
4 Star	8	655	1301
3 Star	17	803	1609
2 Star	36	1428	2783
1 Star	41	919	1921
Non Star	493	7019	14007
Under construction and proposed for register	403	8336	14662
Total	1006	20801	39384

Source : Ministry of Culture, Tourism and Aviation, 2006.

The Table 3 exhibits the scenario of Hotel Industry in Nepal till 2006. The 5 star hotel, 4 star hotel, 3 star hotel, 2 star hotel, 1 star hotel, non-star hotel and under construction and proposed for register are 8, 8, 17, 36, 41, 493 and 403 respectively. The total number of hotel is 1006 and the total number of bed capacity in the hotel is 39,384 in 2006.

On November 21, 2006 the much awaited Comprehensive Peace Accord (CPA) was signed between the government of Nepal and the Maoists-Communist Party of Nepal, which is the end of a decade-long armed insurgency–the 'People's War'. It was regarded as the historic Accord promising to chart a new destiny for 'peaceful and democratic' new Nepal. For the development and promotion of tourism in Nepal, the tourism entrepreneurs saluted the agreement. Nepalese tourism industry suffered severely due to conflicts at home and other untoward incidences that took place around the world. Since both the Government and Maoists committed for free movement of tourists and all Nepali in any part of the country can freely go without hindrance. It is hoped that the peace agreement would bring permanent peace in the country which is vital for the growth of tourism industry. But it is still under experiment .

Travel in Terms of Religion and Religious Ethics

Religion and religious ethics could be described as a strong driving force to travel and tourism in the world. People would

Goddess Palanchok Bhagabati

travel to pay homage to different Gods and Goddesses. People devoted their time and money in their religious trips. During the period of Middle Age of human civilisation, pilgrims who would travel for a far distance visited a holy place. A pilgrim father is unknown. But, today we have priest in temple and father in church. Going on pilgrimage is a custom developed in the world. By the end of the Middle Age, a large number of pilgrims travelled in Europe. By Hindu legend, Hinduism is the oldest religion in the world, which has had more than 5,000 years old history. Besides this, there are other religions like Buddhism, Islam and Christinity. The different name such as Krishna, Alha and Christ in religion refer to their God.

Pilgrimage tourism is still going on everywhere in the world. Due to pilgrimage ideology several religion minded people go to the holy land. The ritual practice of pilgrimage flourished travel and tourism from century to century. The concept of religion broke the limited boundry of agrarian society, 'Stay-at-home' atmosphere gave way to open religious areas. The pilgrimage tour exposed the people more in terms of different modern customs, rites, manners and varieties of food and designs of dress. It created the environment in

Boudha Stupa

Namo Buddha

Sight Seeing in Nepal

exchanging ideas and fostered trade and commerce in the world. The idea of pilgrimage made the people united in mind. The concept of religion gradually penetrated into people as Hinduism and Buddhism in Nepal, Buddhism, Islam and Hinduism in Asia and Christianity in Europe and later in America.

Some persons travelled in search of God considering how this universe came into being. A great traveller of Nepal named Gautam (Prince Siddhartha) was in the path of finding truth. Thus, he walked hundred of miles for the discovery of meaning of life. Later on, he learnt truth and got enlightened as Buddha. Lord Buddha travelled from place to place and country to country.

There are many more religious travellers in Nepal, Asia and abroad. The religion minded people like Hindu would go to visit 'Char Dham' in temples of India. Most of Hindu people would come from Asia to pay homage to God Pashupati Nath of Nepal. Similarly, a large number of Muslim group of people would go to Mecca for pilgrimage purpose. The Christian

Pashupatinath Temple

people would prefer to go to Church in different places, such as Vatican and Jerusalem.

The pilgrimage tourism developed in the world has a great value in world tourism market, even in the twenty first century.

In Sanskrit, the concept of tourism was explored in defferent ways. One of them is 'Atam' under which there is a character of pilgrimage concept in tourism.

The great wave of travel and tourism was initiated by religious zeal and enthusiasm in the early Middle Age. When the atmosphere was peaceful in Europe the Church attracted pilgrimages. Jerusalem became the centre for all christian pilgrims. Later on, Rome, Canterbury and Santiago de Campostela were also gradually developed as religious centres. Religious houses were made for pilgrims for food and accommodation. These houses were said as hospices or hospitals. Today we have the derivation of the term hospitality. Monks would provide entertainment and pleasure to guests, chanting legends of the holy spots. The religious places have been gradually developed as social gathering places, sightseeing trips, match making exercise places and marriage arranging holy places for people.

For Hindu, the pilgrimage to the Ganges and Char Dham in India followed shrines in the four corners of India: Badrinath, Jagannath Puri, Dwarka and Rameshwaram. They all are very important. In the Christain world, a visit to Jerusalem or the Vatican is supposed to be the holy duty because the places are considered as important as heaven.

In the Arab-Muslim world, the pilgrimage to Mecca is undertaken to pay homage to Alhaa–The Almighty God.

Travel for Pleasure

Pleasure is a component of purpose of visit by tourists. Tourists would like to visit places for pleasure. Pleasure is very important for making merry in human mind and body. In balancing mind and body, pleasure is a must, which works as a tonic for human beings. The concept of pleasure travel existed in east and west. Pleasure travel in Roman empire was valued

Travel in Unique Temple of Nepal

as highly as other travel. Most probably, Romans were the first pleasure travellers. The network of roads was prepared by recording routes, places, distances and time. Whereever the Romans went, they did the Travel would be comforted by using relays of horses in the routes.

In travel and tourism history, Spas and Seaside resorts developed for pleasure. Spas or medical baths and Seaside resorts were very popular in Roman society. The Spas and Seaside resorts provided amenities for pleasure and entertainment. The visitors would enjoy medicinal bath and different types of entertainments as well. Coming to the half of the eighteenth century, people started understanding medicinal value of sea water and sea bathing. In 1865, several resorts developed in Great Britain, France and Central Europe were the result of demand for vacation travel. Millions of modern pleasure seeker people would go to seaside resorts each year.

The theory of the leisure class published in 1899 and popularised in Europe had linked with propensity to travel.

Pleasure of Temples

Garud Exhibiting in a Beautiful Pillar

Garud

After the First World War (1914-1918), it is, perhaps, the beginning of travel for pleasure as well as the transformation of travel into tourism. The era of managed tourism started by not only travel agencies, but voluntary organisations and municipal councils as well. Next to oil, tourism has been the

Pleasure of Architecture in Nepal

second largest industry in the world.

Tourism is a highly accountable to income elasticity. Travel and tourism research shows that a 1per cent increase in the income level in real terms gives result in 1.5 per cent to 1.8 per cent increase in propensity for travel. There is a positive correlation between leisure-pleasure and tourism. The travel phenomenon is analysed by disposable income and leisure time and pleasure travel.

The growth of pleasure for travel and tourism is due to this Industrial Revolution. It resulted in an increase in wealthy middle class people. Increase in leisure time and travel for pleasure is due to the concept of paid holidays developed in tourism in twentieth century. Leisure time is the time free from all constraints which could be utilised for travel for pleasure. A person's leisure time split between three periods scored as: (a) after work (b) weekends and (c) annual holiday. People tend to travel when the incidence of travel for pleasure increases. Travel and tourism for pleasure is highly connected with transport and communication.

Basically, disposable income, discretionary leisure time and basic tourism amenities and services like accommodation and

Enchanting Art of Nepal

transportation are a subject to travel for pleasure. Besides this, other facilities such as political stability and peace, accepted means of exchange and free access to travel documents are required to keep them in favourable position. All these factors facilitate the growth of travel for pleasure.

Travel and Tourism in Terms of Seasonal Variation of Climate

Travel issues and tourism are relatively dependent on the seasonal variation of climate in the country. As the climate is favourable, tourism will also be in a favourable position supported by circumstances. Seasonality determines a change in demand for tourism in a year.

Most of tourist destinations have peak season and off-season. As per the high demand, the accommodation tariff will be low. In the Northern Hemisphere peak demand refers to the period of spring and summer months of May to August/ September. By contrast, in the Southern Hemisphere peak demand indicates the period of summer months (season) from November/December to March.

In Nepal the three months of October, November and December refer to the tourist season. Nepal's peak season is confined to October to March whereas slack season in Nepal is April to September. Similarly, periodicity refers to a synonymous concept but within a shorter time period, generally a week.

Nepal As a Host and Tourist Destination

We had better understand a host country as a tourist receiving country and a tourist destination. Tourism is an export industry for a developing country like Nepal. It is as means for balance of payment and foreign investment. The tourist generating country that supplies tourists for other countries help the country's economic in different ways. The world economy is highly related to the tourism receipts. Nepal is not an exception to this.

For tourism to develop at a grass root level, the specific concept of village tourism should be developed. It is relatively concerned with village and villager. It is as a major source of income and employment generation, viz.; hotel, trekking, rafting, transportation and so on. As a matter of fact, tourism is an invisible export industry to a host country. In 1990, the developed nation, Spain played host to more than 55 million tourists.

In 1999, Nepal played host to more than 4,91,504 foreign tourists. The country is becoming dependent on tourism as a source of income and jobs. Tourism is today's vital subject to the upliftment of both village economy and national economy.

It seems to be a key concern of each government that expenditure by tourists may be a major income to its revenue generation. For a host country, the concept of balanced growth is a key factor of productivity. Almost two-thirds of total international tourist arrivals and more than 50 per cent of international expenditure on tourism are focused on Europe. The USA accounts for a fifth of tourist arrivals in a quarter of receipts. Asia and Pacific are experienced more than 13 per cent in tourism activity. In the context of Nepal, Nepal accounted

4,63,684 tourist arrivals and US$ 179.94 million (NRS 13146.53 million) foreign exchange earnings in 2004.

References

1. Tulasi Rama Vaidya, et. al, *Social History of Nepal,* Anmol Publications Pvt. Ltd., New Delhi, India, p. 5, 1993.
2. John Whelpton, *A History of Nepal,* University of Cambridge, Cambridge University Press, UK, p. 18, 2005.
3. Daniel Wright, *History of Nepal: With an Introductory Sketch of the Country and People of Nepal,* Cambridge University Press, UK, p. 51, 1877.
4. The Library of Congress, Federal Research Division, *Country Study: Nepal,* 1993.
5. The Third World Encylopedia, *Nepal and Bhutan,* Country Studies.
6. Surendra Bhakta Pradhanang, *Productivity in Tourism Sector,* National Productivity and Economic Development Centre, Kathmandu, Nepal, p. 234, 1999.
7. Sustainable Tourism in Nepal *Kathmandu Research Centre,* NTB, Sustainable Tourism Network, Kathmandu, Nepal, March, 2000.

Chapter 2

Nepal's Village Tourism

SUSTAINABLE TRAVEL INTERNATIONAL™ leave the world a better place™

NEPAL'S VILLAGE TOURISM: A MODEL FOR SUSTAINABLE TOURISM

Nepal is a country of villages, which host 84.5 per cent of its total population, a majority of whom work in agriculture. Though the villages located along the popular trekking routes benefit from tourism, they're in the minority. Nepal's tourism industry is concentrated in city areas and is dominated by the more affluent class. As a result, tourism has not developed in a sustainable manner. One individual aims to change things. His goal is to develop tourism at the village level, empowering villagers to improve their quality of life, and his name is Dr Surendra Bhakta Pradhanang.

In 1976, Dr Pradhanang, a student working on his Master's in Economics/Management went to Dasharathpur Village, Surkhet for National Development Service. After ten months of service, he came up with the low investment high return concept of village tourism in the context of the Nepalese social structure which was largely ignored by the local tourism industry and government of Nepal. Five years later he formally established the Kathmandu Research Centre and conducted research on the potential and sustainability of village tourism in Nepal. From 1992 onward, Dr Pradhanang's work became increasingly popular to the point where it was proposed that village tourism be included in the Nepalese tourism policy in 1995. It was defeated but not for long. Soon thereafter, the National Planning Commission realised the importance of village tourism as a model for sustainable tourism development in Nepal and gave it top priority for the first time in the history of Nepalese tourism policy.

Today, Dr Pradhanang's vision has helped to generate employment and income within rural areas throughout the Kindgom while helping to protect the natural environment and preserve cultural heritage. Village tourism in the Sirubari village, for example, has been very successful. The Sirubari Tourism Village Committee is selling its village tourism product in the international market and is attracting many groups of tourists. The 35 village households involved have directly benefited in terms of income and employment generation, environmental protection, improved cleanliness, cultural heritage promotion, and a rise in living standards. In total, from 1998-2005 more than 1000 international tourists visited and enjoyed Nepal's village tourism product. The net result is that the direct and indirect economic benefits of tourism have increased by 70 per cent. Now, especially since the political climate in Nepal has stabilised, a majority of the total population would like to take advantage of the benefits of village tourism.

Dr Pradhanang's village tourism concept has been a very successful model for sustainable tourism development. It's now being embraced by governmental agencies, NGO's and private tourism companies around the world. For these reasons, Dr Pradhanang was awarded the title 'Father of Village Tourism in Nepal'. (STI, 2006)

Promotion of Nepal Village Tourism

France Radio Broadcasting has promoted Nepal's Village Tourism in France. Nepal's Village Tourism concept propounded by Dr Surendra Bhakta Pradhanang is found as a model for developing countries like Nepal.

Radio France interviewed Dr Surendra Bhakta Pradhanang, the chairman of Kathmandu Research Centre and advocator of Village Tourism in Nepal on Nepal's Village Tourism Concept and Economy. On the France Radio Broadcasting, Dr Pradhanang highlighted the concept and importance of Nepal's Village Tourism as its own originality and speciality developed in tourism industry of Nepal . He gave the stress on the proper implementation of the concept for developing villages of Nepal and national economy.

Nepal's Village Tourism has been promoted in New York along with the celebration of 2550th Anniversary of Lord Buddha organized by the United Sherpa Association, USA. The programme held at Five Star Banquet and Restaurant in Long Island City, New York highlighted the teaching and messages of Buddha. The participants spoke out the importance of Buddha's teaching for maintaining peace and prosperity in the world.

On the occasion, Dr Surendra Bhakta Pradhanang, the chairman of Kathmandu Research Centre and Village Tourism Expert spoke about the importance and role of Nepal's Village Tourism in maintaining peace and economic development in Nepal. (STN/Nepal, 2006)

Dr Pradhanang and His Village Tourism Concept Growing Popularity in Nepal and Abroad

Dr Pradhanang and his concept of Village Tourism growing popularity more in Nepal and abroad has been today's concern for twenty first century tourism agenda. Nepal's Village Tourism Concept which has been the part and parcel for world tourism industry cannot be ignored by the world tourism community. By and large, every country of the world is being awaked with Dr Pradhanang's Village Tourism concept and his advocacy. The developing and developed countries of the world have to follow it as the basic needs for socio-economic development. In Nepal more than 80 percent of total population is in support of Dr Pradhanang and his concept of Village Tourism developed for people and national welfare. Village Tourism, if effectively implicated in Nepal, can play the significant role in the upliftment of national economy. Due to his commitment on invention and development of Village

Tourism in Nepal, he was appreciated and awarded with 'Father of Village Tourism and Discoverer of Scientific Tourism'. His concept seems to be highly potential and invaluable in order to develop Village Nepal.

Nepal's Village Tourism is the concept propounded by Dr Surendra Bhakta Pradhanang of Nepal. His concept being useful and innovative is most popular in Nepal and abroad. It is his brainchild logged in the Nepalese social structure and economic phenomenon. Dr Pradhanang when stayed at Dashrathpur Village of Surkhet and involved in the National Development Service in 1974 brainstormed the concept of Village Tourism in Nepal. He is the first man of Village Tourism Provocation in Nepal who spoke out the concept and significance of village tourism in favour of national development especially villages of Nepal. His mastermind sketched the road map of village tourism development in the national development plan and strategy. At the outset, no one believed his concept and disregarded his idea and him.

Due to his untiring devotion and effort and continuous advocacy, his concept of village tourism has got a top priority listed in the national plan and strategy of Nepal and abroad. Above all, his dream came true. Lots of people got benefits through income and employment generation. They have had the smiling face with income and job opportunities and are today happy in playing with village tourism.

Dr Pradhanang categorised in an extraordinary and outstanding quality is the pioneer of Nepal's village tourism concept propagated in the specific, scientific and original terminology. His theory of Village Tourism for economic development in Nepal is as true as scientific principle the earth is round. After his exposure on village tourism, by and large, the government of Nepal and people including tourism experts, planners, intellectuals, entrepreneurs and foreign donors began to follow his concept of village tourism. Dr Pradhanang's concept is very simple, but most effective in the country of villages like Nepal.

Once it was neglected as 'Sauta Paryatan' (revival tourism) by the Nepalese tourism entrepreneurs and the government of

Nepal. The high ranked government officers including secretary, joint-secretary and under-secretary of Culture, Tourism and Civil Aviation were against Dr Pradhanang's village tourism concept. Now all of them realised their mistakes as misunderstanding. Dr Pradhanang's Theory and Practice wonderfully introduced as his new and innovative thought in the tourism world. Watched and witnessed the popularity and usefulness of Dr Pradhanang and his Village Tourism concept, the Ministry of Culture, Tourism and Civil Aviation started developing pilot project as TRAP aided by SNV, DFID and UNDP. Surprisingly, those three donors accepted and donated millions of dollars in a single project in terms of one and same project.

Dr Pradhanang who is the first Ph.D. holder from Tribhuvan University in Tourism Economics stands for as village tourism development representative and popular village tourism figure in Nepal. Dr Pradhanang says, 'Nepal need not to have foreign aid if village tourism is carefully implicated in villages of Nepal. But it is much shocked to us that village tourism in Nepal is being undesirably operated by foreign aid. On the contrary of Nepal's Village tourism Theory and Ideology, the government of Nepal is mistakenly under the donar's dependence and pressure.' He further says, 'Nepal is being paralyzed in its economic strength and socio-economic activity by extending unnecessary foreign aids.' For revolutionary change in Nepal's Tourism and Economy, Dr Pradhanang had struggled since the last 27 years. He tied up his mind and body with his own model of development vision as the best strategy for national development in Nepal. In fact, he raised his curious mind in the field of tourism economics for nation instead of dreadful weapon in political economics or politics. The sound of weapon is easily heard and explored, but the sound of mind cannot be easily heard.

Dr Pradhanang's publications on Village Tourism are around Nepal and abroad with research findings and visions developed through studies and works. His several write ups in English, Nepali and Newari languages were published in the various magazines and newspapers. More than two hundreds write ups in Newari were published in the popular newspaper The Desaymaru Jhya. The highly conscious and intellectuals of capital city Kathmandu read and followed Dr Pradhanang's thought for national development.

The book ,Village Tourism in Chitwan popularised most in the world is found in UK, USA, China, India, Pakistan, Bangladesh, France, Japan, Germany, Sri Lanka, Maldives, Bhutan, Afghanistan, Nepal, Canada and so on. The book was publicly released by honourable chairman of Rajparisad Standing Committee Dr Keshar Jung Rayamajhi in 2002. The book selling in UK through the Amazon Marketplace sellers is found. The book created a wonderful awareness and held a message in the world tourism that village tourism concept is twenty first century's tourism industry which can accommodate a large number of people for alleviating poverty and generating income and employment at a larger extent.

Dr Pradhanang's Village Tourism Concept has been a national or international recognized entity, attracting attention for every country's village tourist destination. Village is naturally gifted with a diverse topography with pristine beaches, lush forests, beautiful mountains, rivers and waterfalls.

Dr Pradhanang has been showered with praise from none other than Nepali village people and Nepal Rafting Association of Nepal (NARA) and Summiteers Association of Nepal. He is an excellent and outstanding village tourism hero whose fans are in a big surprise and beneficial to the people of the world.

Dr Pradhanang's Village Tourism concept was followed by various countries like Sikkim, Thailand, Bangladesh, Pakistan, India, Vietnam, Laos, Maldives, Bhutan, and Sri Lanka and so on. His concept was exported to different parts of the world especially by foreign donors and international financial institutions which included village tourism development programme in their plans and policies.

Today Dr Pradhanang of Nepal and his Village Tourism concept has been the showcase for village tourism development in Nepal and international arena. Every country of the world gradually began to follow village tourism concept. The European Tourism Network, Asian Tourism Network and

SAARC countries are being awaked to promote Nepal's village tourism concept. Recently, France Radio Broadcasting broadcast the voice of Dr Pradhanang (interview) and his concept of Village Tourism for village tourism development in the world. Now Village Tourism has been every one's concern as hotcake to test. Besides, Career Builder of New York made query about Dr Pradhanang stating, 'Is your resume as brilliant as you are?' Dr Pradhanang, who is the man of the world, seeks welfare and development of developing and developed countries of the world.

Due to his commitment on invention and development of Village Tourism in Nepal, he was appreciated and awarded with 'Father of Village Tourism and Discoverer of Scientific Tourism'. His concept seems to be highly potential and invaluable in order to develop Village Nepal.

Dr Pradhanang is a well known personality and social committed tourism scientist and village tourism thinker who has made the decision to expand his concept in the United States. He has really been the asset to tourism world to the United States and Nepal in the light of his enthusiasm and endeavour. (Dr. Amatya/Peace Journalism, 2006)

Origin

In Tretayug an era described in sanskrit literature, Lord Ram started travelling in the forest and forest land where forest dwellers lived at small huts and cottages. He walked around the forest for 'banabas' for fourteen years. The word 'banabas' narrated as forest stay in the era could be interpreted as a farm of village tourism. The concept of village tourism originated from this era.

The concept of village tourism originated from Nepal has its own background. It has been structured in its original way. The academic inventor of the original concept of village tourism in Nepal is Dr Surendra Bhakta Pradhanang. The concept was institutionally spread by Kathmandu Research Centre. 'The academic inventor of village tourism stresses the necessity of a linkage of tourism with the community, its economy, local resources, local produce and employment.' (Action Aid Nepal, 1999).

In support of different geodemographic, socio-graphic and psychographic parameters of Nepal, village tourism has been a soil based concept. The original characteristics of village that we have are not found anywhere in the world. The heavenly pleasure accommodiated here in Nepal and its soil on the ground of village is village stay tourism or village tourism.

The popular travel magazine, Nepal Trade Report (2005) states, 'the concept of village tourism has been introduced by Dr Pradhanang for the first time and began to gain recognition as a subject of topic since the start of 1979. Kathmandu Research Centre undertook a comprehensive survey on the possibilities of village tourism in Nepal. Nepalese media formally presented the concept of village tourism in public in 1992. After a long struggle of Dr Pradhanang the government of Nepal finally included in 1995 village tourism into its tourism policy. The credit of instituting village tourism concept in Nepal as a new agenda in travel and trade industry goes to Dr Pradhanang, who has also been honoured with the title of 'Father of village tourism'.

Due to the people's desire and interest, the thirst of village tourism increased in society. To quench the thirst, the concept of village tourism was introduced. Nepal opened its door to foreign tourists for mountaineering expedition in 1941. Since then, the people of different countries came to Nepal as mountaineering tourists. They trekked through Everest village in their to climb Mount Everest. Nepal, being the country of villages, started tourism from village and enjoyed unidentified village tourism. Obviously, Nepal gave birth to twin concept of tourism namely Mountaineering tourism and village tourism. Unknowingly, village tourism had been started since 1941. With Everest expedition, tourists stayed at villages and climbed Everest and Annapurna. Later village tourism went into oblivion. It got missed for a long time. It remained not known to anyone else. None cared for it and searched it. In 1976 Dr Pradhanang went to Dashrathpur village, Lekhpharsa VDC in Surkhet district as a student of National Development Service (NDS). He got so involved in the village that he discovered the potentiality of the village developed and the village tourism concept. This later became his outstanding contribution to the tourism world.

Nature

Village tourism carries a school of thought that is linked with microeconomic power to macroeconomic growth.

The feature of village tourism is very natural and it has a broad concept.

1. Village tourism creates a reality from the world of immagination and state of wonder.
2. Village tourism tends to minimize destruction of nature.
3. Village tourism leads 'village first' concept.
4. Village tourism is a humanitarian concept that provides benefits to people and country.
5. It is more than community based tourism.
6. It is a multidisciplinary approach developing a self-standing economy.

Peculiarities

The original base and heavenly pleasure are endowed nowhere in the world other than Nepal. On the ground of hospitality, Nepal's village tourism concept holds some pecularities:

1. Mahi (curd juice), hot water is offered to visitors in order to quench their thirst free of cost, shows supremacy of Nepalese hospitality service.
2. Experience of original life in tourism-village.
3. A visitor asking for shelter is regarded as God and given accommodation.
4. Village tourism opens new world in village.
5. Regeneration of family values and family love.
6. Establishment of tourism democracy in the world.

Dr Pradhanang's Theory of Village Tourism

The thinker, Dr Pradhanang is able to sit down with a slate and pencil to plan out a new model of village tourism amidst the conflict situation caused by Maoists' people war since 1996 in Nepal. Nepal carrying war affected ill economy requires peace as medicine and progress as economic development. He says that village tourism, if implemented, can guarantee food and work to young Nepali nationals. It can be a peace making concept. Society evolves from village to urban environment. The universal theory of evolution grants that every society does not necessarily go through the same fixed stages of development. It argues that the culture of mankind taken as a whole has followed a definite line of evolution. Man had progressed from small groups to large and from simple to compound and doubly compound, or, in more general terms, from the homogeneous to the heterogeneous.

Today growth economics has been an integral part of modern economic theory. While the classical economist Marx was concerned with growth. Later on, the modern revival Roy Harrod (1938) and Evsey Domar (1946) came with growth model. After the Second World War, the War-damaged economics were being reconstructed fast. Basically, growth is everybody's concern and economists are trying to design the new economic growth model.

Based on modern tourism development, Dr Pradhanang's Theory of Village Tourism is primarily concerned with a function of village as an investment elaborated for productive capacity in the village economy.

On his theoretical ground, the demand for village tourism for business travel and tourism and tourism relates to the consumption of investment good and service not a consumption good. The functional relationship for the growth of village tourism in terms of demand for business in village travel is determined by various parameters. Demand effect initiates further activity for generation of extra incomes. Likewise, supply effect initiates the creation of additional productive capacity which leads to increased output. The capacity should be utilised for the growth of a given economy. The simple village tourism development function for international travel and tourism can be expressed as follows:

$$VT = f(V, V_r, T, H) \text{ Eq. (i)}$$

where,

VT is village tourism

F is function

V_r is villager

T is tourist

H is hospitality

VT shows village tourism development in village, which has the development functional relationship with various parameters. V is the village used for village tourism development in the form of consumption of investment.

$$VT = f(V_c, H_v, V_t, H_s) \text{ Eq. (ii)}$$

where,

VT is village tourism

V_c is village capital

H_v is host villager

V_t is village tourist

H_s is hospitality service

VT has the functional relationship with various parameters. Here, V_c is used as village capital for developing village economy.

$$VT = f(V_{ci}, H_v, V_t, H_{sm}) \text{ Eq. (iii)}$$

where,

V_{ci} is village capital investment

H_v is host villager

V_t is village tourist

H_{sm} is hospitality service management

$$VT = f(V_{ci}, H_v, V_t, H_{sm}, N_r) \text{ Eq. (iv)}$$

where,

V_{ci} is village capital investment

H_v is host villager

V_t is village tourist

H_{sm} is hospitality service management

N_r is natural resources.

$$\Delta VT = f(\Delta V_{ci}, \Delta H_v, \Delta V_t, \Delta H_{sm}, \Delta N_r) \text{ Eq. (v)}$$

$$\Delta Y = f(\Delta V_{ci}, \Delta H_r, \Delta V_t, \Delta H_{sm}, \Delta N_r) \text{ Eq. (vi)}$$

where,

ΔVT is change in village tourism that follows development.

ΔV_{ci} is change in village capital investment.

ΔH_v is change in host villager.

ΔV_t is change in village tourist.

ΔH_{sm} is change in hospitality service mangement.

ΔN_r is change in natural resources.

Δ is change

ΔY = change in output

In operation of village tourism (VT), development equations (iii) and (iv) show the fundamental ground for developing village economy. Most obviously, village capital (V_{ci}) uses as investment for increasing village productivity. Hospitality service management (H_{sm}) is specifically presented as excellent service to tourist as uniqueness of Nepalese villages. Natural resources of village (N_r) are utilised as village tourism products for tourist attraction

In equation (v) assuming that change in village tourism development in terms of demand is a function of changes in village capital investment, host villager, village tourist, hospitality service management and natural resources. The variables might be known as development variables of economic growth. Village is very beautiful endowed with magnetic attraction. Village people are kind hearted with noble character and lovely conduct. Hospitality is unique in quality. These are basic parameters to boost up the economy.

Hence, VT (Village tourism) is that takes changes (ΔVT) as economic development in the village. Development takes place through the change or increase in output (ΔY) as shown in the equation (vi). Here, village tourism (VT) assumed as output (Y) is in village level of development or productivity.

Economics Growth

$$VT = Y = E_G$$

Assuming VT as output (Y) and output (Y) as economics growth, we have the simple equation that shows economics growth.

$$E_G = \frac{R_i}{C_{or}} \quad \text{Eq. (i)}$$

where,
E_G is Economics growth
R_i is Rate of investment
C_{or} is Capital-output ratio

$$E'_G = \frac{R_i}{C_{or}} \quad \text{Eq. (ii)}$$

where,
E'_G is Extended economic growth
R_i is Rate of investment
C_{or} is Value of the increment of capital-output ratio

The equation (i) and equation (ii) show the economics growth (E_G) and Extended economics growth (E'_G). In the initial year, the growth will be steady. In the second or third year, the growth will be fast.

The rate of investment (R_i) is the fraction of income and the value of the increment of capital-output ratio (C_{or}) includes all goods (circulating and fixed capital village).

Numerically supposing that 10per cent of income was saved and invested and the capital-output ratio (capital coefficient) per annum was 4. Then the growth rate would be 2.5 per cent per annum.

By and large, the mulitplier effect takes over the village by the initial income received from village tourism in income and employment generation. The effect of investment can be assessed in different ways, viz., (a) income effect (b) capacity effect (c) Demand effect (d) supply effect and so on.

Village as Capital Investment

Dr Pradhanang states that in functional equations village as capital used for investment implies the significant variable. Investment is done for creating pleasure and facilities to tourists and thereby generates output to the village economy.

There are villages identified in terms of village as capital investment pattern. Assuming that villages of Nepal are justified in the following terminology:

$$V \begin{matrix} >1 \\ =0 \\ <1 \end{matrix}$$

where

V stands for village.

If V is > 1, the village is considered as touched and partially exploded. The village capitalised with some infrastructure development and amenities included is on the way of developing tourism village. Since the wave of modernisation spread in the world, the village cannot be exceptional. It tends to move towards urbanisation. The modern culture damages the natural shape of village. This type of village affected by the modern culture and lifestyle requires comparatively more capital investment that lies the category under V > 1.

The village environment which is partially natural and partially artificial does not meet the speciality, but feasible to those normal tourists who are city loving and city based. In such village, village-city partnership tourism can be enhanced as per the tourist's desire and demand to drive the village tourism. Hence, village as capital is used for investment.

If V = 0, the village is considered as naturally prepared. The village is natural and unique, which is the zone of relaxation and peace. It is nature's paradise and culture's appetite creating design as 'Wonder of the world', which is not imagined by tourists nor expected to have wonderful experience in life. Inclusively, the village will touch upon the heart of tourists. The village treasured with unknown pearls of love, magnificient beauty of nature, unforgettable hospitality service is naturally capitalised. There is no need of actual investment other than normal cost for living and as mangement. Here, village as capital is fully used for investment

This is tourism village invested almost zero capital that results high output to the village economics growth.

If V is < 1, the village is assumed as unprepared and underutilised. Some capital for infrastructure development is needed. The unexplored and virgin villages should be wisefully kept on pipeline as village capital stock for investment. To develop tourism village, the seed capital has to be initially invested in terms of preparation phase. By and large, the village as capital can be used for investment. Later on, the village is capitalised for economics growth.

Dr Pradhanang is of the opinion that talks of creating design view of village tourism on the ground of exciting expression of thought as 'Ah! What a magnificent village look and lovely village!!'.

The tourism village look should attract tourists with magnetic power. This attraction creates interest and demands for tourism village.

Dr Pradhanang says that free and ideal capital cannot create income. Creating demand for utilising village capital is necessary. The growth of village tourism is relatively dependent on supply and demand. At the outset, the supply product has to be more active for displaying modality in the tourism market on the basis of designed and tasted product demand increases. Thus tourism village model is needed to meet supply and demand. He elaborately points out that the village resource Mt. Everest has greater economic power estimating potential business transaction equivalent to those of Ford Company of USA, General Motor Company Toyota of Japan and Sixteen TATA Iron & Steel companies of India, village tourism brings the best reward in terms of income or output (Pradhanang, The Gorkhapatra, Magh 28, 2053).

Besides this, village tourism is the means of developing various economic activities linking several industries and business. It has to be grown by supporting village industries and professions.

The economic linkage growth can be expressed as:

$$VT = f(L)$$

where

L stands for forward and backward linkage in various sectoral activities/industries of village economy.

f stands for function.

Village tourism (VT) is the function of linkage (L) with different village industries associated with tourism. It can relatively boost the village economy.

Considering economics growth, investment is made

possible only when there will be saving in the economy. Saving can help as well as hamper growth. Saving, if unutilised in time, causes a decrease in demand of same value. Consequently, a slackness in the market will be created. Similarly, saving, if invested, creates extra productive capacity. A proper rate of growth depends on the role played by the rate of saving and rate of investment. Thus growth is considered as a payroll flow of two streams-consumption and saving

The national income comes from investment and investment depends on saving. Technically, the rate of growth of national income depends on the rate of saving and the productivity of investment or capital-output ratio. Greater investment leads the greater output.

Hence, the rate of growth of saving and investment in terms of national income determine the balanced growth of the economy.

In conclusion, Dr Pradhanang suggests the policy of investment more in terms of village capital goods and less in consumption goods to the growth be adopted and village economy be developed. As consequence of it, village tourism created 'rainfall of wealth' and baring about revolution in village Nepal. Dr Pradhanang fits Nepal's village model in terms of economic growth model for village development. This is a purely new school of thought created from Nepal. The mastermind of all these concepts is Dr Pradhanang.

VILLAGE TOURISM TODAY

Tourism village branding concept patronises tourist. There is a talk on developing and planning tourism villages including more information on the use and structure of feasibility study of village tourism. The business is a new product.

From the standpoint of international perspective, village tourism is an innovative industry known in the international tourism market. Today tourism, being the largest industry in the world trade, contributes more than 12 per cent of the world's gross national product and employs more than 100 million people. Village tourists are gradually growing up in the international arena.

A molecule of village tourism has a close relationship with two atoms international tourism and domestic tourism. When two atoms get together, they react or produce village tourism as water. Thus, the significance of village tourism can be valued as water for living beings. A study of village life is no more considered to be a romantic narration-full of natural life, hills and forests, streams and rivers and folklores and folktales. The village life has today reached a stage where the glamour of urban life has made inroads inside the village life. But the urban life is nothing but an extension of village life.

The village actors incorporate customs and traditions by planning strategy to develop village tourism. The autonomous growth of small tourism village must be supported and enhanced by national and international organisations and tourism actors. Soon a day will come when the international tourism is marketed by village tourism actors and planners.

Applied Village Tourism Research

Village tourism research is required for economic development especially for village based country like Nepal. Implications of village tourism for regional development and benefits to people are urged. We need statistics for analysing market research and demand for tourism.

The local government Village Development Committee (VDC) and central government should go together for developing village tourism. Likewise, the urban tourism enterprises in relation to Village Tourism Committee have to develop network for planning tourism villages of Nepal on the following considerations:

1. Ratio of village tourism with reference to total tourist flow in the country.
2. Effect of tourism expenditure on employment, income and balance of payments.
3. Tourist expenditure pattern in city and village areas of Nepal.
4. Economic values of village tourism to the national economy and village economy.
5. Trends of village tourists, domestic tourists and

international tourists.

6. Behaviour and interest of village tourists and international tourists.
7. Information and feedback collection on tourism village and its hospitality service and product.
8. Psychological test on village tourism from tourists, tourism enterprises and governments.

Data on village tourist and tourist flow are collected at VDCs, DDCs and airports. Tourist expenditure on travel within the tourist destination, payment to international carriers and import content should also be recorded for analysis.

Tourist Characteristics

Information on tourist characteristics has to be compiled for tourism analysis. The following points are specially important:

1. Purpose of visit
2. Country of origin
3. Age
4. Gender or sex
5. Profession
6. Tourist arrivals via India/Bangkok
7. Tourist arrivals by direct destination, espicially American visitors
8. Number of visit
9. Accommodation used
10. Transport used
11. Tourism village
12. Comments.

Statistics on tourist characteristics are recorded for marketing plan and strategy for developing tourism villages of Nepal. Tourism research is conducted in terms of the split between village tourism and international tourism. Tourism analysis is conducted on the basis of socio-economic values.

Market research is also conducted on consumer or tourism demand and supply side of tourism or tourism product research. Information is collected either by primary source or by secondary source.

Part II : Height of Village Tourism

Chapter 3

Village Tourism in Global Context

Village tourism is a thought – piece for introducing village as a beautiful tourist destination. People would like to get away from the humdrum of day to day busy life and move to villages, mountains and beautiful areas. Village tourism exemplified by Nepal and Nepalese is the showpiece in the global context of travel and tourism agenda. It is focused as powerful economic and social drive in the world. There are various village based resources illustrated as scenary resources, people, natural attractions, cultural diversities and wildlife animals and plants in village world. Thus, village tourism is an appropriate means of collecting foreign capital.

Globally, village tourism is defined as 'the household tourism inserted into the mind of people with simple social life and love to breathe fresh air, to stay at natural setting, to enjoy cultural life, to enter into the tension free world and to relax in happy and cheerful mood coming out of the sophisticated and busy schedule of life provides win–win benefits to host and tourist' (Dr Pradhanang, 2005).

Specifically, village tourism is growing up as a universal industry as well as business in the globe. The magnetic power of village travel and tourism is to generate love, friendship and understanding in the world. The tourists having similar interest and demand are in search of tourism villages.

Dr Pradhanang says, 'Visiting tourism village is being a lifestyle of people in the world.' Today people who are motivated not by money but rather by a human pride of adventure want to be in new and unexplored villages of the world. The affluent tourists do not purchase more amenities, but purchase wonderful experience as quality service.

As commerce and industry are shifted and marketed from urban areas to rural, suburban and airport areas, several world renowned hotel builders and hotel companies, viz., Hilton, Sheraton and Marriott showed their interest to develop their hotel brands in those places. As the 1990s progressed, the industry emphasised innovation and new business strategies implemented by many hotel chains to increase their market share. Acutally, the concept was not new. Hilton and Sheraton each had established hotel and inns division 30 years ago. The hotels were in cities, the inns in suburbs at airport and off highways. The segmentation changed the mode not on location, but on market.

This market development trend attracts tourism village of Nepal towards the international market. Hence, travel opportunities are being searched in tourism village in the world.

Nepal's Village Tourism and Global Agenda 21

Village Tourism concept developed in Nepal is a new agenda in travel and tour industry institutionally propounded by Kathmandu Research Centre. The concept is Nepal's own creativity and innovation developed from the Nepalese soil. Nepal sought the new vision enlightening village tourism industry. It goes hand in hand with village and villager. It is village tourism promoted on the fantastic model of new tourist destinations in the country of villages.

Nepal's village Tourism being a totally new concept can lead the global tourism village development to the whole world at the largest extent. One hundred and eighty two countries of the world participated and discussed at the United Nations Conference on Environment and Tourism Development. But none of the nation could understand the concept and importance of village tourism neither His Majesty's Government of Nepal (the government of Nepal) could provoke it and nor World Travel and Tourism Council, World Tourism Organisation and Earth's Council could introduce village tourism concept.

Furthermore, all those who represented the world conference including tourism entrepreneurs, national tourism authorities and administrations failed to brainstorm and include village tourism in the Global Agenda 21 due to lack of clear vision, knowledge and understanding on village tourism concept. Kathmandu Research Centre started developing village tourism as a fulfilment of gap and a new dimension in the world tourism industry. But it seems in reality that Agenda 21 for Travel and Tourism Industry is incomplete without village tourism.

Agenda 21 is a comprehensive programme of action followed by 182 governments of the world at the United Nations Conference on Environment and Development. It is concerned with the sustainable future of the planet from now into twenty-first century.

Based on the Rio Declaration on Environment and Development in 1992, the following guidelines for Travel and Tourism Industry have been taken into consideration:

1. Travel and Tourism should assist people in leading healthy and productive lives in harmony with nature.
2. Travel and Tourism should contribute to the conservation, protection and restoration of the earth's ecosystem.
3. Travel and Tourism should be based on sustainable pattern of production and consumption.
4. Protectionism in trade in Travel and Tourism services should be halted or reversed.
5. Environmental protection should constitute an integral part of the tourism development process
6. Tourism development issues should be handled with the participation of concerned citizens, with planning decisions being adopted at local level.
7. Nations will warn one another of natural disasters that could affect tourists or tourist areas. Travel and Tourism should use its capacity to create employment for women and indigenous people to the fullest extent.

8. Tourism development should recognise and support the identity, culture, and interests of indigenous people.
9. International laws protecting the environment should be respected by the Travel and Tourism Industry.

The aim of Global Agenda 21 is to eradicate poverty by facilitating poor people more access to the resources they urgently need to live more sustainably. Adopting the Agenda 21 in the international arena, the advanced countries realised that they have a significant role to play in cleaning up the environment than poor nations, who does relatively less environmental degradation and pollution. The richer nations also showed their interest and committed to help for more funding in order to decrease negative environmental impacts in the world. Understandingly, village tourism entrepreneurship is a latest model car to drive the international tourism at the right direction of environmentalism and sustainability as per the direction needed to supply and demand situation in the tourism market.

Historically, village tourism era starting in the twenty-first century has to develop village tourism destinations in terms of environmental resources and tourism attraction and accommodation as global tourism village product. The current knowledge deficit on village tourism development in the public sector is a big weakness and blockage to sustainable tourism development in Global Agenda 21. Hence developing new forms of tourism village destination in terms of public-private sector friendship and partnership is a must in global tourism.

Village Tourism in the World

Village tourism newly created from Nepal is very special and above all the Nepal style tourism, which provides modality as its speciality to the world. It has higher degree of uniqueness and charming hospitality differentiated from other, which are nowhere found in the world.

There is, however no dearth of village tourism literature found in the world. After the implication of Nepal's village tourism, the message of tourism village has spread throughout the world. As a result, the literature on village tourism has gradually grown. The literature shows the synonym of village tourism in other countries.

After the Second World War, tourist villages were developed in some European countries. Located at warm sea sides, Italy and Spain established tourist villages in support of club, social organisations and tourist organisations. The village complex as a centre of accommodation is used for sporting and recreational facilities. The village provides board and lodging. The environment is kept informal as far as possible. In the Spanish island of Majorca in 1950 vacation village was started. Initially 2,500 vacationers slept in army tents. The staffs were trained to work as vacationer's friends and hosts rather than as hotel employees.

Recently, the activities in the villages are being diversified to resort type. Those countries which have tourist village remind of 'tent village' in Majorca.

Similarly, the tourist villages developed in the Australian Alps and Central Australian were the examples in this respect. A feasibility study report prepared for a new tourist village site of Yulara outside the National Park area is the development starting in Australia. Buildings and facilities for tourists were sited away from Ayers Rock and the Olgas outside the National Park. Park managers used to control the flows and tourist arrivals for the protection of park area.

The tourist village area provides all kinds of amenities from camping to interntional standard resort hotels. In this area, solar power, native plants are used in garden landscapping and the distinctive red sand colours of the desert have been used for helping the aesthetics of the buildings. Consequently, visitor employment and attraction, have been heightened by exploring untouched natural beauty in Australia (Jackson, 1997).

Located in Senegal, West Africa, Lower Casamance started village tourism in 1976. The clay house made but not accepted by tourists had no standard for accommodation. Despite, tourists stayed in camps for pleasure. Many officials and villages thought the lodging should be constructed of modern materials and be faciliated by hotel amenities. The first camp was made and opened for tourists in 1974. The initial four camps were completed by 1976.

The management of lodging designed camps for village tourism. Some of the guests staying at the beach resorts would take tours of the Casamance and make overnight stays. To diversify tourist markets, national tourism office encouraged travel agencies to sell tours that include the Casamance camps. Accommodation is limited to 20–30 beds in each camp. By the early 1990s, a considerable number of camps were developed in the name of village tourism. It started in practice camp in village or camping tourism in village.

Global Village and Global Tourism Village

Global Village

Tourism is a global product which has to be bought to please mind. Unlike manufactured products, we cannot buy hospitality but can see and feel it. The new technology can present to tourism customers 'virtual reality' of the tourism product on a computer.

The world people would like to know about others who are being separted by distance, they can form a good relationship in the form of a global village. This is a media – saturated world. Global village is an exciting place, a good place for people enjoying increased contact and increased involvement with one another aided by electronic technology. The world has been a single global village due to the advancement of communications. One can talk with other from one country to another within a minute. The electronic media would permit the 'human tribe' to make 'one family'. The global village is a world in which people encounter each other in depth all the time (Mc Luchan, 1967). The communication technologies permit people to become increasingly involved in other's lives. Thus, village tourism can connect with the whole world with the network of global village.

Global Tourism Village

Global tourism village is a new concept propounded by Dr Pradhanang with a view to heightening tourism villages of the world.

Geographically, all people are from a single origin. Today people cannot remain restless but they cannot live in a particular place for a long time. The world is one and same linked and united by Global tourism village force. It comes back from one to one is the philosophy of global tourism village. Going to the global from one to many and vice versa is its literature.

Conceptually, 'Global tourism village is the extension of world from one country's tourism village to other country's tourism village to develop village link with village people and village destinations, and to create a separate tourism village world as its new identity.' (Dr Pradhanang). The principle of global tourism village is to build 'one country one global tourism village'. To observe global tourism village, we have to click on travel and tourism agenda from village to village. Truly, global tourism village can be implicated to dehumanise and standardise the village people who live in. The idea of global tourism village provides the basis for developing villages as macro level in the international tourism market. Really, it will be a new tourism product in the history of tourism evolution. Villages we generally neglect will disappear when the global tourism society pushes up the bottom. Consequently, the social justice agenda for village might be opened forward. The widening disparity, between the village haves and have-nots is not desirable and the village gap in the world is extensively large. There is need of a separate tourism village conference in the world. Today we need representative and deliberative village. A chosen body of citizens of the countries of world whose patriotism and love of justice will be saved by developing global tourism village. The heavy migration shocked from village to city will be checked if global tourism village concept is considered. Included in every country's socio-economic development agenda, global tourism village can play the vital role in network preparation of world tourism *development* union. Each global tourism village exhibits countrywise tourism village from different parts of the world partially or fully. For example, global tourism village of Asia, North America, South & Central America, Western Europe, Eastern Europe, Australia & Pacific and Africa can be new and wonderful products introduced for world tourism development.

Despite the sophisticated life of many big cities, the erosion of village sovereignty loses its values in national representation and development. Village citizens have little need to examine their own biases and they should not be isolated in a village alone. China has more than a billion people living in more than a million hamlets, villages and cities. As the developed countries promote increasingly urbanised and large percentages of the population stay their daily lives in man-made environment, greater numbers of these city dwellers would seek natural settings for their leisure time (Jackson, 1997).

Hence,the concept of global tourism village represents the whole villages of the world it gives identity as a separate tourism village world to harmonise village power in the world.

Village Tourism Growth and Development in the World

Village tourism, developed in some parts of the world is limited to 'bed and break fast service'. It is narrowed down generally

Tharu Women

in deserts, rainforests, wetland regions, coastal sand dunes and other natural areas. It has spread in 25 countries, of which Nepal has a varied and distinct type of village tourism having its own style and concept. Thus Nepal's village tourism is very special in the map of village tourism.

Village tourism observed in the world is in the form of 'reservation camp' where indigeneous people are resided and displayed to visitors. Folk village in South Korea and Red Indian camp in USA are examples of ancient villages. The Folk village located at Suwan city is a preserved village that highlights the ancient culture of South Korea. There are other villages like Andung village and Jeju island.

Present Status of Village Tourism in the Interntional Tourism

Village tourism is adventure based tourism which is growing more popular day by day. People would like to experience new things. The world tourism is inclined to the adventure holiday.

Tourist Enjoying with Sages

Enjoying Stone-tap

That is why the position of village tourism in the international market is very high. Similarly, people seek free tension environment getting rid of humdrum of everyday life and start travelling to beautiful villages, beaches, mountains and scenic areas. People are also interested to know about the culture, lifestyle of the people, historical monuments, pilgrimage areas, museums, art gallarries and so on. All these desired products are endowed in village tourism.

The international travel and tourism in the world is in favour of recreation, adventure and culture. Today many countries of the world would enjoy and experience the progress made in post industrial society. The elasticity of demand for village tourism is positive. Consequently, it attracts more visitors in the international market. A large number of people would go for holiday and relaxation countinues for every year as vacation. The major vacation is chosen for a long distance for 2 week long holiday or more. This is the trend of world travel and tourism that can be occupied by village tourism.

South Asia Regional Economic Cooperation (in May 26, 2004) decided to develop village tourism in the region. For

Tourist Studying Lifestyle of Sages

common benefits of four member countries, Nepal, Bhutan, Bangladesh and India commited to its development. Likewise, Nepal–Japan AOTS Alumni Association Society organised the seminar cum workshop on village tourism development in Nepal in 2003 for participants from SAARC region. Dr Pradhanang highlighted Nepal's village tourism concept and its importance and encouraged and suggested it be adopted in the SAARC region. Kathmandu Research Centre (KRC) explored Nepal's village tourism concept in WTO Conference on Tourism Leaders of the World held at Osaka, Japan in 2002. In the same way, KRC exposed the village tourism concept in Matsumoto city, Japan and suggested to the Japanese intellectuals and government to develop Hakuba village as tourism village.

There are some tourism villages developed in the world such as Kawaza village tourism in Zambia and Daintree village on the bank of magnificent Daintree river and Mossmon river north of Cairns in Tropical North Queensland.

Foreign advisors came to Nepal from different countries

and officially stayed at UNDP, SNV, DFID, ICIMOD, Asian Development Bank, World Bank, Action Aid Nepal and so on. Those advisors who were surprised to see village tourism development in Nepal and learnt Nepal's village tourism concept and its modality. The foreign advisors instantly whitewashed Nepal's village tourism concept and its model and exported it to Sikkim, Vietnam, Lagos, Thailand, India, Bangladesh, Pakistan and so on. Village tourism started in those countries is the result of demonstration-effect of Nepal, which is a glory to Nepal and Nepali people.

Chapter 4

Concept of Village Tourism

INTRODUCTION

Tourist in village is village tourism. The perception, if agreed, is an appraisal that village tourism is a common thought of tourist going and coming to villages. Village is the common site, walking everytime and available everywhere in the world. But for relaxation in village and developing village economy, village tourism has the special meaning and importance.

Tourist staying in village has greater meaning to village tourism in real term. Village tourism starts from village stay concept. Village tourism is in favour of village stay tourism that explores the unknown things, endangered species, inexperienced adventures and never-imagined products hidden in village.

There are generally four attributes, viz., differentiation, uniqueness, speciality and peculiarity in village tourism.

Regarding the concept of village tourism some tourism experts and tourism related organisations defined it: 'Village tourism is known in WWF as the image of tourism expert Dr Surendra B. Pradhanang who has been advocating it for a long time. Though the concept seems to be interesting, the only example appears to be Sirubari, Syangja. In the opinion of Ukesh Bhuju replication will not be possible just anywhere. For the way the concept has been implemented in Sirubari, the whole community has to be mobilised and coordination and organisation capacity within the community must be very strong. Also the involvement of outsiders to handle the marketing of such a new product is inevitable.'

'The concept of village tourism is not well-defined in the documents of NTB. Mr Dangi and Mr Prasai see it as village based tourism benefiting the local population. At this moment the big and the only example is Sirubari village. The concept of home-stays as opposed to lodges is the central new product of this village. Tourists do not see local culture in lodges and local culture can be conserved in homestays.'

'In the opinion of SNV, the concept of village tourism in Nepal has become exemplified by Sirubari. Village tourism is now understood as tourism to local villages providing homestays and cultral shows. However, this example offers a very limited vision on tourism to villages and rural areas'.

The concept of village tourism emerged as Dr Pradhanang found in it seeds of scientific tourism, 23 years ago while he was working with National Development Service and providing social service for ten months at village. At that time anothropologists used to take the village for their research and the idea was born that scientists in some way are also tourists. This perception evolved over time in the concept of village tourism and the opportunities that it gives to rural economic development. In his perception, village tourism is grass root level tourism. The objective of village tourism is to enhance the economy of the village, utilisation of the village resources, development and promotion of handicrafts and to exchange and learn the knowledge views and culture from the tourists.

According to Bijaya Amatya, Marketing Manager of Yeti Travel Pvt Ltd, the concept of village tourism is still very new in our country. It needs to be watched. Whether it will be successful or not. In the perspective of Raijit Subha, Island Jungle Resort, 'Village tourism is a new and good concept of tourism, by which local people get immediate benefits. It however does not apply to hotels, but entails with homestays.' In the vision of Bhaskar Thapa, Programme officer Terai region, King Mahendra Trust for Nature Conservation, 'Village tourism is community managed, cultural and social comptible to local, traditions and benefits should go to the community.' In veiw of Tara Gurung, tourism officer, Annapurna Conservation Area Project, 'ACAP would think village tourism as tourism that brings proportionate equal benefits to a village. The concept is nice, but is difficult to implement because of the social structure of Nepali villages.' One of the Sirubari tourism village community members an ex-member of parliament and former employer of the ministry of tourism and civil aviation said, 'the development of tourism in the village started about two years back of tourism in January 1997. Through the ministry of tourism he had heard of the concept of Dr Surendra Bhakta Pradhanang, the academic inventor of the concept. Then the community of Sirubari itself brought up the idea of developing tourism in the village wih the concept of village tourism.' (Action Aid, Nepal, 1999).

Shankar Prasad Koirala, the joint secretary of Ministry of Culture,Tourism and Civil Aviation, HMG says, "Dr Surendra Bhakta Pradhanang is the father of village tourism. He came up with the concept of village tourism in village level, national level and international forum. Initially, we could not understand his concept due to the new concept introduced in Nepal. Consequently, we misunderstood him and conflict developed for a while' (Speech by Koirala in Book Release Programme, 2001).

Rajendra Bantawa, the former president of Trekking Agents Association of Nepal (TAAN) says, 'Village tourism is Dr Surendra Bhakta Pradhanang's brainchild and he propounded the concept of village tourism in Nepal. His mastermind on village tourism brought a revolution in the concept of tourism industry' (Bantawa, Comments on Village Tourism, 1999).

By definition, 'Village tourism is a grassroot level of tourism designated at its own Nepali village style, mobilized by Nepali people themselves, their skill and resources displayed as village lifestyle and environment, involved by groups of village tourists, assigned by Nepali adult authorities positively within its balance of social and environmental function and strengthened the village and village economy' (Dr Pradhanang, 1992).

In other words, village tourism is a common bridge in between domestic tourism and international tourism industry.

In fact, it is an integrated approach on tourism development. Village tourism is a major component of scientific tourism that creates the self-sustaining and self-standing economy. It is a process of rooted tourism germinating its seed under the ground. To view the nature and complexity, village tourism is a non-foreign aid requiring concept.

Obviously, village tourism is an economic plan for developing village economy. It is based on low investment and high productivity theory.

As far as the focus of Nepalese tourism is concerned, the villages have an important role as every expedition team has to go through the villages in their bid to reach the peaks that they have the aim of scaling. The villages are the places where the expedition teams interact with local people. However, the villages in the past had not received any benefit as the expedition teams had their own porters, cooks and path finders and whatever they required.

To remove this anomaly the concept of village tourism came to the fore. Dr Surendra Bhakta Pradhanang, a propounder of village tourism has been working over the years for promoting tourism industry in Nepal especially with regard to 'low investment, maximum return' village tourism. The concept of village tourism has gained weightage in Nepal during the past decade.

The focus has been on the villages for tourism promotion because the majority of the people live in villages and Nepal as a country is host to diversity in culture and tradition from one area to another and, thereby it has the essential ingredients to attract tourtists.

Dr Pradhanang considers village tourism concept as a new economic model of Nepal that aims and challenges at focussing on the villages as a means and opportunity to uplift the living standard of the local people through their mobilisation in tourist related activities. He also says that the investments are very low unlike in the tourism flourishing now with big hotels and big money on décor and other things.

The villages themselves have been the inspiration to see that they become more prosperous. Looking in other things the villages could be developed to attract foreign visitors who want a taste of the original culture, tradition and an informal interaction with the local people. Dr Pradhanang says, 'Nepalese village is the second heaven in the earth we can enjoy, see, touch and experience in live. The first heaven which we imagine is very far and may or may not be experienced after death.'

Every village has its own uniqueness that can benefit it economically. But the potentials have been realised but not tapped so far. And it is this very potentials that must be tapped so that the socio-economic conditions of the local people can be enhanced in the context. A significant percentage of the people get their basic needs fulfilled.

When the villagers themselves generate employment through village tourism, two objectives can be achieved. First their prosperity is guaranteed and secondly, the gifts endowed by Nature and the world famous hospitality of the Nepalese can be enjoyed by the visitors, he stresses.

He further says that the village tourism concept was formally recognised in 1995. It was also included in the Ninth Plan with a budgetary allocation of NRS 4 million in 1997. It has to be considered us a golden plan or the new inventory plan. The real recognition came in 2004.

For any new concept to gain acceptance is not easy. This is especially true when the concept comes in conflict with the established pattern and amidst a lack of understanding by the existing stakeholders. This may be the late acceptable reason for the village tourism concept.

The tourism entrepreneurs now realise that as urban tourism is viable, village tourism too can make significant contributions. It has 'both forward/backward linkages' and that is considered as its main benefit. It can also be said it is 'one to all concept' totally organised, managed and operated by villagers and their associated bodies and, hence, no foreign aid and assistance from outside is necessary except the initial theoretical preparation. It is 'self-sustaining and self-motivation'.

He further says that if properly developed, village tourism can contribute 40 per cent to the Gross Domestic Product (GDP) considering the fact that at present only 15 per cent of the tourist expenditure go to the villages which is an unequal distrubution of tourism earnigns. The villagers hardly get anything.

Once the economic condition improves it can lead to the end of violence and conflict. If there is job or work and the returns it will lead to an end of violence because of the prosperity it offers and set up peace in the environment. It also means that we do not have to talk of poverty alleviation in isolation. An economic growth will naturally lead to an end to economic disparity with village tourism concept implementation, Dr Pradhanang asserts.

Now 50 villages are being developed according to village tourism concept and more than 25 village tourism development committees have been formed. The successful village to operate according to concept is Sirubari in Panchamool Village Development Committee of Syangja district in Gandaki zone. It is Gurung settlement with a population of 600. Its success story is interesting enough as the statistics reveal (TRN, 2005).

Chapter 5

Scope of Village Tourism

Village tourism, as we understand it today, is a village first concept. In the eye of tourism, the world has been small. Due to the advancement of information and technology, everyone is nearer and dearer from one place to other. We can see the world in the map very near and travel for pleasure and knowledge is also tabulated.

Village has greater scope in international and domestic tourism. It creates several economic activities in the world. It is a smokeless industry without chimneys that generates more income and employment opportunities.

Subject Matter of Village Tourism

Village tourism has a subject matter of its own. The subject matter of village tourism is widened from its definition given. Village tourism studies village and villagers of every country of the world. How to utilise village resources and skill for the development of tourism in village or local level is its scope. The basic subject matter of village tourism is to develop village economy. It teaches villagers to mobilise village resources, village culture and tradition as village tourism products. It is also concerned with conservation of nature and environment.

Village Tourism Activities

We see village world and village tourism activities around us. Tourism activities concern with village tourism related works in different fields, viz.; rafting, trekking, mountaineering, poultry farming, handicraft production, food and lodging. When the people are working in tourism activities, they earn money. There will be different business in tourism sector. Village households promote tourism accommodation.

A village will be active as a host destination. It will be economic place for business activities. A villager will be an economic man who starts earning only when he will come under the circumference of village tourism industry. This is what we say the subject matter of village tourism.

To sum up, villager-village-village economy leads village development in village level or a grass root level.

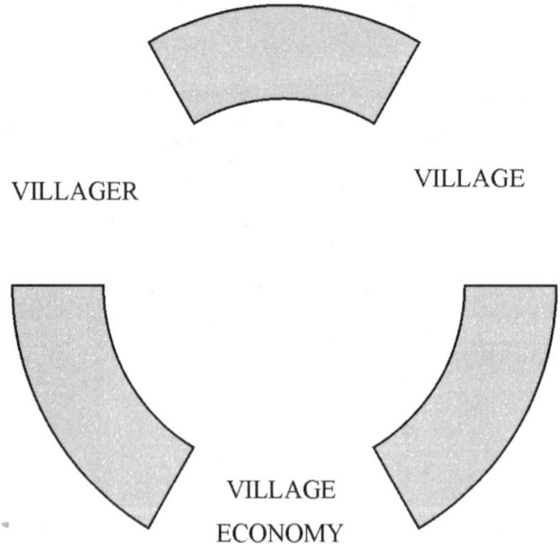

Figure 1: *Village-Villager-Village Economy Relationship*

The Figure 1 exhibits Village-Villager-Village Economy relationship. The economic development starts from the attraction of village and then villager's effort continues for utilisation of village resources and skills. On the ground of effort, village economic development takes place as an ultimate satisfaction. Hence, they have a good relationship with one to another.

The diagram shows tourism activities around the circle. By function, the interrelationship among village, villager and village economy is activised. When village tourism starts earning, wage, rent, interest and profit will be accumulated. They are determined under tourism activity. Then the subject matter of village tourism shifts to tourist consumption, production and distribution.

Hence, the basic subject matter of village tourism is 'Family values' in the village society. The subject, village tourism is concentrated on village which is a part of economics, viz.; price theory or microeconomics. But in the age of globalization, the scope or the subject matter of village tourism is very wide in terms of factors like national income, saving, investment, general price level, output, employment and so on. All these combined together show macroeconomics. Thus we study streamlines of economics both microeconomics and macroeconomics. But in the modern age of tourism, microeconomics is underlined on village tourism development while macroeconomics is on the front line of tourism development as a whole. We give the new creation in the economy as tourism economics in macro level.

Most recently, economists are concerned with the model of economic development with respect to the economic growth theory. It is subject under discussion how the underdeveloped countries get progress into developed economies and the developed economics get progress into boom. Economics is, therefore, the study of economic growth.

In the subject matter of tourism economics, village tourism development in micro level is very important while distribution of income, income and employment theory and economic growth theory are further significant in macro level of economics.

Scope of Village Tourism

The scope of village tourism is very wide and important to national development. The scope enlarges more in development and expansion of tourism in village level.

Basically, the scope of village tourism is relatively widened with the following considerations:

1. The subject matter of village tourism
2. Village tourism is a social science
3. Village tourism is a natural science and art.

Village Tourism–A Social Science

Village tourism studies village and villager. It attracts village tourists who want village environment, village culture, village nature, village sight seeing and so on. It also concerns with the ethnic group of people in the community. Thus village tourism is a social science that makes up the economy as a whole. Tourism village cannot remain isolated, but it is linked with the society for its benefits.

Village Tourism–A Natural Science or Art

A science is a systematised body of knowledge. Some facts collected and analysed result into cause and effect. For instance, a rise in price of the international ticket results generally in decrease in demand of tourism. There is a high correlation between price and demand which shows cause and effect in tourism business. The 'cause and effect relationship' is a natural science. The law or general principle governs the facts of the science. Science shows the common principle of cause and effect that guides tourism business. Village tourism is concerned with the natural art too.

The scope of village tourism and village tourism economics is very advanced subject widening a broader field of science and art. By nature, it is a field of never-ending and ever-growing concept.

Undoubtedly, village tourism provokes village and villager in relation to nation's benefit and development as a whole. It explores village and villager's values to the tourism world. Similarly, it starts research and discovers natural truths with social obligations and a code of conduct and judges what is right and wrong to be practiced in the village society and nation as a whole. Hence, village tourism is both normative science and positive science.

The scope of village tourism widening in the world in the global tourism village. Today the whole world is coming under the umbrella of global village. Due to the invention of aeroplanes and jambu jets, the world has been very close. A person can have his breakfast in New York, lunch in Tokyo and dinner in Kathmandu. The concept of travel and tourism has been penetrated in the society. The industrial revolution made a wonderful change in human lifestyle. Every company of the business world globally initiates to travel at least once a year in the world. Today travel and tourism is in boon all over the world. Every year 5,000 million people take holiday trips in the world. Of these, 698 million people travelled in 2000 exceeding 7.4 per cent as growth rate over 1999. Furthermore, international tourists spent US$ 476 billion on travel and tourism that was 4.5 per cent growth over 1999. World Tourism Organisation (WTO) estimated international tourist arrivals increase by 1600 million by 2020. The growth of tourism industry generates more new employment opportunities in the village and township. Consequently, the people of the world are coming and living together with one other. But it is not possible, if there is no peace in the world. Disturbance of peace hurts or damages international tourism industry as we witnessed the negative impact of Gulf War in 1991, American war on Afghanistan in 2001 and Maoist's people war in Nepal (1996-2006).

Chapter 6

Relation with Economics, History, Anthropology, Politics, Sociology, Culture and Agriculture

Village tourism has a good relation with different fields of subject concerned with the well being of people and society. It is a micro-component in the structure of the national development planning and politico-culture consciousness.

Village Tourism and Sociology

Here we find a relation between village tourism and sociology. The discipline of sociology is the study of companions related with what goes on when people get together in groups and discuss with one another. Talking about rural or village sociology, the study of rural sociology goes back to the origin of society itself. Whatever advanced societies we have, whether US or UK, they originated from the base of village society. Gradually village society turned into city, mega city and metropolitan community.

Today the world is very ambitious to study village life. It can be looked forward through the means of village tourism concept. Thus there is a positive correlation between village tourism and sociology. Village tourism is a new natural science that grows interest among social thinkers and planners today. Village tourism highlights the significance of village society pointing out ancient law and ancient society in the tourism world with full of enthusiasm and zeal. Village tourism and village social life trace out the picturesque of grass root people living in highlands, forests and small villages.

Village Tourism and Economics

Village tourism and economics are closely attached with one another. All social and national issues come from economic crises. Every one needs money as income more at hand. The deprived and marginalised groups of people are in hue and cry for their economic benefits. The unequal distribution of wealth is the cause of poverty. Village tourism is the backbone of national economy.

Tourism contributes more to national economy. Tourism contributes more in national income by balancing regional economic growth. Village tourism provides tourism economic activities in village level and strengthens village economy through employment and income generation.

Hence, village tourism has a positive correlation with economics, which is very important signal for national development.

Village Tourism and Politics

Village tourism and politics have a good relationship. All political constraints and problems are due to lack of an appropriate plan and strategy for national development. Basically, in most countries of the world the development plans are highly focused on the city. They ignore village areas development. That is why there is a conflict in politicians. One sided plan in the name of national planning cannot be accepted by all people. The fruit of development plan should be equally distributed to all. Thus the political leaders would come forward for people oriented plan and strategy. Politics plays the vital role in this respect and draws the essentials of the people and country. Village tourism, being the village related concept, pushes up village politics and political leaders in far oar of village development. Thus village tourism has a good relation with politics.

Village Tourism and History

Village tourism is concerned with the history of human civilisation. Man has a long history with different lifestyles and living standards. Village tourism explores the history of groups of people in the society. In village tourism the historical background of various ethnic groups of people are considered as a major part and an attraction too. By evolution, man himself forgot his nature set up by his ancestors. Village tourism always deals with the background history of man. History is very useful and relative subject to the development of village tourism. Village tourism will be incomplete unless it discusses the history of man and earth. Hence, village tourism cannot be fruitful unless it touches upon the history.

Village Tourism and Anthropology

Village tourism and anthropology are two related subjects of big pillars of society. Anthropology relates to the knowledge about human beings in society. It is in fact, a study of comparison of cultural and social life of people. Village tourism displays the lifestyle and social behaviour of group of people as village tourism product as well as tourism attraction while anthropology initiates and invites people for observation of those attractions in the field or tourist destination. It is very difficult to define anthropology in words but it has to be experienced in practicality through observation and destination visit. Basically, social anthropology accounts for various ways of human existence and interrelationships as village or a colony. It is, in other words, a comparative micro society of social system and human relationship. Relatively, village tourism and anthropology have the basic agenda of culture. There is a good relationship between them.

Village Tourism and Culture

Village tourism and culture are highly related with each other. Village tourism plays as the best actor of culture. The cultural environment plays the vital role in the society. The cultural pattern forms a wonderful behaviour which indirectly selects the high quality of unique personality.

Village society with village culture forms a very common society which is much closer to nature. Village people have different festivals, fairs, folksongs and folktales that have all resemblance of their agriculture. The folk-literature in the world is very rich and heart touching. In Nepal, village has a wonderful village folk-literature that is the treasure house of village and ancestors. The simple nature of village folks shows a manifestation in folk-literature.

Similarly, the tribal villages are also important products for village tourism development. The presentation of folk-songs and folk-dances of tribal villages brings the mastermind of art and literature in the field of culture. It enhances village tourism and village culture side by side.

Village Tourism and Agriculture

Village tourism and agriculture are also related subjects in the tourism development in village level. In fact, agriculture is the main occupation of villagers and the major source of village income. Since village tourism development is as our national strategy in terms of poverty alleviation and economic development, problems in agriculture should be eliminated as far as practicable.

Village tourism and agriculture should go together hand in hand. The development of village tourism will automatically promote agriculture. The agricultural output has to be used in village tourism industry as village tourism product. By promotion of agriculture, green revolution in village can be planned as the best strategy for increasing national productivity and economic development. Tourists enjoy to watch rice plantation by villagers and also would take interest to participate in this event.

Importance of Village Tourism

Village tourism is useful to all sectors. It plays a vital role in the village economy as well as national economy. Nepal is in front line of developing village tourism business. It is the village based invisible export industry, which creates direct and indirect job opportunities for a large number of people. It generates earnings for several people categorised into various occupations, viz.; village milkmen, village flute-players, village masters, craftmen, farmers, travel agents, trekking agents, tour operators, transport agencies, trekking and village guides, airlines, shoemakers, souvenir-sellers, curio shops, handicraft producers, etc. The benefits to village and villager are shared by all. Tourism has gradually transformed the impoverished and backward village into a prosperous and forward looking village.

Tourism can yield more revenue. Village young boys and girls can get job opportunities to earn more. By human nature, people normally do not like to miss travel opportunity so that they travel at least once in a year. Village tourism can grasp this opportunity to attract tourists from different countries of the world. Tourism, being the mobile industry, does not go into recession even at the time of recessionary period of economy.

We have village tourism that has theoretical, practical and developmental importance discussed below:

Theoretical Importance

Village tourism has theoretical importance. It teaches villagers to deal with village tourists coming from different parts of the world. They can understand people's desire and interest in tourism business. As a result, villagers can successfully handle village tourism business. Theoretically, village tourism makes people skilled in human communication and behaviour.

Tourism Awareness

Village tourism makes people more aware of tourism business. Tourism, being the people's hospitality industry has to create village as a best tourism destination. How to attract people at the places is the moot question all should take answer. Hence, it is tourism business that makes people more aware. Tourism is not the story of king Midas's power of golden touch, but it is the touch that practically concentrates on hospitality service and creates opportunities for attraction and satisfaction.

Understanding Village Tourism

The study and implication of village tourism can be understood by village people. How to run village tourism industry in village has to be known by the village people. Village tourism business can be smoothened when it starts with its mechanism. Gradually, village tourism system adjusts in villages of Nepal.

Mutual Benefit

Village tourism provides mutual benefit to villagers. It is the village associated industry benefiting the community. The economic activities in village will be run through several tourism services and products presented to tourists. This function creates more jobs and income to villagers.

Tourism Minded People

The study of village tourism makes people more conscious at the grass root level. Even small children can easily understand the importance of village tourism. The economic problem of the village and national level can be solved through village tourism development. The villager can realise in time that village tourism is an appropriate economic instrument for village development. Either a student of tourism or a tourism entrepreneur can get knowledge on village tourism. The knowledge of village tourism pushes up everyone in the village to do work for village as an obligation.

Practical Importance

Village tourism has greater practical value in society. It is a science studied closely about life and lifestyle.

Useful to Professionals

Village tourism has greater professional values to several grades of professional. In fact, village tourism is useful to businessmen, agriculturists, barbers, trekking agencies, industrialists, business entrepreneurs and so on. Everyone can multiply one's business smoothly. Tourist money creates multiplier effects in all professions related directly and indirectly.

Household in Village Tourism

Village household can actively get involved in village tourism development. Village household itself can be a good tourism product in developing village tourism. The indigenous household of different communities can be modeled as typical accommodation centre for village tourists. The rational that household can get benefit from village tourism in village is derived from this. Every household can meet its expenditure from village tourism development.

Useful to Village Leader/Social Mobiliser

Every village leader as well as social mobiliser can lead villagers towards the objective of developing village tourism industry in village. Village tourism being based on public welfare theory can drive village people into the right path of development. Village leader and social mobiliser ought to think of villager's problems and constraints. Most importantly, village youth requires job opportunities to meet their expenditure and livelihood. That is why village leader can tackle the issues and create environment to involve in village tourism industry for upliftment of village economy.

Development Importance

The concept of village tourism has a special place in the development concept. The development is the buzz word used for welfare of mankind. Everyone works for development and everyone talks for progress. The effort what we make today is for national development in the macroeconomic model. We need development strategy and plan to meet our goal. In this development aspect, first comes the developing country which requires socio-economic progress. The major problem of developing country is poverty, unemployment, low living standard and low income level. These issues can be solved through the implication of village tourism. A majority of poor living in villages is necessary to follow up this national strategy. Hence, village tourism can be a determinant factor for development.

Proletarian Class of People

Most cultures have ideas of rich and poor and middle that do not generally conform to simple population distribution.

Talking about the proletarian class of people, the labour or worker is the proletariat, who includes any body and exists through his / her livelihood by selling his / her labour power and is being paid a wage or salary for labour time.

Village tourism, protecting proletarian class of people, is not a threat to any capitalism nor other systems of societal domination. It is a kind of struggle for income and employment generation even for the common class of people which hardly threatens the status quo. In other words, it is for the economic struggle for all categories of people particularly working class.

The term, proletariat was extracted from Latin Proles, offspring and used to identify a lower social class. A member of such a class is proletarian. Originally, it was explained as those people who had no wealth other than their sons. Initially, it was used in a derogatory sense until Karl Marx used referring to the 'working class'.[1]

In the Marxist theory, the proletariat is that class of society which does not have ownership of the means of production. Proletarians are wage-workers or salariats. However, wage labour may involve in getting a salary rather than a wage per se.

The proletariat is the object of history as it is its labour that shapes the world's history.

Here this author uses the proletarian class of people for those village people who are economically poor and socially backward and who are unable to grasp the opportunities in economic activities for their income and employment generation and living standard. For economism of villages and villagers, village tourism is a must.

Importance for Proletarian Class of People

Village tourism progressively proclaims as a developmental factor, which is good to proletarian class of people. It assists and protects the grass root level people for their livelihood by generating income and employment opportunities. Land, utilized for industrialisation, is going down as scarce commodity day by day. The high technology adopted in agriculture is beneficial to only big peasants. Consequently, the small peasants are out of reach to meet technicality in agriculture. This situation has compelled the poor peasantry to remain as simple agriculture labour, wage earner and wage paid worker. They remain below poverty line. The common persons living in the village are proletarian class. The slogan-land to the tiller coming from the proletarian class of people may cause conflict and violence to the affluent societies. The voice raised by marginal land holders and small farmers can disturb the national political economy.

Under these circumstances the plight of village proletarians requires an appropriate development strategy and plan for their livelihood. The economic development scheme we apply should be addressed most effectively and applicably to the problems of village proletarians. Hence, the implication of concept of village tourism can safeguard and generate income and employment in village. In the developing countries of Asia, Africa, and Latin America a new strategy of village agriculture development has emerged. All these countries involved in the emergence of nation-building are achieving the developmental objectivity. Thus village sociologists, economists, tourism experts, and anthropologists are urged to pay deeper considerations in this regard. As a matter of fact, village tourism industry is the study and implication for grass root people as proletarian class living in highlands, hillocks, forests and small villages.

Importance for Village/Villager

Village tourism is blessing of nature and it is for village and villager. It is the natural product that can be a natural tourist destination where villagers themselves can be the hero of village development. It can also be displayed as a separate model of development area.

The power of village can be disseminated to village people themselves, if they are productive. Today the sole economic and political power which is at the hand of landlord can slowly go down of common villagers' hand. The history of village development programme is very long. But the development fruit could not have reached at the hand of village people. The real development in the life of villagers could not have harvested at all.

The study of village environment is no longer a common theme, it is the subject of the full of natural life, hills, forests, streams, rivers, folk-lores and folk tales. The village land tilled commonly produces the output which is divided among members of the village community. Similarly, spanning and weaving work is done by each family as subsidiary industry.

The village has its own special environment endowed with different cultures and systems. The chief inhabitant works as judge, the holy Brahmin holds talk on religion and the calendar-Brahmin (astrologer) tells about good luck and bad luck. This type of environment we see in the natural village is a wonderful tradition for today's modern society. The village uniqueness can be nicely presented as village speciality to those tourists who would come as holiday makers. Hence, village tourism provides greater importance to village and villager.

Importance to Nation

A country's responsibility is to uplift villages that seem as its own organs of the body. In quest of basic needs, people are in demand of consumption goods and services. The basic necessities consist of food, clothes, water and health care, without which people cannot survive. When any one of them is absent, the country is said to be in absolute under-development.

Development is a value-quoted concept that reveals opening up the potential powers implied a change at the desirable place and time. The cultural milieu may be valued at different degrees of acceptance. At best, development conceptualised as a set of desirable societal objectivity and value is cherished by each individual and community in a special way. The village development connotes small farmers, tenants and the landless villagers. It represents the whole villages of the nation, which should understand the implication of village tourism as time based strategy.

References

1. Wikipedia, *The Free Encyclopedia*, 2005.

Chapter 7

Need of Village Tourism

As already mentioned, at present the need of village tourism is unquestionable. Tourists are attracted to natural villages where the beauty of nature can be tasted. Due to industrial revolution, the economic power of people has increased. As a result, millions of tourists are spending holidays in different places like resorts, mountain treks, wildlife jungles, etc. considering this trend, village tourism has to be tapped.

Tourism Village Development

Tourism is the fastest growing industry leading to a great boom. But mass tourism development damages environment. Environmentally, the earth is for everyone's need but not for everyone's greed. Village tourism in its environment is nature based and culture based. Naturally gifted village tourism development is an emerging sector for village tourists. All these tourism products such as prestine natural areas, unique man-made environments cultural heritages are valued. The mandate given by village tourism is to enjoy village as the best tourist destination and make it more presentable as evergreen tourism industry for many young adventure tourists.

Demographically, Nepal is a country of villages, where 3912 VDCs are lying as ideal aggregate of villages. Today we need to turn those villages into tourism economic villages. Nepal is enriched in resources having bio-diversity in nature and diversity in culture. God seems to have spent His time and effort

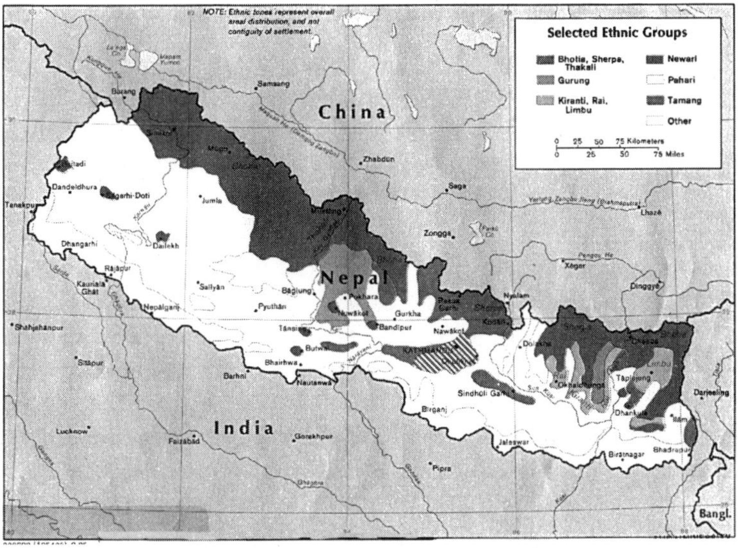

Map of Nepal by Major Ethnic Groups

to make Nepal as a number one natural superdeluxe destination in the earth. The creativity of Nepalese village calculated into economic values will be hundred times greater than the riches collected by USA. As per the demographic position of the country, village tourism strategy should be adopted. Geographically, Nepal is the land locked country. Nepalese leaders and even government tend to reiterate that due to land lockedness, the country remains underdeveloped. Land lockedness by nature is the creativity of God as a uniqueness for village tourism development in Nepal. Village tourism development concept, using those natural uniqueness and attraction in terms of Nepal's land lockedness creates a land of pleasant destination in the world where tourists can accommodiate with pleasure, relaxation, adventure and above all, tourism village brand. God laid down the knotted bag full of gold, jewellery and diamond at the walking road, Nepalese struck at it thought to be an accident but could not recognise what it really is. This is village tourism – the optimistic tool of management in distribution of wealth from city to village and rich to poor.

Identity of Tourism Village Attraction

Today the world tourism market is getting on by leaps and bounds. The qualitative tourists would not like to look upon the modern buildings cemented. The tourism environment has to be out of dusty, dirty and smoking placement.

Nepal focused as village Nepal is due to its occupied by 0.1 per cent on world map. Village Nepal has 2 per cent of all the flowering plants in world, 8 per cent of the world's population of birds (more than 848 species), 4 per cent of mammals on earth, 11 of the world's 15 families of butterflies (more than 500 species). Furthermore, it has 600 indigenous plant families and 319 species of exotic orchids. Nepal has a variety of village based adventure and it is trekker's paradise preferred by adventure seekers. The physical feature of Nepal is a composition of mountains, hills and terai. The distribution of land is as 15 per cent (220281 sq kilometers) occupied by Himalaya, 68 per cent (100080 sq kilometers) by hill and 17 per cent (25620 sq kilometers) occupied by terai. Nepal has a total area of 147181 sq kilometers land. Trekking in Nepal is experienced in terms of cultural and natural values with the Himalayan villages and views. One who passes mountains can see charming villages such inhabited by various diverse ethnic groups of people. Landscape and ethnicity vary from land to land, mountain to mountain and village to village. The world's highest peak Mt. Everest (8848 meter) is in Nepal is a major attraction. Likewise, jungle safari holiday is next interesting tourism activity. There are ten National Parks listed as Royal Chitwan National Park, Royal Bardiya National Park, Sagarmatha National Park, Langtang National Park, Rara National Park, Shey-Phoksundo National Park, Khaptad National Park, Makalu-Barun National Park, Shivapuri National Park and Royal Suklaphanta National Park in Nepal. A close-up view of the top of the world, Everest can be seen from various parts. The magnificent views of Mt. Everest, Annapurna peak and many other beautiful peaks are so panoramic that act in their own way to promote village tourism.

Nepal has more than 102 ethnic groups of people living in different villages of Nepal. The ethnic groups are village attractions which can be promoted to tourism village such as Tamang village, Sherpa village, Newar village, Magar village, Gurung village, Rai village, Tharu village, Rajbansi village, Satar village, etc. We can create 'Mini Nepal' as composition of various ethnic groups of people. Since Nepalese village is not homogeneous, a cluster of village is quite different from one to other.

For example, Nar and Phu villages of Manang district come forward as distinct villages. A trek to Nar and Phu is nearly a 12 days walk from Bisisahar.

Village view

The trek can be carried out in summer and autumn seasons. Nar and Phu located at an attitude of 4240 meter and 4190 meter respectively. These villages are known as the 'Village of monasteries' certainly, village tourist would like them very much.

Mobilization of Tourism Village Resources

Considerably, village tourism is a specific factor in a number of historical, physical, social and cultural factors of development. The village areas, if carefully planned into village tourism destinations, can be the revenue villages. Villages within forest

Unique Picturesque of Village

areas popularised by identity brand are systematically spelled out, tourism village will be more saleable in the tourism market.

In the course of village tourism development, a network of mobilisation of village resources has to be worked out. It should include rivers, forests, herbs, lands, villages, bamboos, lakes, temples, mountains and so on. Forest as a village tourism product can be used for tourist attraction. Forest is a renewable resource utilised for villager's livelihood. Bamboo is utilised for producing souvenior goods and weighted measurement tools as Manapathi. For instance, Pyanjgaun (Pyanj village) located at Lalitpur district is popular for bamboo products. This village can be capitalised by developing tourism village. Pyanjgaun, a bamboo product centre can be illustrated as a model for village resource mobilisation village. The river or river village (Kalkale village) can be utilised for generating micro hydropower and for operating water mill, saw mill, rice mill and so on.

Lakes located at village can be promoted as tourism product for boating and fishing. Tourists enjoy different village indigenous products. Land can be utilised for horticulture and sheep farming. 'Autography of rice' as a mobilisation of tourism village resource can be exhibited as an interesting village product. The process of rice production as from seedling, planting, reaping, banding, drying to storing can be an exhibition to tourists. The agriculture calendar operation has to be introduced for enhancing this product. Similarly, a show of the mother has taking care of her chicks can be displayed as village product. It is the matter of surprise to watch loving young chickens nursed by their mother-hen. There is hen-house to sleep, hen-coop to live and hen-ground to play in village house and its ground. This is very simple village product, but it has deeper love hidden as the bird family. Of course, tourists enjoy the live picture of mother-hen and her chicks. Likewise, bannana village, corn village, orange village, apple village, etc. can be developed and promoted by extending village products. As the study conducted and observed by KRC in the United States of America, 96 per cent American people would prefer bannana to eat. Hence, for example, the bannana village may be a good tourism village in practice.

Boosting Village Economy

The stress given to the development of village economy is the wave of political and economic thought in the developing countries. Nepal has adopted village tourism industry as a leading economic plan and strategy for national development. Today national planners or developers have to pay attention to the domain of village tourism.

The best economy refers to the position held in a country where goods are produced and people are employed with fair wages and salaries. There will be overwhelming the source of employment and production in the national economy. People work, earn and raise their living standard in the developed economy when they are satisfied with their professions. Thus village economy has to be promoted through agricultural outputs which should be marketed in terms of export promotion business. Today we are attaining to the modern economy with the fittest economic model. As per the soil of the country, Nepal has adopted tourism economy suited to the environment.

In the quest of democracy, village tourism provides tourism democracy to all people including villagers who can start tourism in accordance with their capacity. Village tourism, being a labour intensive technique, provides job opportunities to all villagers in the village. The national income has to be distributed to all. It has to be distributed on the basis of the Marxian principle 'from each according to his ability, to each according to his needs'. But the principles of equity and human justice should be followed in distribution of national product.

To boost up the village economy the national economic policy is essential to be moulded in dualistic economy giving priority to villages of Nepal where 84.4 per cent of the total population live. The bottom up economic policy is viable to operate as development strategy. In other words, the 'trickle down' principle is better to implicate to boosting up village economy.

Tourism Village as a Common Global Travel Agenda

Tourism village development as a common global travel agenda is concerned with the developing countries as a whole. Every nation must think to develop village as tourist destination, but the question is how village can be developed as 'tourism village'.

Every National Tourist Organisation has to be alerted in developing tourism village. It should make strategy to include village tourism for village development as well as balanced economy. Besides, travel agencies have to promote this product in travel agenda for package tour. In 1841, Thomas Cook started travel agenda as a package tour. In the same way, this moment New Thomas Cook ought to start village tourism package tour as a special travel agenda in the world. The village tourism market has to be extensively broadened for its development. This is demand push tourism which should be desired by tourists. Demand for village tourism has to be elastic. For example, demand for village tourism in Nepal seems positive. After the successful implementation of Sirubari tourism village in Syangja district, several international and domestic tourist tasted tourism village and learnt what village tourism is. Likewise, several planners, developers, tourism experts, tourism entrepreneurs, government agencies, non-governmental organisations, Action Aid Nepal, UNDP, SNV, DFID and many other national and international intellectuals visited and experienced Sirubari tourism village. Now is the high time to start supply push tourism village in Nepal. The villagers of Nepal, local governments (VDCs), intellectuals and tourism entrepreneurs have to come forward for enhancing village tourism as a global travel and tourism agenda.

Chapter 8

Supremacy of Village Tourism

Village tourism has higher degree of supremacy in its concept and operation. It holds 'village first' principle that guides the people and country to right direction. 'Save your origin and originality' is the message provided by the concept to the modern world. It provides greater values to village and villager empowering them for today's modern civilisation and development. That the history of mankind and his society existed in village is obvious.

Here is supremacy of village tourism in terms of natural face vs ugly face and natural development vs ugly development. We see make-up appearance as modern culture and modernisation, but it is not natural. In addition, there is conflict created between natural process and artificial process and organic product and inorganic product. Nepal is rightly focused as village Nepal that has the wonderful representation of natural life and its own values to modern life of the people.

On the other side, the beauty of village tourism is to create tourism democracy providing equal opportunities to all the people including low income groups of people. It provides tourism business environment to those villagers who are deprived of tourism benefits.

Growth of a Simple Self-Sustained Economy

Village tourism develops self-sustaining economy. The consumption goods used in daily life will be mostly local products. Villagers generally get involved in agriculture and allied activities such as animal husbandry, crop husbandry, dairying, forestry, poultry, fisheries, and so on. The non-agricultural sub-sector follows small and cottage industry, village industry, handicraft, etc. Similarly, village business refers to trading of common goods, micro enterprises, petty trades and small shops. The service sector refers to transport, communication, banking, marketing of farm and non-farm products. The major stakeholders of village are farmers, traders, moneylenders and labourers.

Village tourism gives stress to produce more in village and generally pushes up the village people to stand on the self-sustained economy. The village skill and village product have to go together side by side. The domestic goods produced within the country should be prioritised to consume. Basically, the village products have to be listed by the name as a special product of village. The imported goods are discouraged. The glamour of urban life has to be stopped into village life. A code of village tourism is necessary to rule over the village and villager. Pollution free environment has to be maintained for incoming tourists. The Village Tourism Development Committee (VTDC) and village government, VDC have to be

Beauty of Riverside view

responsible for aggregate demand for consumption. The distribution and production system should be well balanced for village tourism development.

In village consumption pattern of goods and services, the international village tourists are free to have their choice for their entertainment and the system of self-participatory consumption. This system will be launched as a new village tourism programme introduced in the village environment. Milking cows, granding oilseeds, growing apples in the tree, reaping crops and picking up maizes are the village activities relating to self-sustaining economy.

Agro-Tourism Development

Agro-tourism is a new terminology used in village tourism. In village tourism, agriculture is a major activity followed by village people. 65.7 per cent of the population are involved in agriculture. Thus agriculture is termed as the backbone of Nepalese economy. The role of agriculture in village tourism cannot be minimised nor can it be kept in isolation. Village tourism without agriculture is not possible. Due to the lack of clear-cut strategy in agriculture, its productivity is low. 'A progressively agricultural country is unprogressive even in its agriculture' (Galbrath). Hence, agriculture linked with village tourism is the best stretegy for development.

We have a long experience that agriculture alone cannot boost up national development. Every year in the annual budget National Planning Commission gave the high priority to agriculture, but its development is minimal.

'Agro-tourism is defined as a branch of village tourism linked with agriculture in order to show its consequence as high output and productivity to both tourism and agriculture sectors in terms of national income, employment and development' (Dr Pradhanang, 1998).

The agriculture sector with new farm inputs and services merging with non-agriculture sector – village tourism creates high output in agriculture and tourism. Today we should think in dynamic way that agriculture cannot develop in isolation. It needs the development partner. The establishment of micro and less capital intensive industrial enterprises along with new technology in agriculture in village establishes linkages between agriculture and tourism industry. The strategy adopted by Israel in integrating agricultural and industrial sectors is a good example. In Israel, industrial enterprises were eastablished in villages along with the application of new agricultural technology. At the outset, the industrial enterprises started services and industries with agriculture as agro based industries such as production of tools and various accessories, cottage, tiny, village and small scale manufacturing and agro-processing industries.

Farm planning with respect to village tourism should be considered. The plan has to consist of improved seeds, fertilisers, pesticides, water management and improved implements. Micro planning in agriculture in connection with village tourism is essentially a new step in order to develop agro-tourism. It is an interdisciplinary approach. The technical agricultural scientists, viz., the agronomist, the horticulturist, the agricultural engineer, the social scientist and the village tourism specialist have to urge the agro-tourism concept as far as practicable. The next important thing is the identification of agro-climatic villagers which could be known as agricultural pocket area. Besides this, land and water resource should be utilised on the basis of optimum theory. Here we need cooperation from agronomists and animal scientists for accountability.

In agro-tourism, the farm mangement specialist and village tourism specialist work together with a set of agro-tourism farm management plan for villages. On the ground of agro-tourism farm plan, aggregate output and aggregate supply are estimated. Similarly, economists and tourism specialists work out together and estimate production target on the basis of previous statistical data. On the other side, the farm management researcher and the agricultural specialist analyse the cost-benefit of agro-tourism implicated in villages.

Harmonising agro-tourism farm plan requires the appropriate farming villages. Importantly, infrastructral development is also equally developed for marketing, storing and processing. To achieve the goal of agro-tourism, village people have to determine the criteria as follows:

1. Farm households and land holding in tourism village
2. Landless agro-tourism workers
3. Skilled persons of village.

Regarding farm households and land holding in tourism village, the villagers need technical assistance and guidance for developing agro-tourism in village. Besides this, supply of inputs and institutional seed money are necessarily essential to adopt a new farm technology in the village farm area. Farmers, who adopt farm technology, can increase farm output on the one hand and generate employment on the other.

Similarly, farm households are ugred to manage high value and labour-intensive crops. The output of farm households has to be carefully stored and marketed. Besides crop production, some complementary and supplementary works like dairying, poultry farming, beekeeping, pisciculture and sericulture for additional income generation are required. For landless agro-tourism workers and skilled villagers, cottage and small industries and village craft technology are necessary in terms of technical and economic feasibility and social acceptability. To meet these, job training, raw material management, credit facility and marketing should be managed for village production.

In this way agro-tourism can be developed through the means of combined effort on agriculture and village tourism.

The concept of natural agriculture is essential. Natural agriculture means the system of agricultural production that would be by nature without human intervention. This is concerned with nature as a model for taste of natural thing closer to Dr Pradhanang's village tourism concept. In other words, it is said as agro-tourism follows as per the nature's law the environment is preserved. The recycling process by nature in forming natural resources is that the soil becomes more fertile with the help of microorganisms for example, bacteria and fungi. Agriculture should be practiced not by disturbing the natural elements. The network of natural agriculture farms is initiated and at the same time the farmers are also initiated to understand the vedic farming – nature based farming.

There should be a natural link between agriculture and village tourism. One is to be linked with other as inter-relationship development. The farm station and laboratories are basically required to meet tourism demand of agro-products. The standard agricultural products with brand name are better to enter into the tourism market. The agriculture college and university ought to be more active and mobile for developing agro-tourism. Simultaneously, Nepal Tourism Board (NTB) has to take initiation in this respect. The partnership work and strategy by the Rampur Agriculture Farm and NTB are essentially to lunch together in agro-tourism development.

Based on agro-tourism possibility, the governmental and non-governmental farm stations have to be extensively developed in the villages of Nepal. The National Agriculture Research Centre should come forward in this respect 'Research and Development' is the keynote for enhancing agro-products. Every product has to be tested as a qualitative and standard brand. Considering sloping Agriculture Land Technology in the steep and sloping land in the hill areas of Nepal, agro-tourism development plan is supposed to be viable.

The skill of agro-tourism farmers is better utilised by providing job training opportunities to rural youths especially in agriculture and animal husbandry. The major agricultural outputs essential to commercialise are cash crops and industrial crops.

In order to advance agro-tourism more, Nepalese youths need specific job training from the technically advanced countries like Japan.

Nepal is development-minded, She is predominantly an agricultural country. It needs agriculture farm training for Nepalese youths who could be the national star for agricultural output and productivity sector in Nepal. The youths, who should not be in unemployed state of idealness, are to be diverted towards the need for development of the nation. In fact, youth is the power of the nation and the pillar of the strength. Thus, the youth has to be trained in agricultural farm management with new and scientific technology. Nepal, being the agricultural country, has to build up new agricultural technocrats, horticulturists, agronomists, and skilled farmers. The appropriate training on agriculture farm should be provided in high agricultural technology developed countries like Japan. Some Nepalese young girls are given opportunity for midwives training in Japan. Japan has made more progress on agriculture farm through modern technology. Similarly, it can train manpower in the field of health sector especially midwives and maternity. Hence, Nepal should learn the technology that Japan has adopted.

The proposed new training is concentrated on the anti-poverty programme and employment opportunities for the Nepalese youth. Besides, money earning from Japan will be remitted to Nepal, which assists to the Nepalese economy. The target group consists of the rural poor, small and non-agricultural farmers/agricultural and non-agricultural labourers, rural artisans and craftsmen.

Regarding agricultural activities, 65.7 per cent of its total population involved in agriculture is a big ratio. Similarly, 38.7 per cent of its GDP is tied up in agriculture. In the agricultural land we have inelastic property having no possibility of expanding land for agricultural production in Nepal. It accounts for 27 per cent of the total land of country. The slogan of this country is also development. Obviously, development concerns with saving, investment, output, productivity and balance of payments. The development concept is also related with human resources development especially in agriculture based on the job training through systematic or informal training programmes in employing institutions, adult education programmes, socio-economic and cultural exchange programmes for youth with neighbouring and friendly countries.

The programme on infrastructure development, agricultural technology dessemination, agricultural credit facility, marketing provision, etc. should be enhanced by means of commercial strategy. Training and education to youths of

Nepal is essential to increase productivity in the agricultural sector. Training on irrigation technology such as ground-water management and small surface irrigation with reference to conservation and renovation of canals and water reservoirs should be urgently considered. Based on the agro-ecological environment programmes for the production of foods and cash crops, different fruits, vegetables, sericulture and animal husbandry should be promoted.

The tenth plan of His Majesty's Government of Nepal has also given stress on the training programme and increase in agricultural productivity. The agricultural sector will have the lead role and it will be pushed ahead to alleviate poverty and achieve a sustainable and high economic growth rate. The period of the Tenth and Eleventh plans will be declared as the Agricultural Decade in the context of successful implementations of agriculture perspective plan. Similarly, the government plan has emphasised on the rural youth who have a minimum qualification of having passed S.L.C. will be given agricultural/ livestock occupational training to develop them as the rural level entrepreneur for their self-employment.

To achieve the target of the Tenth plan, the agreement made between H.M.G. of Nepal and Japan international Training Cooperation Organisation (JITCO) should be fruitful. In order to provide training and technical internship training programme for enterprises of Nepal in the Japanese industries, cooperatives, chambers and non-profit organisations, Japan has opened the policy for employing agriculture farm workers and midwives trainees from developing countries like Nepal. Recently, Japan made agreement with Philippines for fulfilling two lakhs trainees on midwives.

Hence, for food industrialisation, consultation training and on-job training is necessary to the optimum use of agriculture consisted as food production, processing, post-harvest technology, commercial development and so on. In general, the more developed a country is, the smaller is the share of agriculture in GDP. For example, Japan has 4 per cent share of agriculture in GDP in 1995. Hence, agro-tourism should be promoted in Nepal.

Less Import-Content

Village tourism has almost zero import content. Utilising local resources at the maximum extent promotes village economy. It brings the village products in front of tourism market. Tourists having high desire to experience village life and village environment are enthusiastic to enjoy village products. They would like to adjust in village environment. What the villagers eat and use in daily life is a source of a new experience for tourists.

Tourism Village Festival

In tourist village, most of the consuming items will be locally prepared with traditional values. The village skill and knowledge indigeneously developed is displayed as village tourism product. For the development of village economy, village product should be utilised as far as practicable. Using local product more means the development of village and country on the ground of self-reliance. The village should produce more goods and services as per the aggregate demand of tourists. The productive capacity, if it is in increasing trend, leads the village to economic growth. Hence, we should attract more tourists to increase consumption goods produced in village. Obviously, production, consumption and distribution should be balanced by promoting village tourism. Consumption is the constituent of aggregate demand. A change in propensity to consume results in a change in income and employment in the village. Hence, minimizing import content is helpful in stopping leakage in economy.

Hotel based tourism is dependent on import content. Several items of goods and services imported from overseas countries do not allow us to retain foreign currency. What we earn from hotels goes back to the foreign land. But in village tourism this can't happen.

High Use of Value Added Goods and Services

Village tourism uses of locally produced goods and services and promotes high use of value added items. In fact, village tourism is a function of per capita quantity of consumption goods preferred by tourists and local villagers. The use of domestic goods and services is saving to the village economy invested as capital. The resources gifted by nature in the bedrock of village are soil, water, mineral oil, mineral ore, coal, natural gas, etc. They are naturally domesticated products to add value added.

The philosophy of village tourism associated with village is on the ground of its rationality. The term, value added as used in village tourism can be extensively explained. Village accommodation is value added. The products used as 'Dal bhat tarkari', 'Makai bhatmas', 'Gundruk', etc. are village items to have value added. Thus value added refers to all those things which are used to consumption goods in village tourism. Basically, in value added components, we can introduce organic products as desired by village tourists. We can also declare as 'Organic tourist village' where organic products are served as tourism village speciality. Wonderfully, seeding of Barsin grass can be utilised in tourism village by promoting six types of local product such as 'Jai' grass in the high hilly areas and eight varieties in the mid hill and Terai as natural decoration to tourism village environment. Regarding local village animals, cow by different species name Lulu, Achhami, Khaila Terai and Pahadi, Sheep by name Lampuchhare, Kaage, Baruwal and Bhyanglung, buffalo by name Lime, Parkote and Gaddi, Goat by name Terai Khari, Sinhal and Chyangra, Pig by name Chwanche, Hurra and Bampudke, Poultry by name Saakini and Ghatikuile are categorised into indigeneous products refered to value added strategy closer to nature to promoting village tourism. In addition, the professional gestures of village blacksmiths, tailors, cobblers, carpenters, pot makers, village doctors, etc. can be exihibited as actors to value added creation.

In the natural world, the natural science can be practised in village tourism. We can go through homoeopathy and naturoeopathy in medical treatment and daily life conduct as our best system developed in Nepal. The different herbs and herbal plants naturally produced or cultivated can be utilised as natural products in support of the value added products. We can generate adequate revenue by utilising those natural

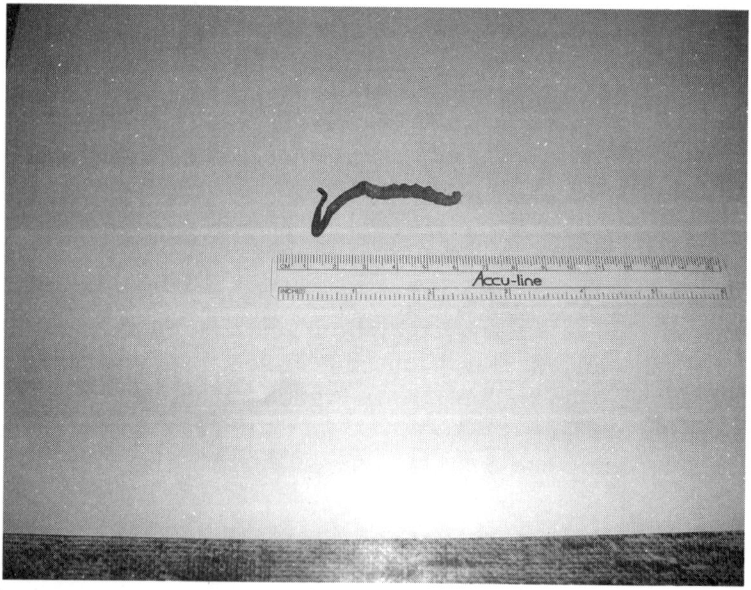

Yarsagumba

products in tourism market. In village Nepal, Humla and Jumla villages can be promoted as ' Yarsagumba tourist village' with regard to value added connotation. In Magar village of Manakamana area, 'Orange village' can be developed by introducing village product.

Similarly, Nepal is water resources endowed country. After Brazil, it has the second position placed in the world. Nepal's Himalayan snow melted water can be formed into the high qualitative mineral water. The international mineral water market is as big oil industry. The natural water of Nepal can be capitalised by low cost investment. As the reasearch study conducted by Earth Policy Institute of USA. The demand for mineral water in the world is increased by 57 per cent within the period of last five years. Its consumption is worth more than US$ 100 billion per annum in the world. The village based water resource of Nepal can be economically utilised and exported to the international mineral water market. On this ground, Nepal can be explored as a mineral water exporting country. Consequently, it can generate more income.

In emerging value added base tourism, demand for village tourism is elastic. The tour operators, trekking agencies and travel agencies successfully sell tourism village package tour in the domestic and international tourism market. We assume tourism village market development in terms of situation analysis as exhibited in the diagram (Tourism Village Tour) on the next page. Supposing that a few tourists are ready to take high price village tourism package tour. But more will be ready if the price of village tourism package is decreased. This situation analysis can be explained by deriving demand curve D which holds the marginal revenue curve MR. These said curves represent village tourism demand for psychic experience. MC denotes marginal costs and AC curve denotes average costs. For successful village tourism package illustrated in Sirubari tourist village, if US $ 180 per tourist were charged, 200 tourists would like to travel. Average cost would be $ 130 leaving the profit margin of $ 50 each or total profit in the first package tour $ 10,000. It would not show the maximum point since marginal cost at the point is above marginal revenue. This point shows MC = MR. At this business situation 150 tourists would like to pay high price $ 250 for the package tour. Here average cost at that situational point (condition) would be $ 160 leaving the profit margin $ 90 each or total profit in the second package tour amounted to $ 13,500. Here the situation analysis shows that if the tour operator would like to earn maximum profit, he should have to sell this package tour to 100 tourists only.

With regard to the expansion of village tourism package second, the tour operator would take interest to hold 200 tourists. These tourists would pay $ 150 each for village tourism package tour. Here the average cost would be $ 110 leaving the profit margin $ 40 or total profit in the third package tour $ 8,000. Again this is not the situation prevailing to maximum profit since marginal revenue is above the marginal curve. At this situational point MC = MR.

Here 250 tourists would like to pay $ 140 each for village tourism package tour. The tour operator would handle 250 tourists. Here, the average cost would be $ 90 leaving the profit margin $ 50 or profit in the package tour $ 12,500. Similarly,

Village Walk

regarding village tourism package third, in the promotion of Sirubari village tourism at the price of $ 90, the tour package would be sold to 530 tourists. The average cost of the package tour would be $ 50, leaving or contributing the profit margin $ 45 or total profit in the package tour $ 23,850.

Following assumption of tour operator, handling in village tourism business, these are the different tour packages developed for village tourism promotion to tourists, which can be programmed for the season. In these circumstances, profit can be earned at the maximum rate by following all three package schedules to tourists where MC = MR.

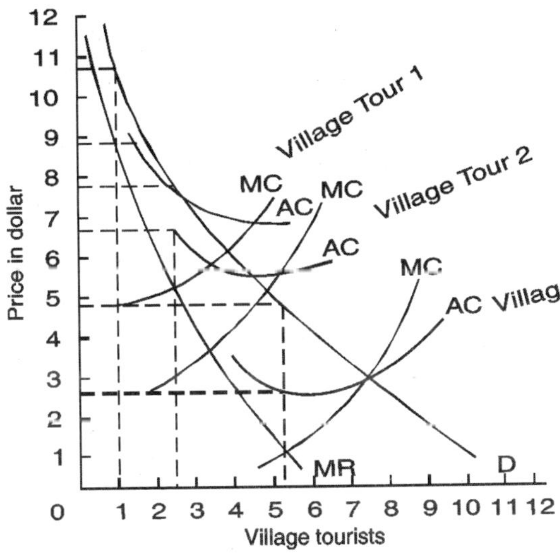

Figure 2: *Tourism Village Tour*

The digram exhibits different village tourism package tours in terms of price. Hence, village tourism package tour first would be provided for 100 tourists, village tourism package tour second for 250 tourists and village tourism package for third for 530 tourists respectively.

Zero or Less Repatriation in Village Tourism Business

Village tourism is far from the normal tourism, which has a special value in the tourism industry. The most striking feature

Watching Village Environment

of village tourism is valued at aesthetic experiences. The village component either in terms of goods or services provides unique product. All components in village tourism have no value at substitution.

Tour operators operate village tourism business in the principle of demand function. Initially, there is no price discrimination in village tourism industry. However, different tariffs can be determined on different grades of tourist as per the situation analysis. This nature shows a high degree on demand for village tourism business due to increase in people's disposable income and budget allocated for travel and tourism.

There is no substitution effect in the village tourism market. However, the internal goods and services are interchangeably presented from time to time in food menu, so that tourists should feel and experience the village tourism products are wonderfully unique in hospitality service. The goods and services imported from outside the country are not generally allowed to use in tourism village with exception to basic needs. The village tourism products are defined to use ought to produce in the village. The village skill and technology have to

Temples Surrounding Pashupatinath

be highly explored by providing development opportunities in village.

Hence, almost zero repatriation situation will be formed in tourism village. In other words, whatever the income generated by village and villager remains at the village as net income, which is said as the setting of less repatriated economy in tourist village. This leads the village and country to self-reliance in the economy.

Balanced Growth and Development in Villages

Village tourism development brings about a rapid change in economic growth and development in the village. It is the multi-sectoral balance of growth undertaken in village development. There are several factors of determinants for example economic, social, institutional, physical and so on. These determinants play the significant role in villages. Depending upon the management system, these factors can create positive as well as negative effect on development. The villages of Nepal, if not

Riverside Green View

wise utilised by village tourism concept, will remain ideal and unproductive. On the other side, the villagers, if properly trained and educated, will be valuable assets and major factors of production and development.

Basically, the economic development in village is a function of utilisation of village resources, village employment, village capital, village technology and village institutions.

The economic growth has to take place through the means of increase in output. It will lead the village to development. The economic growth strategy as a means of development brings in changes in the village. The natural resources should be utilised by villagers for economic development. There are resources, e.g. land, forest, water, mountain, etc. with village, which are strategically to be utilized.

Water is the best natural resource of Nepal. After Brazil, Nepal stands second position in water resource in the world. The major source of water resource is small and big rivers lying in the villages of Nepal. There are more than 6,000 rivers in Nepal supported by glaciers and rainfall. The river spreads at the total length of 45,000 km in the density of 0.3 km per sq km. The major rivers are mainly Koshi, Gandaki and Karnali located in villages of Nepal. Similarly, hydroelectricity is the key resource of Nepal. The hydropower potential is estimated to 83,000 MW, out of which only 0.3 per cent hydropower (253 MW) has been utilised.

In village tourism development, micro hydropower concept is pursued in the plan, so that small village rivers can be utilised in support to the development of village tourism. The village income can be increased by utilising natural resources. This process of development mechanism leads a change in village economy. The labour force of village has to be utilised in the village development. Nepal is a labour surplus country where youths are unemployed at larger extent. Several young people are going to overseas countries for employment opportunities. For the quality of village labour force, skilled and educated manpower should be prepared. The literacy rate scored in the village is very high. At present, in all Nepal 50 per cent of total population are illiterate. There is a positive correlation between the literacy rate and real per capita gross domestic product. As the study conducted in 43 developing countries, the result showed the correlation coefficient between these two parameters was 0.48. Hence, for generating employment, the labour force has to be skillfully trained.

Today in the western world, capital considered as the key player for economic development holds the complex society. With regard to capital formation, the Harrod-Domar model states the school of thought that capital accumulation plays a crucial role in the reading of economic growth. In fact, the rate of economic growth is expressed in terms of saving ratio and outputcapital ratio. So capital formation is the base of economic development. The entire development methodology is largely dependent on capital. An increase in capital stock leads to increase in the marginal productivity of labour. For developing villages, both private and public capital investments are necessary to gear up economy. Tourist money can be accumulated by developing village tourism in village for capital formation, which comes under the village saving and investment terminology. The domestic saving can be worked out as income minus expenditure or less consumption expenditure than income.

The general group of people follows this method of saving and investment to the household economy in the village. But the poor and ultrapoor group of people might not be capable for saving due to hunger and disease. Consequently, these people would spend all the money that they earn. But the rich group of people save their money in terms of insurance premiums, bank accounts, retirement annuities and so on.

The local government VDC can accumulate money for capital formation through village taxes and inflation. Inflation is also a tax on cash balances. In the village economy, those who hold cash balances, purchasing power will be eroded by inflation. Inflation, being a form of taxation, raises funds for government capital formation. Hence, it is way to locally accumulate capital formation in the village through village tourism. In the milieu of social setting, village tourism has to be institunalised in terms of cooperative or public-private partnership organisation or community development organisation.

Chapter 9

Problems and Prospects of Village Tourism

As we see village tourism is floating on the international and domestic tourism market. It has a vivid link with trekking. Village tourism is considered as 'the goose that lays the golden eggs'.

We take up the situation analysis with regard to problems and prospects of village tourism. It concerns with various factors, e.g. market analysis, competition analysis, review of internal data, target customer profile and problems and opportunities. The problem we face is the social conflict in terms of Dalit to the development of village tourism. The marginalised people like Sarki, Kami, Damai, etc. could not be accommodiated in village tourism. The minimum infrastructure and superstructure development has to be faciliated by the government, but the government is keeping silent at all. The concept of village tourism is not being publicised properly. Most of people do not know about village tourism. In absent of rapid development, implementation strategy of village tourism is too slow and moving at the snail's pace.

The situation analysis contains the market of village tourism in both international and domestic tourism. The demand for village tourism should be known for its successful implementation. The study shows that 60 per cent of total tourist arrivals in Nepal would like to visit and experience village and village lifestyle. The village tourism market is viable from the standpoint of tourist's interest and psychology. (KRC, 1998) The correlation between village tourist and tourist arrivals is positive.

Village tourism, being a new product, has no competition market at all. We have very few tourism villages developed in Nepal, e.g. Sirubari tourism village, Ghalegaun tourism village, Kartike Deurali tourism village, Thuloparsel tourism village and so on. For tourism development price, standard of accommodation and average occupancy rate should be carefully analysed. The internal management concerning village food, beverages, sales, handicrafts, etc. has to be in excellent position. For example, metal craft in Nepal is the indigeneous product. The typical and ancestral art of metal craft inherited from generation to generation is today's export goods for earning foreign exchange. The Nepalese craftmanship is very popular in terms of embossing and casting. Analysing customer target brightens the potential of village tourism. In village tourism development prospect, different types of customers are targeted such as the wealthy dreamers, economisers, adventurers and worriers.

The wealthy Indulers are win and confident type of people who are ready to pay for their satisfaction at their will and comfort. These customers would like cruises, resorts and tourist villages. Dreamers are timid type of customers who read and talk about travel and tourism. They have no confidence in travel due to lack of travel skill. But those customers who are ready to travel different places are guided by travel directory. The travel package is accepted by these people as directed by journeymen and tour operators. These customers can be attracted to village tourism setting target as village tourists.

Economisers are travellers who would like to travel for relaxation. They are price minded. These customers are interested in low priced package tours.

Adventurers are adventure-seekers tourists who are young, energetic, confident and independent. They would prefer new experiences, cultures and people, which can be supported by Nepal's village tourism development. Most of them are interested in travel packages to the South Pacific and the orient. In type of tourists, adventure tourists are accounted by 44 per cent in which there are between 18 and 34 age year old. Nepal can attract those adventurers by developing village tourism. Nepal's village tourism can be marketed in the international tourism arena by promoting village tourism packages. The village tourism customer target profile can be prepared from USA, Europe, Japan, South Korea, UK, France and so on.

Worriers are the people who are afraid of flying aeroplane. Half of them are 50 years old. Those people who would believe in well experienced travel agency only are highly conscious in travel management. We can attract them through reputed and experienced travel tour operators. Hence, village tourism has a good potential in tourism market.

The 'problems and opportunities' component is concerned with the strengths and weaknesses of the organisation relating to tourism village development. It opens the genuine problem and opportunity for solution. The small bottle neck of air service is the major problem of Nepalese tourism, so that a large number of tourists cannot come to Nepal. One airport for nationwide tourism development is not adequate. We have to extend other international airport ground in village Nepal in order to accommodate by jet planes. This is a golden opportunity to develop Nepal as a centre for international village tourism in the world.

Apart from this, there is threat as 'Band and dwanda' (strike and conflict) frequently organised by Nepalese political parties and Maoists. This conflict situation is a cause for downfall of national economy. The losses incurred by the country by one day's band is over NRS 1 billion, according to the research conducted by the Kathmandu Research Centre (KRC). It was also found that a day's band meant a decrease in the Gross Domestic Product (GDP) rate. It also has the effect that an individual has to bear an additional burden of NRS 47.59 per band day. Now, it can be understood how serious the impact is. The loss of one billion referred to the direct losses for that one particular band day. One day's band has a multiplier effect in the sense that one day's band leads to a three day effect on the national economy. It means that in real terms the loss turns out to be NRS 3.85 billion. It results in great loss to the nation. For example, the foreign exchange loss amounts to 2.74 per cent because one day's band has a long-term impact. The Table 4 shows the breakdown daily loss from band.

TABLE 4: Daily Loss from Band

Sector	*Loss (in Nepalese Rupees)*
Imports	29,30,50,000
Business, commerce	18,88,70,000
Exports	14,14,30,000
Industry	11,20,50,000
Employment	7,50,00,000
Transport	5,14,50,000
Tourism	3,24,03,840
Education	3,81,65,451
Social services	1,41,20,000
Law and order	3,50,00,000
Revenue collection/customs	12,04,40,000

Source: Kathmandu Research Centre.

Differentiately, the big bosses of Nepalese tourism enterprises consider that village tourism is 'Sauta paryatan' (revival tourism), which is the threat to village tourism.

Nepal is tourist's paradise and the imaginative land of Sangrila. Endowed with immense natural and cultural heritage, Nepal is the land of villages, home of mountains and kingdom of Himalayas. The country showing 79 per cent of its territory under mountainous topography is very beautiful to see. There are 1,310 peaks above 6,000 meters and eight peaks above 8,000 meters including Mt. Everest in Nepal. The other popular mountains are Kanchanjunga, Lhotse, Makalu, Chooyu, Dhaulagiri, Manaslu, Annapurna and so on.

The Himalayas of Nepal gradually attracted several adventure seekers and adventure mountaineers of the world. There are ten over 8,579 m snow peaks and hundreds 4,877 m peaks in Nepal, which are equally challenging to the world mountaineers who have had high ambition climbing the mountains.

The longest Himalayan range begins in Afghanistan, passes through Pakistan, India, Nepal and stops at Bhutan. Nepal has one-third of the total length of the Himalaya which comes out to be 800 km. This area covers almost all the highest mountains of the world.

The importance of mountaineering tourism increases by the attraction of the Himalayas. It is very high from the surface of the sea. Most importantly, scientists say it is the 'third pole' of the world. Topographically, Nepal seems to be the land of nature. There are still more virgin and unexplored peaks of 7,000 m (22,966 ft) left for promotion of mountaineering tourism. These peaks attract world climbers to taste the mountaineering expedition as well as trekking. Basically, all alpinists, lovers of nature and mountaineers from the world can enjoy Nepal based villages, mountains and peaks.

The economy of Nepal can be pushed up by mountaineering tourism and expedition. The income derived from mountaineering expedition is significant. The revenue generated from this sector NRS 44.49 million (1994) which is income elastic. In fact, demand for mountaineering tourism and trekking tourism is highly elastic. Laid on village Nepal, the Himalayan beauty and world highest mountains are the strengths transfering to potential of village tourism.

Villagers with Indigenous Musical Instruments

Welcoming guest in Nepal is a good marker of strength. On a special gesture of welcoming pattern, guests are honoured as God. The ritual practice, that we have is a good asset to tourism. It makes tourists more respectable and comfortable. Nepalese believe 'guest is God'. This perception is the strongest strength and potential for village tourism development in Nepal. Namaste is the most popular and respectable pattern of welcoming guests in Nepal. Offering tika (a mixture of rice, curd and red vermillion) on the forehead with the welcome snack and raksi (Nepali liquor), putting garlands and khadas (white or light blue colour scarf used by Lama/Tamang) and offering bouquets are equally heart touching Nepalese gestures in welcome.

The highly sophisticated welcoming pattern follows national musical instruments such as sarangi, dhime baja, madal, basuri, ek tare, etc. are played in welcoming ceremony. The different ethnic groups of people express their warm welcoming hospitality service with different systems. The Kathmandu valley Newar community has a typical welcoming tradition carrying 'Kota' (worshipping object) at hand in beautifully dressed women in traditional clothes said as Haku Patasi (black cotton saree with red border) stand in a line and give a small wreath of flowers greeting 'Namaste'. Similarly, Tamang ethnic group of people follows a very distinctive style of welcoming ceremony whereby people stood in order in Tibetan monk dress in the cupped hands to the guests followed by traditional Tibetan musical instruments.

Goddesses welcoming to guests are the divine virtue which is known as 'Panchakanya'. This Panchakanya means five symbolic representatives of goddess Mahabidya, Astha Sidhi, Nawa Durga, Sidhidhatri and Maha Gauri. Panchakanya can be announced only maids having 8-10 years of age. Panchakanya is exhibited on special occasion to garland prominent personalities and head of state guests.

Beautifully dressed in chaubandi cholo, sari and sirbandi (gold plated head band), panchakanyas take position by standing admist the playing Naumati bajas (Nine traditional musical instruments). Panchakanyas offer a special garland with

Beauty of Nature in Village

a pleasing smile to each passing guest. This type of welcome is not offered anywhere in the world.

This welcoming pattern of village Nepal is the strength of village tourism that brightens its prospect.

Part III : Partnership and Link Development in Village Tourism

Chapter 10

Public-Private Partnership in Village Tourism

Village tourism cannot be isolated. It needs partnership approach for development. The private sector as well as public sector should go together hand in hand. The history of private sector's involvement in development work has been started since 1980. Basically, private sector was emphasised as per the economic liberalisation policy adopted in 1990. For the development of village tourism activity, village tourism products have to be identified in terms of type of visitors, purpose of visitors and host-visit relationships, thus, it is necessary to create the favourable environment for public-private partnership in developing village tourism in Nepal. The government should take a special initiation with positive steps in establishing public-private partnership culture.

Description of Public-Private Partnership

The Public-Private Partnership (PPP) is a form of procuring and financing infrastructural projects in the public sector. This option ensures sustainable investment and attains development goals in partnership with the private sector. This is the Government's strong confidence in the role of private sector as a development partner.

Government can start PPP projects, namely, housing and environment, wildlife conservation and tourism, University of Science and Technology and so on. It has to identify possible areas where the PPP option can be operated to the nation's benefit and economy. PPP method, if appropriately implicated and utilised, can serve valuable public funds and revenue for other key and instrumental development sectors.

In respect of the private sector, Government has to consider some measures on the one hand, and the private sector, on the other side, should do everything we need to support Government's effort.

'Those at the top of the mountain did not fall there.' This doctrine tells us that we cannot as a nation be taken to higher levels of development by Government's effort alone. We have to challenge ourselves as individual citizens to climb to the capacity to reach even greater heights, if we choose the right way through PPP. Government aims to pursue in earnest reform initiatives that we believe, once tactfully grounded, service delivery will be improved in the public service. A lot of public reform initiatives, geared towards creating an effective public service have therefore to be lunched.

The Public Service is essentially going to be a strategy-focused institution for quality services. In the long run, we see the high productivity and better and scientific management to optimize resource utilization of the country with the PPP approach.

Public Sector Role

Managing village tourism or village destination is today's concern in sustainable tourism development. Sustainability relates setting goals for tourist destination and composing techniques or tools for better tourism management. There is a good prospect for developing ties between the public and private sector in building up partnership on tourism management.

The public sector role means the explanation of regulatory and other powers exercised by local government Village Development Committee (VDC) with support and direction from the central government and tourism agencies. Public sector bodies have statutory obligations and responsibility and political accountability for tourism development. Really, the local government, VDC acts as an agency for implementing agreed regulations and law composed by the government.

The public sector has five major management tools in terms of power use for controlling and managing tourism at village destinations:

1. Land-use planning regulations.
2. Building regulations.
3. Provision of infrastructure, especially access.
4. Investment incentives and fiscal controls and regulations.
5. Influence over tourism demand.

The first four tools are resource-based or supply-side measures and the fifth tool is related with demand.

Central and Local Government Role

Regarding land-use planning in terms of protective action statutory control over land is necessary to manage and promote socio-economic activities of the people. It is considered as an important management tool for the welfare of the people and for the protection of people's health in villages and towns from the bad effect of industrialisation.

Land-use legislation is generally administered by local government,(VDC/municipality) in every form of development and tourism development industry. The permission from local people (villagers) is required for land-use in order to develop land for a holiday village, park, village resort, tourism village and so on. Village tourism as a new phenomenon brings changes over the traditional land-use patterns. It creates inflation, social conflict, speculation and so on. Thus Environmental Impact Assessment (EIA) is conducted by the local authority before granting permission.

We should protect the natural resources and bio-diversity from the changing behaviour of the people and growing scenario of development plans. In the land-use pattern the concept of green belts around villages/towns should be considered by developer and planner. For the protection of areas of special scene and scenery and bio-diversity, the protective land-use regulations have to be operated.

Specially, the tourism sector should regulate through various protection measures on land-use pattern. It is illustrated by designing National Parks such as the Royal Chitwan National Park in Nepal, the Lake District in UK, the Kruger Park in South Africa, the Great Barrier Reef Marine Park in Australia and so on. This sort of protective land-use designation strengthens the land-use regulations in practice. Consequently, the village environment is saved and naturalised.

Considering proactive land-use planning, proactive action is to be implemented. The selected areas of land have to be utilised for promoting tourism industry. In practice, a combined idea of control and incentive over land-use is encouraged for sustainability. Zoning for tourism development is encouraged. For example, planners in Europe, North America and Australia identify zone for housing, parking, golf, etc. as an indicative or proactive land-use planning. Bermuda's land-use pattern is an example with respect to the indicative land-use planning. Bermuda utilised its power to sustain the environment in 1994 and the provision was made for restricting households to have more than one car, prohibit rental cars, restrict the number of cruise ships permitted at any one time in the harbour, impose heavy fines for anglers or boat operators that damage oral reefs and so on (WTTC/WTO/Earth Council, 1996).

Similarly, for reactive measures, positive designation and new development model on uses of land are considered. Some proactive land-use controls are undertaken in the redevelopment plans for protecting environment such as water treatment plant, sewage treatment and waste water disposal, solid wastes management and so on. Protectively, a positive designation relevant to tourism has been achieved by the United Nations Educational Social Cultural Organisation since 1975. UNESCO used to protect over 300 world heritage sites of outstanding universal value in terms of cultural and natural heritage such as the pyramids of Egypt, the Taj Mahal in India, the Great Barrier Reef Marine Park in Australia, the Royal Chitwan National Park, the Durbar Square of Nepal and so on. For better land-use planning some areas of land are given to public authority by transfering the ownership as for reactive measures. As for illustration, traditional inns, buildings, dharmasalas, public squares, etc. are left to the public sector as common property as well as responsibility.

UNESCO has Protected Heritage and the Philosophy Behind it

UNESCO–the United Nation Educational, Scientific and Cultural Organisation was founded on 16, November, 1945. For this specialised United Nations agency, it is not enough to build classrooms in divested countries or to publish scientific breakthroughs. Education, Social and Natural Science, Culture and Communication are the means to achieve a far more ambitious goal and at the same time to build peace in the minds of man.

Today, UNESCO acts as a laboratory of ideas and a standard-setter to forge universal agreements on emerging ethical issues. The organisation also serves as a clearing house–for the dissemination and sharing of information and knowledge–while helping Member states to build their human and institutional capacities in diverse fields.

In sum, UNESCO promotes international cooperation among its 191 Member states and six Associate Members in the fields of education, science, culture and communication in the world.[1]

Regarding Nepal World Heritage Sites, UNESCO declared 10 World Heritage Sites, 7 inside Kathmandu valley are cultural Heritage Sites. These Seven World Sites standing majestically–some of them as old as 2500 years. Furthermore, the ancient heritage Khokana village of Lalitpur district and Panauti Bazar of Kavre district are under the pipelines to add to Nepal World Heritage Sites.

It was in response to the situation that the Cultural Heritage Management and Tourism Model for cooperation among stakeholders project was launched for 1998-2001 with the technical assistance and cooperation of the UNESCO Regional Adviser for Culture in Asia and Pacific and the Nordic World Heritage office, Oslo. The project selected the best site as South East Asian World Heritage Town as working case studies. From the study, UNESCO concluded that an increase in tourist visitation of 40 per cent-60 per cent is not uncommon in the World Heritage Sites.

The project suggested developing sustainable tourism by

discussing with different stakeholders and local communities for preservation and maintenance of heritage sites. It is also recommended to develop workable best practice models for the sustainable preservation of heritage and management of tourism as a local resource, through the win-win benefit amongst stakeholder groups.

Building Regulations

Control over buildings through protective and reactive measures is supply-side tool of local government planning. It relates with buildings for all purpose including travel and tourism. As for land-use there are regulations enacted for new building constructions and for protection of existing ones in the structure of local government planning. As for illustration, new tourism buildings follow the necessary regulations like size of the buildings, height and density of building structures, office building in relation to a site plus access and car parking space.

Building regulations in terms of proactive planning state the specified terms and conditions for landscaping the areas for building constructions. For example, there are building materials specified in terms of fabric and texture, colour, architectural design and so on in Bermuda. At least the rudimentary guidelines published for planners such as beach space required per hundred tourist beds, ratio of parking space and so on are proactive measures for buildings.

The formal designation of buildings regulates the protection by considering the specific obligations and prohibiting significant changes in the historic and modern buildings. Some specific areas may be designed as conservation zones where the proactive planning provisions can be used for protecting all heritage buildings. In these circumstances, 'sticks and carrots' approach can be used for achieving planning goals. Here we follow the regulations which are considered as stick and the grants and subsidies which are considered as carrots. As for examples, Bath or canterbury in the UK, Bruges in Belgium, Prague in the Czech Republic or the Centre of Munich in Germany. The UK alone has had more than 9,000 conservation areas in the late 1990s. In the last decade, tourism in the UK generated more income due to the protection of historic buildings and townscapes, indigeneous villages and huts and cultural sites.

The state, regional or local government can build and protect the specific types of buildings as a planning strategy for tourism development. Examples are taken as convention centres, resorts, theatres, sports and entertainment complexes, houses for socio-economically disadvantaged groups of people and so on. Hence, Nepal has to adopt village house/village building regulations in time for development of village tourism in Nepal. The strict law and order should be maintained for the protection of pristine villages of Nepal.

Provision of Infrastructure in Terms of Access

The provision of infrastructure development for tourist destinations has traditionally been at the hands of the public sector. Broadly speaking, infrastructure concerns with the various aspects such as means of accessibility, use of natural resources, construction of man-made environment and provision of public utilities, e.g. gas, water, electricity, sewerage, drainage and so on belong to the work areas of government.

The local and central governments are likely to jointly plan, fund and operate the development plans. The infrastructure provision is also jointly developed on partnership approach as the target set for developing tourism destinations.

Regarding access to destinations, roads, seaports, airports, railways and terminals for public transport and the provision of car parking spaces and public transport system, they are developed by the local and central governments. In fact, a destination's capacity to receive tourists is largely dependent on public sector's plan and policy. For many tourist destinations, infrastructure development is taken to sustain local economy.

Similarly, the local government can prohibit the heavy size of vehicles such as trucks, tracters, etc. on main roads and areas specified for controlling environments. In some places, it is necessary to close roads to control visitor access by car to environmentally sensitive and fragile areas.

Tourism is relatively dependent on the quality of natural resources and environment such as forests, lakes, mountains, beaches, rivers, parks, gardens, etc. The local government working with central government and its associated agencies is responsible to maintain those natural resources which are procteted by the land-use regulations enforced for enhancing tourism and environment. Skiing development, long-distance walking routes in national parks and garden development funded by the public sector are the important structure environment responsible to the local government.

The role of the public sector with the partnership of commercial enterprises is good for all as per the economic base and future prospects of the local destinations/village destinations.

The local government,VDC manages the provision of various public utilities, e.g. water, electricity, gas, sewerage, waste disposal management, etc. as infrastructure services to the local people and destinations. These are the related services for development of tourism industry. Similarly, golf courses, swimming pools and baths and laundry services are facilities for tourists.

Drinking water in several destinations is a scarce commodity to be fulfilled by the local government. For agriculture also, the local residents frequently demand water supply. Ultimately, the public sector has to manage and control infrastructure of tourist destinations. The capacity of infrastructure determines the capacity of tourism development, it is instrumental in meeting sustainable goals at the hands of the public sector.

Investment Incentives and Fiscal Measures

The public sector has to persuade developers and tourism enterprises through some incentives for enforcing planning regulations. Epitomised in the example from Bermuda, regulations on land-use and building are considered as 'sticks'. Similarly, in village Nepal, we should think about it.

Incentives for all should form the basis of industrial development. They are supposed to provide enlarging subsidies and grants as 'carrots'. In this respect, the local and central governments should pay attention to the development planning strategy. Tourism is an illustration for economic development, which is a modern search for investment. Normally, some incentives are explained below:

1. Grants towards the capital cost of tourism accommodation and attractions.
2. Loans at very favourable rates not available commercially.
3. Public sector acting as guarantors for corporate bank loans.
4. Initial work in clearing land and preparing it for development.
5. Provision of infrastructure services such as access and utilities to the site paid by the public sector.
6. Peppercorn rents for the use of a site for a fixed number of years or until profits reach an agreed level.
7. Tax concessions offered against capital development costs.
8. Exemption for a specified period from corporation tax on profits.
9. Tax holiday for development of village tourism for the period of 10-15 years.
10. Relief from import duties in specific goods and technical equipments if needed to build tourism facilities.
11. Subsidies to developers/tourism village developers for taking on local/village labour.
12. Guarantees to ensure that existing exchange rates are maintained.
13. Training/on job training provision for local labour especially village people and tourism village entrepreneurs.

Fiscal measures are opposite to incentives. The suppliers of tourism industry would charge prices in the commercial sector such as airport taxes, sales taxes, value added taxes levied on accommodation and food, local taxes on buildings and land in tourism destinations and so on. There is a growing practice of 'the polluter pays principle' in which the government levies taxes by specifically identifying forms of pollution. The fiscal method used by the government is effective to control the commercial sector of tourism as a step to ensure good use of environmental resources.

The monetary and fiscal measures are considered as 'sticks and carrots' used to the supportive aspect of land-use controls and building regulation. Hence, the role of public sector in favour of supply-side of tourism is significant to achieve the sustainable goals in villages of Nepal. The public sector influences over tourism demand in terms of price, licensing procedures and marketing and information.

Private Sector

The private sector is a forward-looking firm which concerns with marketing rationale relevant to the important village tourism business practices at local destinations. It is always in calculation of profit maximisation principle. Despite it, the private sector plays the vital role in managing tourism at local destinations. Management tools of the private sector are generally more effective in managing supply system in village tourism than the tools available to the public sector due to the commercial knowledge of customers marketing strategy and demand management system.

The rationale for village tourism practice in the private sector mainly depends on maintaining a good environment of village through the indigeneous technology for energy, waste reduction and excellent hospitality service.

Managing Tools as Price, Product, Promotion, Place and People

There are five major management tools use by the private enterprises in village tourism industry. These tools are basically concerned with marketing in relation to the products that supply at village tourist destinations. Those tools are explained below:

1. Product
2. Price
3. Promotion
4. Place
5. People

The first 'four Ps' are known as marketing mix and fifth P denotes people as employees working in village travel and tourism services. In this regard Kotler (1994) says, 'the marketing mix is defined as the mixture of controllable marketing variables that the firm uses in pursue in the sought level of sales in the target market.' Any commercial organisation can be considered as a car controlled and moved by brake, accelerator, steering, wheel and gear as per the direction needed to supply and demand conditions in the village tourism market.

Elaboration of Four P's

The four P's represent a significant oversimplification of Borden's concept. The four P's are noticed as marketing something for people to buy, finding people who will buy, encouraging people to buy and providing value.

Marketing methods are undertaken by the study of social sciences, particularly economics, psychology and sociology. The four P's must concern with the wants and desires of customers in the village tourism market. The market depends on marketing research both formal and informal to find out what consumers want and what consumers are willing to pay for.

Some aspect of marketing especially promotion is very important. It is a problematic in terms of classical theory, which is based on the assumption of supply and demand. However, product promotion is an attempt coming from the supply side to determine demand. In this way, product market is measured by profit margin which would not be realised under the free market. The argument follows that non-free market is imperfect and lead to production and consumption of sub-optimal amounts of product. Marketing has legitimate uses in connection with goods and services to consumers. Its technique is used to achieve goal of the business.

Marketing is the promotion of products through advertising and branding. The four P's have passed into the language as product management and product marketing aspect with the specifications of the actual goods and services relating to needs and wants. Pricing refers to the process of setting a price for a product including discounts. Promotion includes advertising, sales promotion, publicity and personal selling and refers to the various methods of promoting the product and brand of company. Placement or distribution refers to how the product gets to the customers. The fourth P has also sometimes been called place referring to 'where' a product or service is sold.[2] E. Jerome McCarthy divided marketing into four general sets of activities. His typology has become so universally recognised that his four activities set the Four P's.

In fact, marketing variables seemed to fit typical situations observed by the initiations of the shortlist of four standardised P's. These typical situations can be illustrated as selling consumer's packaged goods in a North American mass market. However, in other markets the infrastructure is to varying degrees different and the products are only partly consumer packaged goods. Basically, the four P's of the marketing mix have been the universal marketing theory and practice.

1. Product

The tourism product is a set of different service items which a visitor consumes from the period of time he or she leaves home to the time of return. A tourism enterprise provides various services such as the services of airlines, tour operators, travel agents, hotels and attractions. It also concerns with the infrastructure development facilitated at village tourist destinations and access to the natural and built environment. Village tourism product is a service-designed for targeted customers. The product has the following characteristics:

(*a*) Design of facilities like selection of tourism village, number of beds/rooms at luxury of economy.

(*b*) Sustainability in tourism.

(*c*) Product presentation consisting access to a destination and atmosphere.

(*d*) Service to customers by employees.
(*e*) Branding designed for the product to communicate and promote targeted customers.

The private sector has to provide all kinds of products needed to tourist destinations. The holiday tourist wants the tourist village holiday destination with facilities like transport, catering, recreational centre, entertainment, art and culture, etc. The supply of the products promotes the potential demand for tourism. Therefore the destination image should be perfectly good by providing excellent services to tourists. Some resorts established as Blackpool in the UK, Gold coast in Australia, Hanolulu in Hawaii are the successful examples.

Hence, the private sector is highly responsible for establishing and designing tourist destinations with respect to the product standardisation.

2. Price

Price is the second important management tool linked with the product design and quality to be delivered. Price denotes the value of products and revenue objectives in relation to the potential customers.

For leisure tourism, price is a determinant factor that attracts tourists at large volume. Price may be calculated by analysing cost benefit. Therefore the price charged for products should be highly logical and acceptable to customers in terms of operating cost, revenue objective and market segmentation. Market segment can be normally known by tour operators who affiliate with visitors. Budget hotels are designed for budget tourists. Tourism villages and luxury resorts are designed for high spending tourists categorised as A and B class tourists.

Thus, price is a key tool for designing products in influencing demand for village tourism. Pricing by commercial opetators is strategically developed as an art of tourism promotion supporting demand for tourism.

3. Promotion

Promotion is an important management tool concerned with marketing mix for managing tourism demand. The promotional activities are taken into account through the various means of publicity. The communication techiques are generally used for influencing customers such as advertising, distribution of brochures, information materials and so on. For international tourism promotion, especially for those visiting tourist destinations for the first time, information materials and motivation stimulated by brochures influence over customer choice of destination product. Tourists get knowledge on a destination's environment that influences their choice.

The local government and private tourism sector take a lead in tourist village destination promotion as local partners in order to implement jointly agreed promotional campaign.

4. Place

Place normally denotes the location or destination where a product is produced and consumed. It symbolises all the places at which a customer can gain access to the product. The provision of easy access is in the marketing mix. A well developed distribution system provides convenient access to customers. The targeted customers should not face any difficulty to find out the products. They desire or demand something and it is available in place.

For tourism village promotion, accessibility is generally provided by marketing channel directly to customers or through retail travel agents. Today the information technology plays the vital role in widening access opportunities and for accessing tourism products.

5. People

Regarding service products, the people or employees working at different levels are important for dealing with customers. The staff-visitor ratio has to be high in order to provide the excellent service to tourists. Tone of voice, selection of words, body language of welcome, appearance and look of staffs, etc. are parts of the tourism product.

Similarly, conveying messages to tourists at right time is experienced as a part of tourism product. Understandably, travel and tourism is a special business where the priority of hospitality service is granted. Guests are welcomed and honoured with the special consideration and management. Staffs represent a company in selling and delivering products and they are considered as the good informers of places that they visit.

Hence, the people or staffs at tourism village destinations are powerful means of modifying customers behaviour especially for environmentally fragile and sensitive places.

Village tourism development in the country is better followed by a cooperative concept of private and public partnership. When joint effort is taken into account, funds are pooled. This type of organisation is known as a 'quasi-governmental association'.

Incentive Based Village Tourism Development

As we understand the village development problem, the pricing system in natural resources is not applied. However, we cannot minimise the value of village development with regard to the village initiation and its protection. Thus pricing the public goods is one of the best alternatives for resource mobilisation. The incentive based village tourism development encourages developers to develop village tourism in villages. Villagers are aware of opportunity costs of utilizing village and its resource in lieu of keeping ideal village.

The incentive-based regulations on village tourism development aims to modify the behaviour of village tourism developers with attraction. Similarly, the developer is encouraged to utilise village resource and skill directly or indirectly. Some of the incentive-based measures are explained here.

Taxes and Subsidies

Valuing resources show the price-based policy for village resources. Taxes and subsidies can be utilised as policy instrument to correct over-pricing or under-pricing of the village resources. Taxes are levied to the utilisers of village resources to unrelated city areas. The city migrants are discouraged by charging taxes. It is argued that tax is an instrument of control over migrants from village to city. But it is difficult to analyse that increase in tax brings decrease in migration. In village tourism, tax structure can be designed as per the situation and targeted goal. Generally, the taxation policy on tourism is operated on the basis of capacity threshold and area development strategy.

Subsidies

There are mainly two types of subsidies namely, unit subsidies and grants for meeting the expenditure of tourist village development. The unit subsidies are reduction on taxes and holiday tax for village tourism development for certain period. The grants, on the other hand are payments made to meet the cost of development village tourism. The tourism industry needs subsidies for purchase of equipments required for water treatment, waste disposal, energy saving and water harvesting. For the promotion of eco-friendly tourism and investment in new areas, subsidy packages should be taken into consideration. Hence, subsidies are used in order to conserve environmental resources, village tourism promotion, traditional art and architecture and historical buildings.

Besides this, tradable permit is next important incentive based investment. The firm in the market will get the liberty to trade as per its permit. It is useful for village tourism destination development, control of wastes and infrastructure development.

Introduction to Actors Essential and Graph

Village tourism cannot go on isolation. It needs involvement of various sectors for development. All actors in village tourism development have their own responsibilities and obligations such as Villagers, Local Government/Village Development Committee, Ministry of Culture, Tourism and Civil Aviation, Nepal Tourism Board/National Tourism Organisation, Trekking and Travel Agencies, Private Sector/ Tourism Entrepreneur and Tourism Research Centre–Kathmandu Research Cer're, Development Funding Agencies–World Bank and Asian Development Bank and Village Tourists. We could discuss the role of actors in village tourism development in the following way:

(A) ***Villagers/Host People***

Villagers are the main actors in developing village tourism. They have to think that village tourism is for villages and villagers. That is why they should specially follow the importance and value of village tourism in Nepal. The village area development through village tourism concept is an appropriate plan and strategy for boosting up village. The village resources and skills–if timely and properly be utilized–make village people and village economy rich and strong. The hospitality service of host is necessarily essential to be excellent and satisfactory.

(B) ***Local Government/Village Development Committee***

The Local Government / Village Development Committee is the main actor of village. The entire local administration is obligatory to it. So it has to think over the village developmental activities. Basically, it should include the village tourism development plan and strategy in its annual plan, so that village tourism can gradually be developed as tourism village destination. In fact, the local government has to be very mindful concerning village tourism advancement.

(C) ***Ministry of Culture, Tourism and Civil Aviation***

The Ministry of Culture, Tourism and Civil Aviation is a central governmental body which has the directive role in developing village tourism. The national tourism development based on village tourism can uplift the country and national economy. Thus the policy of developing village tourism in Nepal has to be promoted by the Ministry. The village tourism model in villages of Nepal should be illustrated by the central government and necessary regulations should also be implemented in time.

(D) ***Nepal Tourism Board/National Tourism Organisation***

Nepal Tourism Board is an autonomous body in promoting tourism industry in the country. It has a sole power and authority to design, operate and market new tourism activities like Nepal's village tourism. It is, in other words, the National Tourism Organisation which is responsible for public awareness, training and education. Hence, Nepal Tourism Board, being National Tourism Organisation should concentrate in public-private partnership tourism development. It is legally and socially accepted organisation for the development and promotion of village tourism in Nepal as a whole.

(E) *Trekking and Travel Agencies*

Trekking and Travel agencies are important promoters of village tourism, which have the significant role in promoting tourism village destination. They are very good actors. For travel and tourism advancement, these agencies contain effective action for village destination with defined objectives and suggested steps. These are in fact the intermediate between the host and guest. The success of tourism business is entirely dependent on them.

(F) *Private Sector/Tourism Entrepreneur and Tourism Research Centre*

Private sector/Tourism Entrepreneur is next key actor in the wave of privatisation. The government alone cannot achieve success in developing village tourism. Today the concept of privatisation has been widened in the world. So the role of private entrepreneur is very significant in the task of village tourism development in Nepal. Basically, tourism in Nepal has already been promoted by the private sector. Besides, tourism based research centre Kathmandu Research Centre has conducted many more important research studies on tourism and economics of Nepal. It has been a prominent key actor in research and findings.

(G) *Development Funding Agencies*

Development Funding Agencies are considered as helping hands to some extent to the Nepalese tourism. For example, World Bank and Asian Development Bank which are aid players in Nepalese economy have dominant role in tourism sector.

But they are to be used not in terms of their interest and plan but of nation's interest, requirement and plan.

In sum, these actors can be categorised into four major sectors. They are as follows:

1. ***Governmental Sector***
   - Local Government/Village Development Committee
   - Ministry of Culture, Tourism and Civil Aviation, Development Funding Agencies
   - Nepal Tourism Board/National Tourism Board
2. ***Non-Governmental Sector***
   - Trekking and Travel agencies
3. ***Private Sector***
   - Villagers/Host people
   - Tourism Entrepreneurs
   - Tourism Research Centre-Kathmandu Research Centre
4. ***Development Funding Agencies***
   - World Bank
   - Asian Development Bank (ADB)

These actors are explained by the following chart:

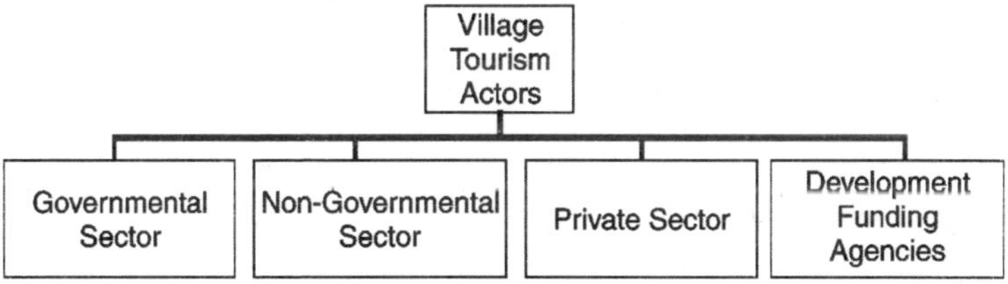

The chart exhibits village tourism actors relating to the governmental sector, non-governmental sector, private sector and development funding agencies. They are highly important holding responsibilities and obligations for village tourism development. Hence, each stakeholder ought to be a responsible builder of village tourism in the country.

References

1. UNESCO, *World Heritage,* 2006.
2. Wikipedia, *The Free Encyclopedia,* 2001

Chapter 11

Village Tourism in Relation to Urban Tourism

We tend to talk about tourism in rural shape and urban shape in generalised form. Specifically, village tourism is introduced with meaningful purpose and product. Today most of the people consider urbanisation is an index of development. So the infrastructural network and capital-intensive industrial enterprises are spreading in urban areas. In the developing countries like Nepal the concept of dualistic economy has come to operate as economics of development. There are two separate sections of economy consisting of urban section and rural section. In the developing countries, both sections are activised in operation. Without these linkages between them, the overall economic development is not possible. One section is auxulliary to other section in operational development aspect. In fact, rural development is the basic ground for national development. This school of thought leads the linked development concept between the rural and urban subsectors of the economy. What is needed is a complementary approach to economic development.

Urban development dilemma is undertaken by industrialisation, which can modernise agriculture in terms of high productivity wage rates and employment. The rural urban partnership strategy should be carried out for development of village tourism and urban tourism in Nepal.

In village development, agriculture is a basic foundation for development, but agriculture cannot develop alone. Thus the non-agricultural sector also should be developed by creating coherence with agriculture. Agriculture and industry should go parallely. The industrial enterprises have to set up in villages by utilising agricultural production.

Considering rural-urban development partnership, village tourism has to develop with coordination and link of development with urban tourism. Most of the hotels developed in Nepal for urban based tourism. Tourists stay in hotels and travel in several city areas where various historical monuments, temples, ancient palaces, natural and cultural heritages, etc. can be watched. Tourists come to Nepal and stay in cities where tourist standard hotels are located. First, travel programme should be given at the maximum extent for a long length of stay. After that village tourism programme should be given to tourists for their holiday making and entertainment. Tourists passing from city to village should be well informed about tourism network. This tourism function creates a good equation for attracting tourists to stay for longer stay in tourism village and city based hotels. The village tourism product should be more attractive, unique and entertaining to tourists. Ultimately, the benefit from tourism has to be shared between village and city. Consequently, village tourism promotes village and villager in terms of tourism economic activities, standard of living and progress while urban tourism supports urban development in urban areas of Nepal. A single coin having two faces which represent village tourism and urban tourism can be programmed.

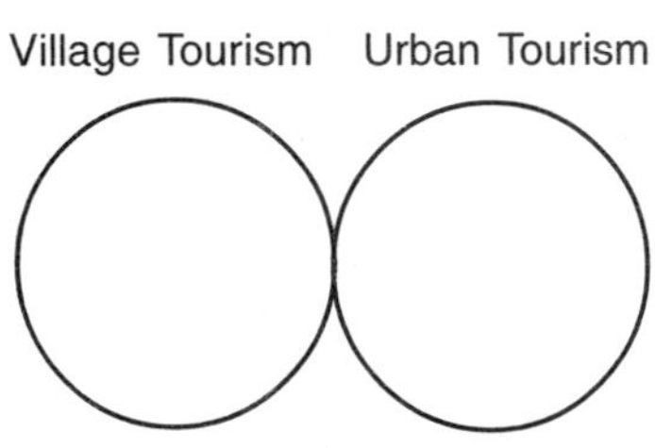

Front Face *Back Face*

Coin in Dollar

Village-Urban Tourism Partnership

Under the 'Partners in Progress' we salute all those who work as part of the complex network that brings tourism development in village and urban areas. The promotion of urban tourism links to the economic regeneration and urban economic development while village tourism initiates new development of village destination in support of village community and village local government.

As a matter of fact, 'village-urban tourism is a single coin having two faces'. Tourism continues to be viewed as a panacea for the economic and social ills of the nation. It is essentially an economic formula to boost up parallel both the village and urban areas. It is an appropriate plan and strategy to be part of a portfolio of strategies to successful village and urban development. But the opportunity costs and factors will vary from village to village and city to city.

Most tourists in village areas are urbanites. The question arises who benefits and who loses from the development of tourism in village and urban areas? Certainly, the debate over the mutual misunderstanding between village and city and the perceived conflict between urban and rural values and importance are taken into consideration. Later the debate goes to politicisation, which is not good and fruitful to the village and town. The Village-Urban tourism is friendly and complimentary to each other. One cannot go further without having support and assistance of other. Both are important from the placement vision and business linkage. Economic factors include income leakage, low multiplier and limited number of entrepreneurs in terms of low volume of business in village. Ironically, the village economy is already weak, since village tourism is likely to generate income and employment. Hence, village tourism is better compliment to urban tourism and for boosting village economy as well.

TABLE 5: Village-Urban Tourism Partnership Programme

Travel and Tourism Package	*Tourism and Destination*	*Tourism Activities*	*Period of Time*
Annapurna circuit or Himalayan Sangrila	Kathmandu -Annapurna -Himalayan Sangrila - Pokhara	Tourist Village experience, Rating Driving, Boating Cultural Knowledge	Autumn and spring 23 days
Everest Base Camp/ Kalapathar Trek	Kathmandu -Everest- Kalapathar Trek-Khumbu	Flight, Trekking, Sightseeing, Camping, Cultural experience	Autumn and spring 16 days

This urban-village tourism partnership programme enhances national tourism industry in Nepal. For example, Table 5 shows the village-urban tourism partnership programme, which follows travel and tourism package, tourism and destination, tourism activities and period of time. Regarding travel and tourism package Annapurna circuit or Himalayan Shangri-La for 23 days and Everest Base Camp/ Kalapathar trek for 16 days have been taken as village-urban tourism partnership programme. The tourism destination is selected from Kathmandu-Annapurna-Himalayan Sangrila-Pokhara followed by tourism activities, tourist village experience, rafting, driving, boating, cultural knowledge and so on.

Beauty of Nature in Village Nepal

Similarly, destination follows Kathmandu-Everest-Kalapathar trek-Khumbu having flight, trekking, sightseeing, camping, cultural experience in the Everest Base Camp/ Kalapathar.

Chapter 12

Relationship

Village tourism has a positive relationship with various tourism related activities. Village travel and tourism provides more unique experience than the normal hotel based tourism. Sensitivity of the interrelationship of the various components with respect to village tourism results in a green signal for economic development. Village tourism and its related sectors have 'pen-paper' relationship. One can normally show the relationship. Just as the relationship exists with the atom and the molecule in physics and with the cell and tissue in biology, in the same way with village and villager the conceptual relationship exists in village tourism. Village tourism has further relation with village based activities that broaden the functional relationship.

The functional relationship with different tourism activities for the promotion of village tourism is given below:

$$VT = f(H_l, T_r, T_k, R, S, W, A)$$

where,

VT is village tourism

F is function

H_l is hotel and lodge

T_r is travel

T_k is trekking

R is rafting

S is sustainability

W is wildlife and nature conservation

A is adventure

Observations on the tourism products, if linked for an aggregate of both pleasure and business travel, all of the parameters given will be complete into the village tourism relationship.

Here we discuss different parameters related with village tourism.

Hotel

Village tourism concerns with hotels where tourists go for accommodation and food. The concept of modern hotels was started from London in 1744. The hotel industry is the global industry affecting economy of countries of the world. Bass Hotels and Resorts located at London operate in 98 countries. The French company Accor has started hotels in 80 countries. Similarly, The Hilton International Chain has carried out hotels in 49 countries. U.S. based Sheraton operates hotels in 53 countries of the world.

In 1960, the development of hotels in new areas expanded in US. Prior to that period of time, hotels were made generally in the heart of city areas and resort areas. As hotel industry expanded, the construction of hotels shifted from urban areas to rural areas, suburban and airport areas. Some hotel companies like Hilton, Sheraton and Marriott started to extend their hotel business in these new locations. In 1970, keen competition among hotel companies started. In 1990, the hotel industry gave stress on innovation and new business strategies and plans. At the end of the twentieth century and the beginning of the twenty-first century, the idea of mergers and joint ventures changed the lodging environment in the world.

Hospitality standardisation is categorised by location. The hotel location categorised by different names is, e.g. center-city, resort, suburban, highway and airway.

Village tourism relates to suburban inns/hotels. Suburb is the distinct place away from the centre of the city. Hotels located in suburban or downtown areas are beautiful. Suburban hotels are typically located as a major chain having 250 to 500 rooms as well as restaurants, bars and other facilities. Characterised as downtown hotel, its main source of income is business meeting/seminar and convention. There are amenities given such as sports, health facilities and swimming pools in the hotel.

In Nepal, Nara Samsher opened Nepal Hotel at Jawalakhel in 1952. Mr Boorish Lissanevitch opened tourist standard hotel, Royal Hotel in 1955. Now we have more star rated hotels, e.g. Hotel Soaltee (Five Star), Everest Sheraton (Five star), Hotel de l' Annapurna, Sherpa Hotel, etc.

Lodges are located in the city areas where budget tourists will stay. There is no facility of food in this guest house type of accommodation. For food service, they have to go to local restaurants.

Dwariks's Hotel at Kathmandu is village type hotel, which represents village culture and environment. Its decoration is full of traditional art and architecture. For example, the hotel serves typical Nepali food from 4 to 16 course ceremonial meal for lunch and dinner to both international and domestic tourists. The Nepali cuisine–a unique food popularised by 'Krishnarpan' is being marketed largely in the hotel. Krishnarpan costs US $ 22 for an international tourist and NRS 999 for a domestic tourist (2005).

The Kathmandu valley has its own speciality and unique food menu itemised in the feast ceremony in different festivals. This is described as below:

The accepted system of the order of the sciences places the social sciences as the last member of a series that begins with Mathematics, Physics, Chemistry, Biology, Zoology and ultimately Sociology. Scientific knowledge begins with the exact sciences and end with the social sciences. Actually speaking, this arrangement generalises the relation between man and society which brings countless traditional performances and responses. In a very real sense everything we call 'natural' or 'human nature' is wholly a product of human social conditioning. We have our religion, traditional values, customs and manners as social pattern.

Considering this, in our country, Nepal has possessed with several traditional performances. Among these the Newars in Nepal have a distinct feature in the world. They are composed with a high degree of material culture and a complex society which is distinctly separated from others.

The Newar is only a phonetic variation of Nepal and it means simply a Nepalese. In other words, the people of Nepal is logically called as Nepal or Nepami. Although the kingdom as a whole is now said as Nepal, the people themselves still use the word to denote only the actual valley, particularly Kathmandu. The Newar has celebration of feast called 'Nepami Bhoya' which is highly concentrated in Kathmandu, Bhaktapur and Patan. It had been in practice since the Malla period. The term, Bhoya is meant feast having a large number of dishes of foods with systematic arrangement in order. Newari feast, it is generally experienced, is not only balanced food but scientific diet as well. The ethnic group of people particularly 'parbate' and tourists are puzzled when they get the opportunity to enjoy Newari feast. The Newar had traditionally practiced the grand arrangement of delicious foods with nutrition along with national culture.

The national culture of Nepal leads various occasional festivals which have scientific and traditional performances. Uttering Newari feast arrangement, the Newars will be quite conscious. They talk and take care of the preparation of flattered rice (bajee) and liquor (Aaila). The Newars attach much importance to these home-made items of foods and drinks because if these are taken from outside, it is generally believed, it looses the prestige of the family. It takes few months to prepare and arrange those items of foods more specifically liquor, Aaila, which is scientifically stored in huge earthen big jars, tepa.

Following the system of Newari feast, guests are asked to seat on the long mat, "Bhoya-Suku', a home-made straw-carpet, as per feast discipline none can leave midway, all should be seated until the last item is served and the feast ends. It takes generally the duration of one to two hours to end feast. First and formost, guests will offer 'Dea-Chha', (an offering with special things prepared to God). Later on, feast is started with Bajee (flattened rice), Achar (pickle), Takha (frozen meat) and Dakogula (soup type of meat) in a lapte, (circle shape leaf flat vessel), Aaila (liquor) is given in a Salicha (a circle shape semi-flat vessel made of soil). The Newari feast which is celebrated in scientific orders, highlights the system of Newari feast through the following table:

Table 6: System of Newari Feast

S. No.	*Serialwise Items of Food*	*English Version*
1.	Bajee	Flattered rice
2.	Achar	Pickle
3.	Takha, Sanya-Takha	Frozen meat, Frozen mixed dry fish, meat soup lemon & Chilli
4.	Dakogula	Soup type of meat
5.	Aaila	Liquor
6.	Chakumahari	Sweets
7.	Aalu Chhong Bhuti	Potato, bamboo shoot, bean mixed
8.	Kauli tarkari	Cauliflower curry
9.	Simpu	Bean
10.	Kaigu	Pea
11.	Bhuti	Bean
12.	Takola:	Roasted Meat:
	(*a*) Duguyagu	(*a*) Goat
	(*b*) Khasiyagu	(*b*) Mutton
	(*c*) Meyagu	(*c*) Buff
13.	Siyala:	Fried Meat:
	(*a*) Takogu	(*a*) Big
	(*b*) Chi-chikogu	(*b*) Small
14.	Aaila	Liquor
15.	Oaucha	Fresh green vegetable
16.	Phasi	Pumpkin
17.	Thow	Liquor made from fomented rice
18.	Paun	Sour in liquid form
19.	Chini	Sugar
20.	Dhau	Curd
21.	Sisaphusa:	Fruit:
	(*a*) Lai	(*a*) Radish
	(*b*) Kera	(*b*) Banana
	(*c*) Syau	(*c*) Apple
	(*d*) Suntala	(*d*) Orange
	(*e*) Kabsi	(*e*) Straberry

S. No.	*Serialwise Items of Food*	*English Version*
	(*f*) Tusi (*g*) Mewa (*h*) Too	(*f*) Cucumber (*g*) Papaya (*h*) Sugarcane
22.	Aaila	Liquor (wine)
23.	Sayaguli	Special type of occasional sweet
24.	Gwa, Goya, Musimahari	(Bettle, Nut, special type of occasional sweet)

In the meantime, the guests are repeatedly honoured with additional foods and Bajee so long as they do not respond as 'Gata-gata'. 'Gata-gata' is symbolised as ultimate end of full satisfaction of guests in feast ceremony. It is the prestigious issue of the organiser, the Newars believe, to satisfy the guests without any criticism.

The above table shows the systematic order of dishes of food in larger varieties in consumption pattern. Dhau (curd) in the feast sequence is the last item of feast whereas Sisaphusa (varieties of fruits) with Aaila (liquor) and Sayaguli (Special type of occasional sweet) are the closing items of feast. Besides these, Gwa (Bettle), Goya (Nut) and Musimahari (a special type

Newari Food

of occasional sweet) with Namaste is not only the ending of feast ceremony but the sign of cordial departure from the guests as well.

The Newari feast is arranged along with various occasional festival, marriage ceremony, religious rites and Guthi institutions. The feast is small or great depending on the significance of occasion. Generally speaking, feasts are nicely arranged in each occasion.

The Newari feast has been experimentally tasted and has resulted in greater scientific values. The feast is a general combination of vitaminous items of food consisting with differential vitamins A, B, C, D and so on. Man has to exit on exogenous supply of vitamins. This is necessarily essential for the growth and development of human body. The people of the world, generally the developing countries are suffering from vitamin deficiency that we call malnutrition in other words. If vitaminous foods are taken into proper amount from the very beginning of life the onset of lession of the connective tissues of man primarily due to deficiency of vitamins can be delayed. Vitamins improve general condition, increase vitality and resistence to infections and retards the aging of the tissues besides other benefits. The vitamin has an appreciable action in prolonging life of human beings. Many reports have pointed out that there are severe deficiency of vitamin A and C simply because of poor food and poor food habit of man.

We talk of vitamin C which is regarded as a wonderful vitamin. Vitamin C in large doses provides a beneficial adjuvant in virus pneumonia, chickenpox, influenza, mumps, measles, etc. There is no report about secondary effect from the use of vitamin C in high doses. That is why the use of vitamin C either in the form of dietary substances or in the form of tablets is most essential. The common dietary substances that contain vitamin C are in onion, cabbage, coriander, radish, cauliflower, tomato, orange, guava, lemon, chillies, papaya, etc. In the recent times, researchers in Yugoslavia indicated that vitamin C possesses preventive action in rabies infection, anti-infectious, anti-toxic effect and virucidal properties.

The need of nutrition for human beings is fulfilled by

adequate supply of food. Newari feast is a fitting answer to it. The Newari feast consists of 20-25 items or dishes of food (excluding Gwa, Goya, Musimahari), in general Achar (pickle) which is a combination of Lai (radish), Hamo (seasameseed), Labsi (a kind of fruit which has a taste of sour) has a good deal of vitamin C. Moreover, 8 varieties of meat, phasi (pumpkin), oaucha (fresh green vegetable), simpu (bean), kaigu (pea), bhuti (bean), pau (sour liquid form made from labsi), dhau (curd), varieties of fruits, etc. have adequate vitamins A, B, C, D and so on.

'Nepami Bhoya' is indeed, scientific and above all, most balanced feast of Nepal. The feast that has no comparison in the country is wonderful, because there is no other system of feast which does so many beneficial effects. As the system of Newari feast shows, the food can be divided into six categories: (1) Flattened rice, (2) Meat, (3) Vegetable, (4) Fruit, (5) Liquor and (6) Miscellaneous.

Today the Nepali people should achieve the Asian standard by the year 2000 more specifically food, clothing, housing, health, education and security. A simple Nepali needs minimum 2250 calories of nutritious food as fixed by National Planning Commission. The objectives of the Seventh Plan were also to fulfil the basic needs of the people along with increase sustained food production, meeting food requirement of the growing population and improving food habits and consumption level of people. With regard to improvement and consumption of Nepali food the First Food and Beverage Festival (1984) held in Nepal hit it off as a big success. It is realised that Nepali food has super quality which is preferred by many tourists and world food experts. Over 1200 people attended the festival held in the Rose Garden at Hotel Soaltee Oberoi. This festival displayed Nepalese products and simultaneously encouraged food industries of Nepal. Furthermore, to maintain standard of Nepali food and to promote catering services, Newari food be declared as Asian Standard Food, though it may be expensive.

However, we have studied very little about Newari people at all. In the nineteenth century very few European scholars like Brian Hodgson, H.A. Oaldfield, Col. W. Kirkpatrick had collected some data on them, but they are still a dearth of literature. In the meantime, German scholars and Kathmandu Research Centre are studying the Newari and the ethnic groups. Thus we need to investigate and study a detailed monograph on the Newari feast and Newars based on actual field work and research more scientifically for village tourism development.

Nepali and Continental Food

Nepali food is popularly known as 'Dal-bhat-tarkari' which is very popular in Nepal. Most of the Nepalese would prefer it as best food in their life. Nepal, being the composition of multi-ethnic groups of people, has various types of traditional and daily food. The people of Terai would take 'Dal-Roti'–lintel and bread. Similarly, the people of Hill would eat 'Dhindo-Gundruk'–husty pudding and fermented vegetable. The people of Kathmandu valley, particularly Newar would take 'Bhoj'–feast.

Regarding Continental food, it includes classic Italian and French highlights served in speciality restaurants and hotels. Several restaurants and hotels also serve German, Mexican, Hungarian and Brazilian food. The continental food sought after are the Italian Pastas, American style Pizzas and Burgers, Chinese Soups and Noodles and Mexican Tortillas. Western style confectionery–chocolate cakes, fudge, cookies and tarts are popular among Indians.

World is a mobile structure where food migrates along with human beings from place to place. Today, we have the concept of globalisation of food, but this globalisation dates back to the human culture and way of life and civilisation. The Western and particularly the American food has been a synonym of the continental food as America has experienced migrants from various countries at the maximum extent. As foreign people come and settle down, they bring their culinary cuisine. For these reasons, most of the soups and baked dishes fall in the category of continental food. Hence, the range of continental food is very vast continuing to increase more and more.

Here is some comparative outlook between the Continental food and that of Nepali food, which is given below:

Comparision Between Continental and Nepali Foods

*Continental Food	**Nepali Food
Cold Side Dishes	*Cold Side Dishes*
3-Bean Salad $3.09 lb American Potato Salad $2.89 lb Broccoli Salad $4.19 lb Broccoli, Carrot, & Raisin Salad $3.29 lb Chicken Salad for Sandwiches $5.49 lb Chicken Salad Mac $5.19 lb Cole Slaw $2.89 lb Dill Macaroni $3.29 lb Fresh Fruit Salad $4.19 lb Grape Slaw $3.29 lb Hawaiian Salad $4.19 lb Macaroni Salad $2.89 lb Marshmallow Fruit Salad $4.19 lb Pasta Parmesan $3.69 lb Pasta Salad $3.09 lb Pea Salad $3.09 lb Tomato Cucumber $3.09 lb Tossed Salad $1.25 pp Baked Potato Salad $3.29 lb Vinegar Cole Slaw $3.09 lb Waldorf Salad $4.19 lb Christmas Crunch $3.59 lb	Frozen Meat, Frozen Mixed Dry Fish, Lemon and Chilly
Hot Side Dishes	*Hot Side Dishes*
Au Gratin Potatoes $3.49 lb Baked Beans $2.89 lb Broccoli Rice Casserole $3.49 lb California Blend Vegetables $3.29 lb Corn, Carrots, Green	Potato, Beam, Bamboo, Rice, Meat Cauliflower, Pea Fried Meat, Pumpkin, Fresh Vegetable, Pickle

Beans $3.29 lb
Creamed Corn $3.29 lb
Dressing $1.99 lb
Garlic Mashed Potatoes $4.39 lb
German Potato Salad $3.49 lb
Gravy $1.99 lb
Green Bean Casserole $3.29 lb
Mac and Cheese $3.49 lb
Mashed Potatoes $3.29 lb
Rice Pilaf $2.49 lb
Wild Rice $2.49 lb
Scalloped Potatoes $3.49 lb
Sweet Potatoes $3.49 lb
Twice Baked Potatoes $2.20 ea
We recommend 4 servings per pound on most salads and meats

Hot Dishes	*Hot Dishes*
Original Roast Beef $7.80 lb	Meat Soup, Potato, Bamboo, Bean Mixed
BBQ Beef $8.00 lb	Cauliflower Curry, Bean, Pea, Roasted
Italian Beef $8.00 lb	Meat, Rice, Lintel, Curry.
BBQ Pulled Pork $8.00 lb	
Baked Chicken (8 pieces per) $7.00 ea	
Baked Haddock Call for Price	
Baked Ham $6.10 lb	
Baked Pork Chops with Onions & Peppers $3.20 ea	
BBQ Chicken $7.50 ea	
BBQ Ribs $4.99 lb	
Beef Stroganoff $5.69 lb	
Beef Tips and Noodles $5.69 lb	
Chicken Cordon Bleu $3.75 ea	
Chicken Kiev $3.75 ea	

Chicken Stuffed Broccoli & Cheese $3.75 ea
Fried Chicken (8 pieces per) $8.00 ea
Hot Chicken Salad $5.29 lb
Italian Sausage with Onions & Peppers $5.99 lb
Lasagna Meat or Vegetable (10 servings) $26.00 ea
Mostaccioli $5.09 lb
Polish Sausage with Kraut $5.99 lb
Prime Rib, Steaks Call for Price
Roast Pork $7.80 lb
Spaghetti/Meat Sauce $4.89 lb
Stuffed Cabbages $1.85 ea
Stuffed Peppers $1.50 ea
Turkey Tetrazzini $5.29 lb
Turkey Breast $6.15 lb
Turkey off the Bone $7.50 lb

Breads & Buns	*Breads & Buns*
Medium Sweet Buns $3.49 dz Hamburger or Hot Dog Buns $3.49 dz Dinner Rolls & Butter $3.49 dz 6″ French Rolls $4.49 dz Kaiser Rolls $4.49 dz Garlic Bread (8-10 people) $4.99 ea 4″ French Rolls $4.29 dz	Jelibi, Khajuri, Nimki, Swarhi, Malpwa.

Desserts	*Desserts*
Fruit or Cream Pies $7.50-10.50 Apple & Cherry Slices	Fruit: Radish, Banana, Apple, Orange, Strabery. Cucumber, Papaya,

$1.10 ea	Sugarcane.
Brownies $1.10 ea	Curd, Sugar, 'Musimahri'–Special Type of Sweet
Cookies or Cake Squares $.60 ea	Bettle, Nut.
Seasonal and Other Options Available	

Prices subject to change without notice
Source: *Reuland Food Service Catering Delicatessen, 115 Oak Avenue, Aurora, Illinois, 1995.
**Kathmandu Research Centre, 1990.

The above mentioned Table exhibits the comparison between Continental food and Nepali food. Regarding Continental food there are several items of food categorised into different dishes. These dishes prepared by Reuland Food Service were as a cottage industry in the 1950's. As the demand of Reuland's unique taste and service grew, the food service was started in the old Fruit Juice House at 115 Avenue in 1971. Its speciality was–roast beef sandwiches on freshly made buns, potato salad and baked beans all remain Reuland classics. Through the years, its food menu selections and service options have expanded greatly. This constant blending of innovative new taste with familiar old favourites is one of its strongest assets. Its roast beef sandwiches on freshly made buns, potato salad and baked beans all remain Reuland classics. Reuland Food Service offers creativity, versatility, and of course, the same wonderful food and friendly service that people have been counting on for over fifty years as valued continental food.

Nepali foods having different dishes are delicious and tasty, which has had Nepal's classics. The Nepali foods are also listed into cold dishes, hot dishes, breads and buns and desserts, which can also be qualified for Continental food valued at Nepalese classics.

Besides this, looking for a romantic Italian restaurant where the food is freshly prepared and value is outstanding.[1] People for pasta course select home-made vegetable ravioli with tomato sauce ($11), fettuccine alla matriciania with pancetta

Kentucky Fried Chicken in U.S.A.

and onion in tomato sauce ($13), seafood linguine ($18) and freshly made white and green noodles with peas, proscuitto

Roasted Turkey & Bacon Ciabatta and Grilled Greek Chicken Salad

Three-Cheese Chicken Penne and Caesar Salad

and cream ($14). Similarly, for a major course, select such house specialities as Zuppa di pesce seafood stew($ 24), veal stuffed with mushrooms, prosciutto and fontina cheese ($23), veal scallopine with marsala wine and mushrooms ($18), chicken breast scarpariello with garlic, lemon, white wine and rosemary ($16), and veal saltimbocca alla Romana with sage and prosciutto ($16).[2]

CafeSalamannca in Jackson Heights is one of the

neighbourhoods most enduring family dining traditions. Start with such appetisers as Spanish sausages ($ 5.75), clams in green sauce ($4.75), mussels in green sauce ($4.75), escargot ($7), Spanish sausage and vegetable soup ($4.50) and shrimps in garlic sauce ($ 6.75). For famous paella valenciana ($13.75), veal chops Salamanca ($ 19.75), mariscada fish stew in spicy Diablo sauce ($ 17.75), chicken in garlic sauce (12.75), grilled shrimps ($13.75) and red or white home-made sangria ($9.50) for a half pitcher, $16.50 for a whole pitcher.[3]

Besides, Kentucky Fried Chicken ($20) is very popular and delicious in New York, USA.

Current Nepali Food

Dal -Bhat and Tarkari (Lentils, Rice and Curried Vegetables)

Appetizers/Snacks[4]

Chatamari (Newari)- food resembles Pizza or Dosa(South Indian),rice flour flat bread cooked over heat with toppings such as minced meat (with or without some vegetables),egg, sugar or no toppings.

Choyla (Newari) - grilled/roasted spicy meat generally eaten as appetizer with liquor.

Gundruk (dried and fermented green vegetables leaves) - Prepared as soup, a slightly sour and slightly tangy are mixed.

Kwati (Newari)- soup with many mixed beans. A special soup prepared in Janepurne festival.

Momo (Newari popular food)–a dumpling filled with minced meat usually buffalo and goat. Served steamed or fried, a very popular and delicious appetizer, afternoon snack or evening meal.

Samay Baji (Newari)–beaten rice with roasted meat, smoked fish, boiled-then-fried egg, black soybeans and diced ginger, generally a ritual food of Newari community.

Sekuwa-grilled meat usually prepared from mutton, duck chicken, buff wild boar.

Sel-donoght-like shaped dessert/snack prepared from rice flour.

Sukuti-spicy dried meat roasted over a charcoal fire.

Alu Tama-Potato made with bamboo shoots.

Takhala-Newari frozen/jello meat soup served cold.

Wo and Bara–(Newari) flour patty made of lentils with or without meat/egg topping. It is usually used in festival as snack.

Dish of Nepal[5]

Alu Acchar (Pickled Potatoes)
Alu Dum
Alu Tama
Alu Tarreko
Babari (Mint) Ko Acchar
Bhat (Cooked Rice)
Chana (Spicy Chickpeas)
Chana Masala (Spicy Chick Peas)
Chatamari
Chiau Ko Tarkari
Chicken Bhutuwa
Chiken Chili
Chicken (Kukhura Ra Pyaj Tareko)
Special Chicken Ko Masu
Grilled Chicken Masala
Chicken Tarkari
Naram Chicken Ko Masu
Dal
Dal Bhat
Dal Fry (Fried Lentil Soup)
Golveda Ra Dhaniya Acchar
Momo
Mula Ko Acchar
Kinama Ko Jhol (Fermented Beans)
Mixed Vegetables Tarkari Soup
Palak Paneer (Spincach with Cottage Cheese)
Phapar Ko Roti (Backwheat Pancakes)
Tandori Chicken
Golveda Ra Tofu (Tafu with Tomato)
Vegetable Pulao
Vegetable Thukpa
Rajma (Kidney Beans) Curry

Desserts and Sweets

Burfi (Milk Burfi)
Doodh Peda (Flat Milk Cake)
Gajar Ko Haluwa (Carrot Pudding)
Kheer (Rice Pudding)
Milk Cheese Cake (Peda)
Rasbari (Milk Balls)
Sel Roti (Crispy Rice Doughuts))
Suji Ko Halwa (Semolina Pudding)

Vegetarian Nepali Food

Alu Acchar (Potato Pickle Salad)
Alu Dum (Curry Potato Stew)
Potato Salad
Cucumber Salad
Dal Bhat (Rice with Lentil Soup)
Golveda Ra Dhaniya Ko Acchar
Mixed Tarkari
Chiau Ko Tarkari (Mushroom Curry)

Nepali Breads

Phapar Ko Roti (Buckwheat Pancakes)

Vegetable Pulao (Fried Vegetable Rice)

These are Continental foods and Nepali Food changing from destination to destination and time to time as demanded by the people's choice and interest. But Nepal ought to exhibit its speciality and standardisation of food dishes and menues in the globalisation of food.

TRAVEL

Village tourism has a close relation with travel. Without travel tourism cannot be imagined. Today 'travel for a holiday' is the people's voting choice in the list of preferences. By nature, human beings, are very mobile, they would like to travel from place to place and from destination to destination. Holiday away from home environment is a priority given to travel and tourism. Now-a-days, travel has been an art of living style. People would like to get rid of humdrum of everyday life. So they want to move for relaxation in mountains, tourist villages and scenic places.

Tourists travel with different purposes described as below:

Recreational Travel

Tourists travel for recreation and pleasure. 'Holiday for pleasure' is the major motto of people who start travelling. In the world, 75 per cent of international travel is managed for pleasure.

Adventure Travel

Adventure travel is growing over time 'People would go for trips for playing golf, tennis, skiing, trekking, mountaineering and village walking, etc. Adventure tourism has a close relationship with village tourism and vice versa. It can be promoted in village Nepal by programming adventure holiday.

Health Travel

People would take trips for health purpose. Tourists visit different places where healthy climate is available. Similarly, for medical treatment people visit special areas for bathing, hot springs and meditation/yoga. Village is non-polluted area and tension free place where tourists can enjoy and spend their holiday happily.

Cultural Travel

Village tourism relates to the cultural travel. Tourists are interested to experience different cultural heritages of people and country. Visiting ancient historical places, religious places, temples, museums, art gallaries, etc. are the prominent objects for culture.

Dead Body Disposing at Ghat

Incentive Travel

The concept of incentive travel is to encourage employees working in the factory through rewards of free holidays within the country or overseas countries. These rewards support meals, hotels, transportation and recreation. People would like and choose holiday rather than gifts. Every year millions of people go for free travel as an incentive travel from different companies in the world. With regard to travel, various companies can recommend free holiday programmes in tourism village where people can enjoy a lot by experiencing village culture, village environment, village sight seeing and village lifestyle. Hence, village tourism has a positive correlation with incentive travel.

Convention Travel

Convention travel is highly demanded in the international tourism market. People would like to participate in different national and international conferences. The convention can be arranged in tourism villages of Nepal where pollution free environment and natural beauty are available. Hence, village tourism has to be promoted as per tourism demand and psychology of tourists. There is a positive correlation between village tourism and convention tourism.

Nepal has to extend its travel and tourism activities from city tourism to village tourism to large extent. The maximum number of tourist arrivals in Nepal recorded 4,91,504 in 1999 is not enough as compared with other countries of the world. For example, Spain having a population of 10 million had 48 million international travellers in 2000. Likewise, Singapore having population of 2.4 million had seven million tourist arrivals in 2000. The population-tourist ratio is 1:4.8 in Spain and 1:2.92 in Singapore.

The government has to play a vital role in developing and planning village tourism. Village tourism, in fact, assists in employment and income generation.

World Tourism Organisation (WTO) is the apex body leading the whole world with respect to tourism industry development. It has 137 countries listed as members. Besides, it possess 350 members as affiliated from sectors such as travel agencies, airlines and so on.

Pacific Asia Travel Association (PATA) is next important organisation related to the pacific region. Established in Hawaii in 1951, it promotes tourism all over the world. PATA/Nepal Chapter has to take initiation on village tourism development. Nepal's village tourism product should be tasted by international tourists.

The Table 7 shows tourist arrivals by purpose of visit from 1995-2000. In 1995 tourist arrivals were recorded for Holiday/ pleasure by 50.4 per cent, for trekking and mountaineering by 23.3 per cent, for business by 6.0 per cent, for pilgrimage by 1.4 per cent, for official by 5.5 per cent, for convention by 1.5 and for others by 11.8 per cent.

Similarly, the tourist arrivals were ensured as the highest by 55.2 per cent in 2000 for holiday/pleasure, for trekking and mountaineering by 25.6 per cent, for business by 6.4 per cent, for pilgrimage by 3.4 per cent, for official by 4.5 per cent, for convention by 1.2 percent and for others by 3.7 per cent.

Trekking

Village tourism has had the brotherly correlation with trekking tourism. It can provide lots of benefits to trekking tourism development and promotion in a new and innovative way. Basically, Nepal's trekking tourism can be modified into a grand and high power of attraction by collaborating with village tourism. By trekking route by route, the new type of village tourism and trekking tourism partnership programme can be introduced to village and trekking tourists. Undesirably, the villagers of Nepal and villages were used as commodities until the concept of village tourism introduced by Dr Pradhanang. Now villagers' mind have been opened for developing village tourism in their villages having understood the concept and significance of village tourism in Nepal. As for best understanding and communicating to the people, villages and villagers are themselves the best means of village tourism products that can be wisefully utilised.

By a new partnership programme between trekking and village tourism industry, we can provide a lot of advantages to villages, villagers and society. More job opportunities and income can be created in local villages. The village products can be utilised by the means of village tourism. The village houses and indigenous huts are utilised as village tourism attraction. The trend of 'Lahur Jane'–going to foreign land particularly India for job opportunities in minimum wages for life existence and 'Lahure Hune'–going to be existed in the foreign land are the malpractices of traditional Nepalese society due to the lack of income and employment opportunities within the village Nepal. Village tourism creates its own local environment for generating income and employment. The ideal villages are going to turn into productive and economic villages when village tourism is apparently implicated. The village community will be slowly advanced and raised its living standard and economy. Earlier this, Sirubari tourism village showed its exemplary successful story of village tourism in this regard. Villages and villagers being the main actors of village tourism development can explore village skills and resources at the best opportunities in the domestic and international tourism market.

Trekking is very amusing adventure in Nepal due to wonderful scene and scenary, diverse flora and fauna and complex culture. The first trekkers were the mountaineers, who in 1950 were permitted access to the peaks of the mountains of Nepal. The early climbers who were Eric Shipton and Bill Tilman from the UK and Toni Hagen from Switzerland experienced the trekking routes by hit and miss.

Trekking tourism was introduced by Colonel Jimmy Roberts, a Gurkha officer and mountaineer, he himself established a trekking company named Mountain Travel. From that time, trekking tourism in Nepal began to develop to a large extent. Today international tourist's purpose of visit to Nepal has been trekking and mountaineering. Trekking business has been massively increased with a large number of trekking companies established in Nepal.

The history of trekking shows that early trekkers would generally use tents for their accommodation and would be accompanied by a large number of porters. This sort of trekking is still running in the remote areas of Nepal. In the trekking routes, one would find the teahouses for trekkers. Consequently, in trekking route, trekkers can travel from teahouse to teahouse. Trekking in Nepal is a relaxing experience. The trekking trails in Nepal, where the absence of the daily routine of home environment, attracts the trekking to relax mentally and physically. The trekking trails of Nepal are rarely flat.

Table 7: Tourist Arrivals by Purpose of Visit

Year	*Holiday/ Pleasure*	*Trekking & Mountaineering*	*Business*	*Pilgrimage*	*Official*	*Convention*	*Others*	*Total*
1995	1,83,207	84,787	21,829	5,257	20,090	5,272	42953	363395
	(50.4%)	(23.3%)	(6.0%)	(1.4%)	(5.5%)	(1.5%)	(11.8%)	(100%)
1996	2,29,377	88,945	25,079	4,802	20,191	6,054	39,165	3,93,613
	(53.2%)	(22.6%)	(6.4%)	(1.2%)	(5.1%)	(1.5%)	(10%)	(100%)
1997	2,49,360	91,525	27,409	4,068	24,106	5,824	19,565	4,21,857
	(53.2%)	(21.7%)	(6.5%)	(1.0%)	(5.7%)	(1.4%)	(4.6%)	(100%)
1998	2,61,347	1,12,644	24,954	16,164	22,123	5,181	21,271	4,63,684
	(59.1%)	(24.3%)	(5.4%)	(3.5%)	(4.8%)	(1.1%)	(4.6%)	(100%)
1999	2,90,862	1,07,960	23,813	19,198	24,132	5,965	19,574	4,91,504
	(59.2%)	(22.0%)	(4.8%)	(3.9%)	(4.9%)	(1.2%)	(4.0%)	(100%)
2000	2,55,889	1,18,780	29,454	15,801	20,832	5,599	17,291	4,63,646
	(55.2%)	(25.6%)	(6.4%)	(3.4%)	(4.5%)	(1.2%)	(3.7%)	(100%)

There are basically two kinds of trekking such as fully organised trekking and teahouse trekking (lodge trekking). The first type concerns with the trekkers who are fully independent local accommodation and food. The entire trekking management is done by trekking company. The trekkers are faciliated with lodging, fooding in tents and trekking guidance. There will be group equipment and food itemised for trekking. The trekker and staff ratio would be 1:3. This type of trekking provides a lot of advantages to trekkers in terms of security, guidance, hygiene, convenience, care and interpretation. Comparatively, it is expensive.

Teahouse trekking, on the other side, is a very popular type, which concerns with small groups of trekkers. This type of trekking is suggested only for the most popular areas where there is better network of teahouse management. Trekkers can independently travel without the help of trekking guide. But it is more risky and disordered. In the tourist season, the independent trekkers may have to face difficulties and crowds of other, trekkers in the teahouse and routes. But it has advantages of cheap cost for trekking to trekkers. The day to day trekking business is in a good order of travel. Generally, a trekker follows five or six hours trekking a day with a break for lunch in the way. The trails are usually maintained in a good way for easy walking. The trekkers generally experienced the village life and environment and magnificent scene and scenary of village Nepal. The trekkers see something in the way and this will be special for their experience and adventure.

Hence, the trekkers should decide to travel by teahouse trekking or camping. If camping is followed, the trekkers have to contact with trekking agency to arrange all groups equipment needed. Regarding trekking areas and mountains, head covering is very important precaution. Peaked caps for sunny days and wool cap for cold are suggested as best combination in trekking trips.

The trek has to use map; it helps trekkers to travel and find out route. The trekkers can enjoy several villages, mountains, rivers and scene and scenary on the way. Delighted with local villagers, tourists enjoy a lot . The trekkers would delight more with the magnificient mountains in trekking period. But they would delight more than double when meeting with villagers appear friendly, hospitable and welcoming. They find the Nepali people, villagers, best of all in the world. All these things can be nicely presented to tourists by developing village tourism industry in village Nepal. That is why the relationship existed between village tourism and trekking can be further enhanced by introducing village tourism and trekking tourism partnership programme.

In trekking advantages of village tourism to villages, villagers and society specially route-wise in brief:

Trekking in Everest Region

Trekking in Everest region is very interesting. Access into this region is possible by aeroplane or on foot. A travel by bus can be made from Kathmandu to Jiri for seven to ten-hours. There is also a new road opening soon to Salleri, the district headquater of Jiri. Alternatively, the trekkers can travel the Everest region via the Arun valley where the major road is Hile.

There are three alternative choice given to fly Everest treks. The most convenient one is Lukla, which provides the regular flight from Kathmandu. The second option is the Phaplu flight from Kathmandu. The last choice is the small flight to Syanboche located above Namche Bazar at the altitude of 3,760 meters.

Everest is the land of Sherpas, which exhibits its majority with distinctive houses and village monasteries. The flora and fauna can be seen in altitude from less than 2,000 meters to the high peaks of the Himalaya at over 8,000 meters. Up to 4,000 meters dense forest can be viewed by flowering rhododendrons, pine, oak and so on. In spring season, the hills between 2,000 and 3,500 meters present themselves in a riot of colours.

Birds can be seen in this region including the national bird of Nepal, Danfe (the impeyan pheasant) commonly found in Namche Bazar. Land animals like Mountain goats (Himalayan Tahr) are also seen in this region. The peak season lies in the months of October/November and March/May. The spring season is pleasant for watching wildflowers paricularly rhododendrons.

One of the pleasant trekking areas in Nepal is Everest Base camp, which is normally visited for two week trek. Namche Bazar was once a small village, but today it has been a centre of trekking and major junction of the Sherpas. There are many villages for visiting tourists in and around Everest region. Passing through Namche Bazar one can see the beautiful valley of Imjakhola where the mountains like Thamserku, Kangtega and Ama Dablam, Everest and Lhotse show their majesty. The most amazing night to stop after Namche Bazar is at Thyangboche, which is the place of Buddhist monasteries in Solukhumbu. There is very famous landmark of Kala Patter above Gorak shep. Alternatively, Kumjung is an interesting place next to Namche Bazar if trekkers would like free of hustle and bustle of the bazar.

Trekking in the Gokyo valley is also interesting, which is dominated at its head by Chooyu at 8,153 meters (the eight highest peak in the world). The distinctive feature this valley is the rocky hill above the third lake recognised as Gokyo Ri or Gokyo Kala Pattar. It takes at least two hours to climb the hill. The trekkers can see better panoramic views from this hill than from the Kala Pattar. It takes at least two hours to climb the hill. The trekkers can see better panoramic view from this hill than from the Kala Pattar at Gorek shep.

There are two major high passes going through the Gokyo valley such as Cho La pass that connects with the Khumbu valley Lobuche and other is the Renjo La Pass which passes the trail between Thame and Nangpa La. Trekking Gokyo valley is more pleasant after visiting Everest.

Trekking from Jiri to Lukla

Trekkers can travel to Jiri by bus. The service from Kathmandu to Jiri completed in seven to ten hours. The trek from Jiri to Lukla takes on average seven days. On the route, Lamjura La Pass located at 3530 meters is the highest point that can exhibit beautiful pink and lilac rhododendrons in spring season.

Trekking from Jiri, the night halts can be taken at villages like Deurali, Kenja, Sete, Lamjura, Junibesi, Tragsindho, Khari Khola and surkhe, etc. The trek passes through the areas of

Solukhumbu which are backward as compared with Namche Bazar. The trail passes through several settlements of ethnic groups of people like Tamang, Jirel, Rai, Chhetri, Brahmin, Sherpa and so on. The most pleasant village destination is Jundbesi, the indigeneous Sherpa settlement in Solu. The southern area of Solukhumbu attracts more trekkers with its magnificient natural beauty and culture. The trek of nine day's period of time normally starts from Jiri and ends with a flight back to Kathmandu from Phaplu. Optionally, the trek can be continued from Phaplu to Everest trek at Ringmo, the village below the Tragsindho La Pass. Traveling Pike Danda is pleasant trek, trekkers should follow the Jiri to Lukla trek nearby Likhu Khola before Kinja. The sacred Lake named Dudh Kunda is next attraction of Everest region, which lies at the base of Mt. Numbur. The trail to Dudh Kunda begins at Ringmo on the route between Junbesi and Tragsindho La. Trek to Salleri is also interesting.

As for on the short trek, the Choilsa-chiwong circuit is interesting. Treks extend the ridge above Salleri to the east. The ridge, Ratnongi Danda attracts trekkers with beautiful mountains through Makalu Barun National Park and long distance view of Everest. The route passes the ridge on northern side at Trogsindho. Trekkers travel Rolwaling with Khumbu from east to west. The Everest trek can either begin or end by trekking the Arun valley in the east Nepal. By road, the starting place can be fixed at Hille or Tumlingtar for flight.

Trekking in Annapurna Region

The Annapurna region is the best trekking destination in Nepal and abroad. It is most popular destination preferred by tourists. Between Annapurna I and Dhaulagiri at 8,000 meter, the valley of the Kali Gandaki river lies in this place, which is the deepest gorge on earth. Combined with fertile land, natural forest and ethnic groups of people, trekkers can experience the diversity and uniqueness in trekking.

For trekking in this region, Pokhara is the point for starting or ending of trekker's trek. Pokhara located at 200 km, west of Kathmandu can be reached by bus in five to six hours or by

Panorama of Himalaya

aeroplane in 30 minutes duration from capital city. There are major three Lakes in Pokhara valley namely, Fewa Lake, Rupa Lake and Begnas Lake. Among the three, the largest one is Fewa Lake which is very popular Lake side tourist destination

Rhododendron

preferred by tourists. There is a large number of restaurants, hotels, travel agencies, shopping centres and different amenities in Lakeside and Damside. For trekking in the eastern part of the Annapurna massif, Besishahar is the starting gear, which is the district headquarter of Lamjung district.

A variety of flora and fauna can be watched in this region. Due to the tropical climate, the area is famous for orange production, which can be bought fresh oranges on the way and trails in the foot hills. Pokhara and Besishahar are located at less than 100 meter elevation. Several birds and animals can be seen such as pike blue sheep, Himalayan Tahr, etc.

Trekking routes developed in the Annapurna region are serviced by teahouses. The popular treks like the Jomsom trek, the Annapurna circuit trek and the Annapurna Base Camp trek are service-oriented treks by locals.

The Annapurna circuit is felt very long day to trekkers while crossing the high pass of Thorong La. The major group of people living in the Annapurna region are the Gurung, Thakali and Manangba. The Gurungs distributed from Gorkha to Palpa are in majority in this region. The Thakalis who are from the upper Kali Gandaki valley around Jomsom operate restaurant and

Pretty Flower

hotels business. Gurung's culture is very rich and preferred by tourists. Trekking in this region is suitable in the spring and autumn seasons. Spring is the season for flowering rhododendrons.

Annapurna circuit is the classic trek popularly known as 'Annapurna world class trek'. The task of Annapurna circuit has been completed since the mid 1980s when the Manang destination was officially declared as free trek for foreign trekkers. This mode of trekking is good for all in experiencing Nepalese culture and nature. For trekker's attraction, orange trees are laden with fresh and ripe fruit and fragrant frangipani blossoms cast their scent throughout the whole trails of the region.

This is a challenging trek in adventure. There are some risk factors crossing Thorang La generally unexpected snowfall. The trek is completed within a minimum of fifteen days or more. The trek can be started from Kathmandu and ended in Pokhara. For this trek, an entry permit to Annapurna Conservation Area Project is necessary.

The trek starts from Kathmandu to Besishahar by bus, which takes five or six hours duration. The trail from Besishahar follows Kuldi, which is the small market town of the locality and the trail at Bhul Bhule. The trek follows the Marshyangdi where the Gurung community stays. The Himalayan Rescue Association clinic located in Manang village serves tourist

Hosting Tourist in Village

protect themselves preserving from high altitude mountain sickness.

Trekkers to Muktinath is a pilgrimage site for Buddhists and Hindus after crossing Thorong La. From Muktinath the panoromic scene and scenary is seen. The trail follows villages inhabited by the banks of the Kali Gandaki River, the home of the Thakali ethnic group of people. It is also interesting to trek the high altitude Lake at Tilicho that takes four days for trek.

Annapurna Sanctuary

The trek to the Annapurna sanctuary is also interesting. It is classic trek based upon the site of the base camp. The short trek that can be completed in eight days from Pokhara is an additional pleasure to trekkers. The trek to Annapurna Base Camp combines with the most spectacular mountain view and life of Nepali villagers of middle hill. The favourable time to visit the sanctuary is spring and autumn season. But trekkers should be aware of snowfall and avalanches. The trek normally starts from Pokhara and ends at the same point. But it can also be a part of the Annapurna circuit or the Jomsom trek by trekking from Tatopani to Ghorepani and Tadpani, which joins

Panoramic of Himalaya

the main sanctuary trail at Chomrong. It takes twelve or fourteen days duration for enjoying the sanctuary and enroute areas Ghorepani and Poon Hill.

The trek follows the Gurung village settlements such as Dhampus, Pothana, Landrung and Ghandrung which are known as 'enroute Annapurna tourist villages'. The magnificent scene of steep snow-clad ridges falling from Hiunchuli on the left and the Machhapuchhre on the right give formation of the entrance gate to the sanctuary where a solid wall of snow capped peaks named Annapurna I, II, III and IV plus the fish tailed spire of Machhapuchhre can be seen. For refreshment to trekkers, teahouses are available at Machhapuchhre Base Camp, just inside the sanctuary or at Annapurna Base Camp.

Annapurna Foothills

Annapurna foothill is next attraction to trekkers. There is a number of short treks in the foothills to the north of Pokhara. Ghandrung and Ghorepani are the best tourism spots for trekkers. Ghandrung is a traditional Gurung tourism village while Ghorepani is the settlement below Poon Hill from where trekkers can watch the scenary of the central Himalayan range. For trekker's convenience, several teahouses are available on the way. Trek crossing the Modi Khola at Naya Pul and trek passing through Birethanti to Syauli Bazar and its adjoining cultivated land and small villages and river are pleasant foothill treks. At Syauli Bazar the trail passes steeply to Ghandrung tourism village. From Ghandrung the major trail passes through Tadapani to Ghorepani where Poon Hill is located above three hundred meters.

From Ghorepani there are basically three alternative choices to be taken as routes for trekking. The first one is the route dropping down through the villages of Ulleri and Terkedhunga to Birethanti. It is the original starting point for trekking during the peak season.

The second option is further to follow Ghorepani to the Kali Gandaki at Tatopani. The third choice is trekking along the ridge that starts at Poon Hill.

Trek to Jomson and Muktinath

The Jomsom trek is highly related with village tourism in Nepal. Most probably, it is the single most popular trek in Nepal in terms of diverse landscapes, cultures and way of life of village people. The trekkers can watch the marvellous living style of villages on the trekking route. The major pleasant walk through the gorge carved by the Kali Gandaki River carrying water from the Tibetan Plateau to mix with the Ganges in India.

Trekkers travel from Jomsom to Muktinath known as pilgrimage site for both Buddhist and Hindus. Muktinath literally means the place of salvation for Hindus. Brahma, the God of creator lit the eternal flames that still burn at Muktinath. Guru Rinpoche (Padmasambhava) who meditated in Muktinath, is the great sage of Buddhist philosophy. It is the place of enchanting Shaligrams. In science, Shaligrams are considered as fossilised ammoities found in the Kali Gandaki river. The inhabitant of this area is a composition of Gurung and Magar. The trekkers can watch the customs and dresses wore by the local villages. In Muktinath, the annual horse race

Muktinath Temple

Image of God at Manang Village

popularly known as yartung is wonderfully organised in terms of unique culture in Tibetan style.

Dramatically, the scenary varies between Tatopani and Lete Khola Pine forests are beautifully laid on the train and villages seem quite wonderful appearance. The layout of the villages and style of village houses are unique and different in this area. For example, Marpha village can be a model tourism village where unique architecture is found. It is a two-hour walking distance below Jomsom. The Marpha village environment is stone flagged streets with underground drainage system and the flat roofed houses having the central courtyard. By production, it is an 'apple village' illustrated for horticulture development in the village. Trek in the village of Kagbeni may be an alternative destination to Jomsom. Kagbeni is much quietar than Jomsom.

Established by the Annapurna Conservation Project Area (ACAP) in the Gurung village of Silklis, a model trekking village was developed. It is located to the north east of Pokhara at 2,000 meters elevation in Annapurna II and Lamjung Himal. Here, well preserved Gurung village is seen in the form of traditional

Beauty of Himalaya

Gurung culture. There is Rishing Danda above the village from where panoramic-scene of Annapurna II and Lamjung can be seen. The Ghantu dance performed by young girls Gurung culture is most popular.

Treks from Besishahar to the villagers of Ghalegaun, Bhujung are pleasant to trekkers. Ghalegaun was recently developed as a model tourism village of Lamjung district. The village people of Lamjung followed Dr Pradhanang's concept of village tourism for exploration of villages of Lamjung.

The next adventurious trek is the circuit of the Dhaulagiri massif to adventure seeking trekkers. The route passes the remote areas. The Dhaulagiri trail follows the Myagdi Khola and massif passing through the settlements of Darbang and Muri where scattered villages and farming land are located. Trek to upper Mustang is rarely experienced by trekkers. They can experience the real people of Nepal in terms of geography, culture and living pattern. Until 1950, Mustang was a separate kingdom followed by the ancient capital, Lo Manthang, it takes a minimum of nine days duration trek here.

Short treks can be organised around Pokhara. The southern part of Phewa Lake is interesting to trek for two-five days. Similarly, Panchase, the west of Pokhara, is at 2,500 meter height

Himalayan Panoramic Peaks

from the sea level. This hill provides the Himalayan panoramic views to trekkers. Access to Panchase is easy from the village of Badauri that can be reached from Naudanda in Baglung.

Trekking in Langtang Area

Trek in Langtang area is another interesting option to trekkers. Access to Helambu is easy through Sundarijal. Optionally, trekkers can start from Budhanilkantha, Kakani and Melamchi Pul. After that a four-hour bus ride is to be followed at east of Kathmandu.

For Langtang and Ganesh Himal trek, one should use the bus from Kathmandu to Trisuli. Trisuli road leads to Dhunche from where trek to Langtang and Gosaikunda can start and continue to Syabrubesi where trekking programme to Ganesh Himal and Langtang can be organised. But service from Kathmandu to Syabrubesi takes a day drive. Trekking routes in Helambu facilitated with teahouses. The people are Sherpas who originated from Tibet but they are quite different from those of Solukhumbu. Trek in Langtang is suitable in spring (February to late April) and autumn (late September to late November).

Trekking Adventure

Trek to the Langtang valley is more delightful to trekkers. The best trek starts either from Dhunche or from Syabrubesi. Syabrubesi follows the north bank of the Langtang Khola passing through the villages of Khangjung and Syarpa Gaun. The trail passes through cultivated and grass land, grassy slope and forests of rhododendron, bamboo and oak which have very

Image of God

beautiful scene and environment.

Gosaikund is the largest among the three major lakes. The two lakes consist of Saraswotikund and Bhairabkund. As the Hindu legend states that the lakes were created by God Shiva when He plunged His Trisul (tident) in the ground for water. By name, the Trisuli River has its source in these lakes.

Helambu circuit is the short trek close to Kathmandu. It takes seven days to complete the circuit. In Helambu, trekkers can see the local inhabitants such as Tamang and Sherpa. There are villages like Melamchigaun, Tarkeghayang and Sharmanthong. The trek is mostly in a low altitude of 3,000

Riverside Beauty

Himalayan View

meters and trekkers can experience snow at the time of trekking season. The route to Ganja La begins from Kyangin Gompa environment in the Langtang valley. The pass is distinctly seen from Kyangjin. The trek from Ganesh Himal to Trisuli at Dhading is the remote area suitable for fully equipped trekkers. The Ganesh Himal spreads ranging several peaks over 7,000 meters. The route follows the old trail to Paldor Base Camp.

Trekking Around Manaslu and Gorkha

Trekking around Manaslu and Gorkha is wonderful and unspoiled areas. The view and splendid place to the east of the Annapurna massif point out several peaks of Manaslu.

The Manaslu circuit is one of the best trekking areas in terms of remote treks. The route developed with some teahouses attracts trekkers. There is the Conservation Area Project that encourages trekkers to trek. It takes 18 days duration to complete the circuit. The trekkers can see the rugged gorge of the Budhi Gandaki for the first 12 days until they cross the Larkya Pass and Marshyangdi Khola. Occasionally, the trekkers have to face heavy snow that distrubs the route difficult situation.

Gorkha is the historical village of Nepal, where Prithivinarayan Shah, the great was born and he unified Nepal into an independent country. The trekkers can see cultivated land and beautiful villages. From Gorkha trail passes for joining the Budhi Gandaki at Arughat village. The village is inhabited by Gurung community in the upper reaches until Nambru where villagers experience by influence of the Tibetan culture. Nambru is close to Tibet.

After passing the village of Samdu, the trekkers cannot see the permanent habitat until Bimtang. A large stone is seen at Larkya Phedi, which provides shelter to trekkers. As the pass is forwarded, the scenary of Manaslu looks stunning. The stunning scenary compels visitors to pause for a while until they go down to Bimtang. After Bimtang the trail follows the Dudh Khola valley consisting blue pine and rhodondendron. From this point, the trek can be joined with the major Annapurna circuit trail at Dharapani on the Marshyangdi River.

Cable Car Service and Visitors

Manokamana Temple

Besides this, trek from Manakamana to Gorkha including the temple of Manakamana is very attractive. To reach Manakamana a short cable car from Kurintar to Manakamana can be entertained for 10 minutes. Apart from this, the stunning

Cable Car Station Area

Natural Beauty Surrounding Cable Car Service Area

view of Manaslu and Annapurna can be enjoyed by trekkers. The meditation cab of Lakan Thapa can also be watched by the visitors.

The trek to Manaslu foothills is next part of village trekking relationship. Mostly, the trek passes through the villages like Dharchya and Gorkha. With regard to trekking management, the starting point can be fixed at Dharchya and ending at Gorkha. The trekkers can experience unspoiled trails and villages. On the trekking route, Barpak village dominated by Gurung culture can be visited by bypass trekking. This is a relatively low altitude trek exhibiting the middle hill environment and living pattern of the people inhabited.

The far East: Kanchenjunga Base Camp Trek

The trek to Kanchenjunga Base Camp lying at the far east is one of the difficult treks in Nepal. Kanchenjunga situated at the altitude of 8586 meters is the third highest mountain in the world. The trekkers coming to Nepal can experience never boaring wonderful remote villages at Kanchenjunga trekking route. Visiting base camp requires at least twenty six days duration. For complete package tour, generally the trek starts from Basantapur and ends at Taplejung.

River and Mountain View

For going to Basantapur, the visitor should follow the route via Dharan and Hile. Alternatively, it can be shortened by aeroplane from Kathamandu to Biratnagar and bus service taken. The trekking trail passes the bazar of Basantapur and several communities such as Chauki, Gupha Pokhari and so on. Gupha Pokhari is very interesting pond located at the ridge top with spectacular distant scenary of the Himalaya consisting Makalu and Kanchenjunga.

In Taplejung natural gorge and small villages are beautifully seen. The trail follows the ever-narrowing gorge of the Tamur River and several small villages resided by the Limbu and Chhetri ethnic groups of people. The village of Chirwa popularly known as 'Tongba making village' where the wooden pots are utilised for drinking the fermented millet drink. In the rocky walls, several wild bee hives are harvested by the villagers. The trail passes the dense forest which is the home of wildlife, e.g. leopard, deer and so on.

Besides, Ghunsa is resided by the people of Tibetan origin and it shows their skill development in a traditionally

Enjoying Nature

developed carpet industry. There is a big wooden Buddhist monastry built in the unique form. It takes three days duration to reach the north part of Kanchenjunga base camp located at Pang Pema. No permanent settlement above Ghunsa is available but simple shelter can be accommodiated at Kambachen which is a summer grazing place. Wonderfully, the landscape varies shortly above Ghunsa. The pine forest provides the stunted alpine bushes. The last camp made in Lahnok is a sheltered place for trekkers.

Kanchenjunga Foothills

The trek in Kanchenjunga foothills is interesting in the lower hills around this world of the third highest mountain. The trekkers follow the trail to Kharang and Chainpur from Tumlingtar. The Chainpur bazar developed as the production centre of typical 'Karuwa' (water pot of Nepali style) and other brass ware is trekker's destination for adventure. This bazar is well popularised by using the Nepali phrase 'Chainpurko Karuwa'. From Chainpur the trail passes the valley of the Piluwa Khola that connects the Milke Danda ridge. In the spring season, the area will be a riot of colour from the blooms of the rhododendrons, which is very popular in the trekker's adventure tour. There is a beautiful pond-village named Gupha Pokhari at the southern part of the Milke Danda. The village having wonderful scenary and natural beauty is good for developing tourism village as well as trekker's paradise centre. Staying at the village, trekkers can watch most splendid views of the distant Himalaya from Everest through Kanchenjunga. The trekkers can enjoy the natural beauty from Gupha Pokhari to the Tamur River at Dobhan. The trail passes lush forest and cultivated land. In this locality, cardamon is produced and it is an important cash crop for villagers. Following the Tamur River, the trekkers can see the small villages of Mitlung and Chirwa. From Chirwa they can visit Pathibhara and Suketar.

Milke Danda is the 'zone of rhododendrons and star hill of national flower'. It is world famous for flowering rhododendrons. After passing the Gupha Pokhari, the rugged and isolated Jaljale Himal can be enjoyed by visitors. The trail from Basantapur to Gupha Pokhari is a component of Milke Danda exhibited the settlements of village in pristine habit. The ridge top of the Milke Danda forest with beautiful rhododendrons provides 32 varieties of rhododendrons. After passing Milke Danda from the west, trekkers can see and enjoy Arun valley and back to Tumlingtar.

Some selected trekking package tours

TABLE 8: Some Selected Areas Generating
Income and Employment

Trekking		Employ-ment	Estimated Income For Trekking Agencies Per Person Per Package Tour
Area	*Package*		*Nrs*
Everest/Khumbu	Everest BC/Kala-pathar	10	27,250
Annapurna	Annapurna Circuit of Himalayan Sangrila	14	40,700
Annapurna	Annapurna Sanctuary Trek of MBC& ABC of Himalaya Wonder	6	24,050
Western Nepal	Poon Hill Trek	10	31,450
Annapurna	Muktinath	8	25,500
Annapurna	Pokhara-Dhampus-Pokhara Trek	10	27,7500
Annapurna	Pokhara-Ghandruk-Pokhara Trek	10	18,500
Mid Hill	Panchase	8	22,000
	Total	76	2,71,023

Source : Sample Study

Notes : *Estimated Cost per Package per Tourist from NRS 16,137- NRS 40,700.
*Employment Generation Estimated From 6 Persons-15 Persons per Package on the Basis of the Group of Tourists.
*Trekking Starts from Kathmandu to Pokhara.
*Estimated Duration of Trek 8 Days-23 Days.
*Adventure Based Activities-Trekking, Camping, Rafting, Boating, Cultural Show, Nature Trek, Sight Seeing, etc.

The Table 8 exhibits some selected trekking areas generating income and employment.

The trekking areas with packages are selected as Everest Base Camp/Kalapathar, Annapurna Circuit of Himalaya Sangrila, Annapurna Sanctuary Trek, Rara Lake, Poon-Hill, Muktinath, Pokhara-Dhampus, Pokhara-Ghandruk and Panchase. The estimated duration of trek having adventure based activities like rafting, boating, camping, sighting, cultural show; nature trek and so on is for 8 days to 23 days. From trekking the businessmen or trekking agencies generating income per package is estimated to NRS 16,137-NRS 40,700. The total income is amounted to NRS 2, 71,023.

Rafting

Village tourism has a good relation to rafting. It connects with each other in terms of wilderness experience and adventure. Characterised as a soft and tamed wilderness with white sandy beaches for camping, rivers compel friendly village people to have relationship. Specifically, rafting developed in Nepal is highly likened by rafters. Due to the magnificent nature and beautiful scenary, tourists are attracted by enjoying rafting. River lovers say, 'Nepal is a wonderful country having warm welcome and hospitality to the rafters and kayakers'. Rafting, having a good relationship with village tourism, is as a part of village tourism. The rafting villages are plenty in number nearby rivers of Nepal. Understandably, Nepal is a river runner's paradise that provides unexpected pleasure and entertainment.

The story of rafting states that the first crazy river runners were seen in Nepal in 1960. In 1968 two French men rafted in Sun Koshi as experiment in the Nepalese river. Standardised as one of the top ten rivers of the world, the Sun Koshi river attracted rafters.

Basically, the history of rafting and kayaking in Nepal started from 1970. The commercial trip was handled in 1974 for 15 tourists by promoting different rivers of Nepal. The trip was highly succeeded by taking interest in Nepalese rafting. The rafters were very pleased with the standard of Nepalese rafting. Associated with Tiger Tops Mr. Al Kid, an American national started rafting regularly in Trisuli and Sunkoshi under the direction of Mike Yager who trained some Nepali rafting guides and explored the rivers of Nepal as rafting tourism business. Further, he organised training cum workshop programmes including a friendly tour in the USA. In 1976, Himalaya River Exploration was formally registered in His Majesty's Government of Nepal (the government of Nepal), which was the first commercial river rafting company in Asia. Popularised as world class professionals, Nepali rafters were invited for expeditions in other countries of the world.

Selection of Rafting Sites

Rafting in Nepal is an adventure creating water based activity. The rivers of Nepal having perennial source emerging from the glaciers of the top mountains passing through the plateaus of the Himalayas provide wonderful pleasure to tourists. Nepal is a watery and riverian paradise created the nature. Nepal is the world famous top tourist destination where varieties of charming tourism product can be enjoyed. Rafting holds a number of beautiful things like flora and fauna, majestic landscape, water-fall, lifestyle of the people, etc.

Rafting is a river based village tourism which can be developed in a special style. The selection of rafting sites can be done on the basis of river system. In Nepal there are basically three major river systems consisted as Sapta Koshi, Sapta Gandaki and Karnali. The best, selection of rafting sides are Karnali, Tamur and Sun Koshi. They are categorised as 'World classic type' in the international rafting market. The very interesting and superqualitative white water trips can be organised in these rivers. Similarly, the best and interesting rivers for wildlife tourism and fishing are Baabai, Bheri, Karnali and Mahakali.

The experience of Nepal's rivers shows the best rivers for rafting and kayaking. The best white water trips can be programmed in rivers like Marsyandi, Kali and Tamur for 3-6 days. The next best sites are Trisuli and Bhote Koshi for 1-3 days white water trips. The best easy water trips can be scored as Bheri for 4-5 days and upper Sun Koshi, Seti, Babai, Trisuli

Trek and Nature

for 1-3 days. Similarly the best combination of trekking and rafting can be introduced side by side as a new tourism product/trip in Tamur and Marsyangdi.

The site selection for short white water rafting can be suggested as Bhote Koshi. The best selection for family trips can be accounted as upper Sun Koshi, Seti and Trisuli. From the stand-point of budget tourism, trips in Trisuli, Kali and Sun Koshi can be choosen as the best in water tourism.

Consideration to Select Rafting Site

Rafting, being the most adventurous tourism, is related to various interesting things for tourists. Rafters should enjoy the beautiful scene and scenery and culture of the rafting villages. To make rafting more enjoyable and to select rafting site, the following considerations should be taken into account:

1. Unspoiled Natural Heritage

The rating site should be selected on the basis of unspoiled natural heritage. The natural scenery and cultural heritage are most effective tourism products to attract tourists. Rafting

Nepalese Village with Nature

provides not only water, but it also provides several things like temples, rural people, villages, living style of the people, culture and so on.

2. Tourism Village

The rafting site should possess tourism villages where rafters can enjoy the villages spending nights as a good centre for accommodation and food, locally prepared in the indigeneous style. The rafters staying at the tourism village will get high relaxation and wonderful Nepal's village hospitality which will be unforgetable in life. The villages of Nepal are unique in attraction so that the international rafters can enjoy with high aspiration.

3. *Trekking Route*

The rafting site should be selected in terms of the importance of trekking route. The tourist can enjoy the river and river side views on the one hand, and different sight seeing, environmentally soft activities like hiking, trekking, nature observation and nature photography on the other hand. Thus, the rafting site should be chosen from the standpoint of the prospects of trekking route.

4. *Experience Geography*

The rafting site should have a great scope of geography. Rafters can experience the geography of the rafting destination and nature. The study of national geography is a great enchanting activity preferred by a large number of people. The national geography can be explored through rafting adeventure and water tourism development. Tourists want the unexplored destinations that can be made accessible by rafting.

5. *Land of Paradise*

The land of the rafting site should be very interesting. To select rafting site the image of land should have a teriseatable position. Nepal is the land of paradise where the highest snow mountains, deepest gorge, majestic scene and scenary are surrounding. Thus rafting can be promoted as an appropriate tourism business in Nepal. As a result, the people and country can get more benefits from rafting.

Rafting is a very good tourism product which should be commercially promoted in the international tourism market. As per the demand of the tourists, the world class rafting professionals should be promoted to support expeditions and adventure based tourism industry.

Safety and Precautionary Measures in Rafting:

The rafting business is increasing at a faster rate in Nepal. Rafting, being most interesting job, can generate income and employment opportunity. About 6 per cent of the total tourists come to Nepal for rafting purpose.

Some safety and precautionary measures shoud be taken in rafting. They are explained below:

1. *Life Jacket*

Life jacket is the most important equipment for safety of life. The modern life jackets are good and comfortable. The best type of jacket having a minimum weight of 7 kg for an adult is prescribed for entertainment.

2. *Cater-Raft*

Cater-raft is used for carrying equipment for camping in long rafting trips. It is basically taken for precautionary measures.

3. *Self-Bailing Raft*

The self-draining raft having an inflatable floor is known as self-bailing raft. It is used for precautionary measures against challenging rivers.

4. *Helmet*

Helmet is compulsory in any white water trips. The possible danger is saved from helmets. One who falls down from the raft will be saved by wearing the helmet.

5. *Paddle*

Paddle is the most important equipment used for rafting. The best paddle made of plastic and alloy will be comfortable and has precautionary safety for rafters.

6. *First-Aid and Repairing Kits*

In rafting there is need of carrying first-aid and repairing kits for precautionary measures of life.

7. *Water Proof Container*

The water proof container is used for protecting cameras and valuable goods of tourists from the viewpoint of safety measures.

8. Water Proof Bag

Water proof bag is used for keeping clothes and sleeping bags for tourist's facility as precautionary and safety measures.

9. Harness

Harness is the belt used to tie different goods in rafting activity.

10. Camping Gear and Cooking Gear

Camping gears and cooking gears should be taken for being self-sufficient in rafting.

SUSTAINABILITY

Village tourism is concerned with sustainability. Sustainability is hidden within the concept of village tourism. Village tourism is the second name for sustainable tourism. There is a close relationship between village tourism and sustainability. In 1972, the Stockholm Conference on the Human Environment gave the message for environmental protection. Report on 'Our Common Future' brought a significant environmental awareness in the developmental process.

Development with continuity and a balance in environment is characterised as sustainability. The World Commision on Environment and Development (WCED) introduced the term, sustainable development emphasising the supremacy of ecology over human needs. The term, sustainable developoment is defined as 'development that meets the needs of the present generation without compromising the ability of future generations to meet their own needs' (WCED, 1987). The concept of sustainability is related to a wide area ranging from development to population and covers every component of social, economic, cultural and ecological aspects of citizen, this should actually be taken as a special 'beat' by the media. The time frame that sustainability has in its vision is so broad that it covers the whole of present and most of future.

Regarding sustainable tourism development, 'sustainable tourism development meets the needs of the present tourists and host regions while protecting and enhancing opportunity for the future. It is envisaged as leading to management of all resources in such a way that economic, social and aesthetic needs can be fulfilled while maintaining cultural integrity, essential ecological processes, biological diversity and life support systems.' (WTO, 1991).

The developing countries like Nepal have primary sector based economies where natural resource in terms of value added ratio is high with a higher output elasticity of natural resources. The value added in terms of local resources utilisation brings in comparatively more sustainable development in the country. Based on growth, equity and environment, sustainable development proceeds ahead. Fundamentally, the holistic approach of sustainable development concerns with three-approach like economy, environment and society.

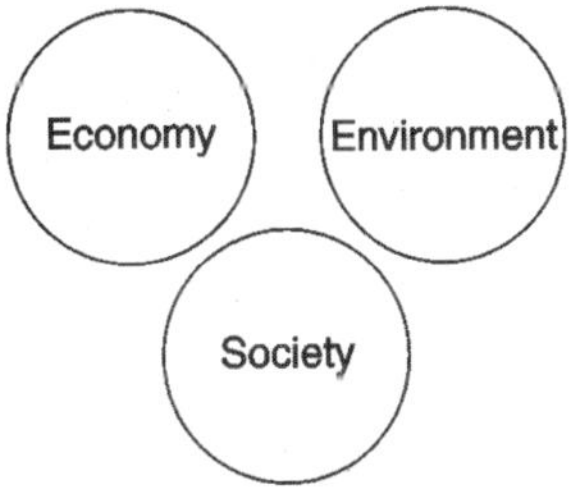

The community showing as three separate unrelated components

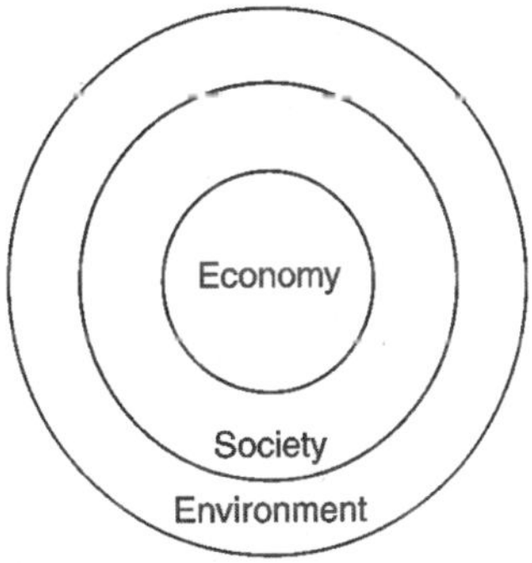

The community showing as three concentric circles.

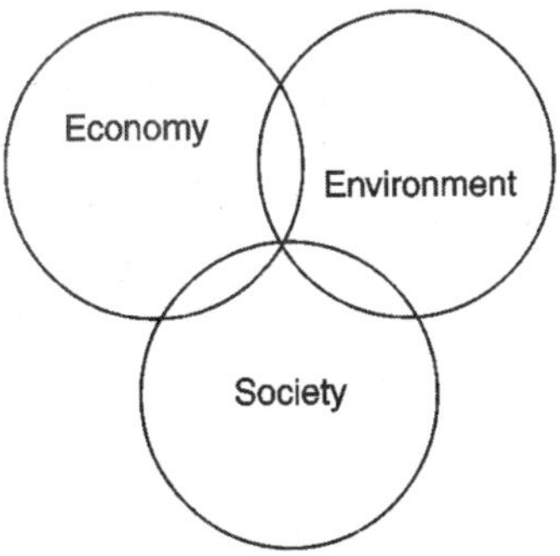

The diagram exhibits that the economy exists within society and both the economy and society exist within the environment

The diagram stating community shows the linkages among its three components economy, environment and society.

Village tourism links with sustainability through the vision as such:

(*a*) living pattern within the limits and discipline.

(*b*) implementation by understanding the interconnections among economy, society and environment.

(*c*) Equitable distribution of resources and opportunities to all including village and villager.

Village tourism relating to sustainability pushes up village and villager for economic development with several linkages. Hence, village tourism and sustainability have positive correlation. The value attributed to the natural world and rights of animal are respected by developing relationship between village tourism and sustainability. Too much concentration on environment cannot result sustainability without links developed with society in terms of livelihood, economic benefit, equal distribution of wealth and so on. The high output elasticity of natural resources results positive correlation by utilising and pushing up value added goods and services through village tourism industry. This village tourism is sustainable and in it equal justice, could be ensured equity, village economy, nature conservation and environment are also preserved in the prolers.

WILDLIFE AND NATURE CONSERVATION

Village tourism associated with wildlife and nature is much closer to nature conservation. Wildlife as an ornament is valued in terms of conserved nature. Village tourism plays with nature and natural products. That is why it has a close relationship with them.

Nepal is very rich in bio-diversity conserving nature. Embarked on a new era of wildlife conservation, the National Parks and wildlife conservation Act 2029 has been implemented (NDPWC, 2002). Conserving wildlife such as rhino and tiger species with the safeguard and control of Royal Nepalese Army in the National Parks and Wildlife Reserves since 1975 is good for all. The Department of National Parks and Wildlife Conservation, (DNPWC) has set its objectives for conserving wildlife species and habitats preservation with regard to integrated wildlife management. But DNPWC could not have succeeded in its management approach had it no involved local people as participants in conservation objectives. The inter-linkage between village tourism and nature conservation is highly prioritised.

Realising the need of village tourism concept in terms of villager's benefit and economic development along with wildlife and nature conservation, conservation strategy has been undertaken through community participation. Considering the new idea of village tourism, the buffer zone can be enhanced as tourism village keeping in view local village and villagers' development. Harmonising nature conservation for livelihood with reference to village tourism is the challenge and opportunity for national development especially villages of Nepal. Nepal is famous for its participatory nature conservation adopted to the approach of highlighting landscape. The nature conservation concerns with ecosystems, unique natural and cultural heritages, wonderful landscapes and endangered wildlife species. All of them should be preserved by respecting nature for better environment.

Nepal is a landlocked country located at the Himalayas spreading at 800 km east-west in rectangular form. Its altitude climatically differs from the flat lowland of the terai region at 60 m to the top of the world, Mt. Everest at 8848 m. It has 2.2 percent of the world's flowering plants.Nepal is rich in biodiversity.The following table exhibits the nature of biodiversity in Nepal.

TABLE 9: Glimpse of Biodiversity in Nepal

S.No.	*Category Given*	*No. of Species*	*Category Given*	*No. of Species*	*Category Given*	*No. of Species*
1.	Flowering plants	7,066	Amphi-bians	43	Fungi and Molds	1666
2.	Mammal	181	Fish	135	Lichen	465
3.	Birds	859	Butterflies	635	Algae	687
4.	Reptiles	100	insects	5052		

Source : Department of National Park & Wildlife Conservation, 2061.

The Table 9 shows the biodiversity by category in different species. Flowering plants consist of 7,066 species, Amphibians posses 43 species and Fungi and Molds have 1666 species. Similarly, Reptiles and insects have 100 and 5052 species respectively.

Besides, more than 700 medicinal plants and 200 plant species are use for domestic medical consumption. There are 375 endemic flowering plants in Nepal.

In accordance with NPWC Act 2029, parks and reserves were established in 1973. Historically, six protected areas spreading 4376 sq km were formed such as Royal Chitwan National Park, Langtang National Park, Sagarmatha National Park, Rara National Park, Kosti Tappu Wildlife Reserve and Royal Suklaphanta Wildlife Reserve. In addition to it, other six protected areas Shey Phoksundo National Park, Khaptad National Park, Parsa Wildlife Reserve, Shivpuri Watershed and Wildlife Reserve (Shivpuri National Park,2002), Dhorpatan Hunting Reserve and Royal Bardia National Park covering 671 sq km were established. The next important conservation areas like Annapurna Conservation Area Project, Makalu Barun National Park, Kanchanjunga Conservation Area and Manasulu Conservation Area covering 8.17 percent land area in the country were established. Similarly, the buffer zones,covering 2777 sq km in and around RCNP, RBNP, LNP, SPNP and MBNP were declared. The buffer zones in Sagarmatha National Park and Royal Suklaphanta Wildlife Reserve were also declared.The following table displays the protected areas in Nepal.

TABLE 10: Protected Areas of Nepal

S. No.	*Protected Area*	*Established Date*	*Area Covered in Sq km*
1.	Royal Chitwan National Park	1973	932
2.	Rara National Park	1976	106
3.	Sagarmatha National Park	1976	1148
4.	Langtang National Park	1976	1710
5.	Royal Suklaphanta Wildlife Reserve	1976	305
6.	Koshi Tappu Wildlife Reserve	1976	175
7.	Royal Bardia National Park	1984	968
8.	Shey Phoksundo National Park	1984	3555
9.	Khaptad National Park	1984	225

S. No.	*Protected Area*	*Established Date*	*Area Covered in Sq km*
10.	Makalu Barun National Park	1991	1500
11.	Parsa Wildlife Reserve	1984	499
12.	Dhorpatan Hunting Reserve	1987	1325
13.	Kanchanjunga Conservation Area	1997	2035
14.	Annapurna Conservation Area	1992	7629
15.	Manaslu Conservation Area	1998	1663
16.	Shivpuri National Park	2002	144
	Total Area		23,919

Source: DNPWC, Biodiversity Conservation Efforts in Nepal, 2061.

The above Table 10 exhibits protected areas in Nepal. There are 16 protected areas declared from 1973 to 2002. The total area covers 23,919 sq km.

TABLE 11: Buffer Zone in Nepal

S.No.	*Protected Area*	*Declared Year*	*Area (sq km)*
1.	Royal Chitwan National Park	1996	750
2.	Royal Bardia National Park	1996	328
3.	Shey Phoksundo National Park	1998	449
4.	Langtang National Park	1998	420
5.	Makalu Barun National Park	1999	830
6.	Sagarmatha National Park	2002	275
7.	Royal Suklaphanta Wildlife Reserve	2004	243.5
8.	Total		3295.5

Source: Department of National Park and Wildlife Conservation, 2061.

The above Table 11 shows buffer zone declared from 1996 to 2004 in Nepal. There are seven buffer zones identified in conservation area. The total area of the buffer zone covers 3295.5 sq km.

TABLE 12: Revenue Generation and Tourist Arrivals in Protected Areas of Nepal

Year	*Revenue*	*Tourist Arrival*
1994/95	6,48,53,584	90086
1995/96	7,65,31,973	111211
1996/97	7,23,95,882	152262

Year	*Revenue*	*Tourist Arrival*
1997/98	7,92,47,548	139286
1998/99	8,95,99,892	148317
1999/2000	9,35,02,138	163574
2000/2001	13,40,98,496	161020
2001/2002	7,11,83,709	84484
2002/2003	6,08,13,796	80891

Source: DNPWC, 2061
Notes: *Not included revenue from Annapurna Conservation Area and Manaslu Conservation Area.

The above Table 12 exhibits the revenue generated from different protected areas and tourist arrivals from 1994/95 to 2002/2003. Under these protected areas, there are hundred Village Development Committees (VDCs) having thousand of villages. The adjoining villages in the protected areas and buffer zone can get benefits in terms of income and employment. The villagers get more job opportunities when several tourists would visit the areas. The employment generated in terms of culture show, local guide porter, and naturalist and so on. As exhibited in the Table 12, revenue generated NRS 6,48,53,584 in 1994/95 is the significant amount, which can be used for the welfare of villages and villagers. In 2002/2003 revenue generated in the protected areas was NRS 6,08,13,796 and the tourist arrivals were 80,891.

The above mentioned Table 10 and Table 12 indicate the linkages of economic benefit to village and government in terms of revenue and tourist arrivals and employment creation, which is very important in relation to village tourism development.

Nepal is in the direction of community based organisation as partners and key players in the conservation of biodivesity and environment. It experienced Community Forest Development as applied in the Annapurna Conservation Area Project with the participating approach of local people. Nepal has started enacting buffer zone policy in 1996 along with the application of community based biodiversity conservation purpose. Hundred Village Developoment Committees (VDCS) involved in buffer zone development.

Historically, Nepal's biodiversity conservation started from 1950. Established as a Rhino Sanctuary in Chitwan in 1956, the sanctuary's objective was to protect one-horned rhinoceros. The international NGOs like WWF, UNDP-PPP, CARE-Nepal and IUCN are in support to mobilise local community in biodiversity conservation. Today Nepal has been able to protect 80 ecosystems out of a total of 118 ecosystems through the protected network.

The national commitment on behalf of government shows ample measures for conservation and sustainable utilisation of biodiversity in Nepal. There are several protection laws enforced in Nepal such as the constitution of the kingdom of Nepal 1990, Environment Protection Act 1996, National Parks and Wildlife Conservation Act 1973, Forest Act 1993 and Water Resource Act 1992. Furthermore, Nepal is a signatory to the five important international conventions as treaties related to the biodiversity conservation such as the convention on Biodiversity Conservation, the conservation on the International Trade in Endangered Species of Wild Fauna and Flora, the Ramsar Convention and the World Heritage Convention and the United Nation's Convention to Combat Desertification. Nepal also has adopted the National Wetland Policy that followed the Ramsar Sites like the Koshi Tappu Wildlife Reserve, Bish Hazari Tal, Ghodaghodi Tal, Jagasdishpur Reservoir. Included two national parks namely Royal Chitwan National Park and Sagarmatha National Park under World Heritage Sites, Nepal seems to be more dedicated to Nature Conservation.

Hence, the relationship developed and extended more between village tourism and nature conservation brings a good reward for national development and economic growth.

Adventure

Adventure in Nepal is most exciting product, which is related to village tourism. The varied landscapes creating adventurious activities lie in village Nepal. Adventures like trekking, mountaineering and sporting are most popular in Nepal. The other prospects have been explored as new development in adventure tourism with relation to village tourism. For example, rafting, biking, fishing, rock climbing, paragliding, ultra-light aircraft, hot air ballooning, mountain flight, boating, ponytrek, jet scooter, boating and bungy jumping are additional items for adventure.

Hot air ballooning is an interesting sport based activity. In its flight, adventure seeking tourists can enjoy the most spectacular view of the Kathmandu valley, beautiful villages, carpeted land with green grasses, Himalayan ranges and so on. Tourists feel that they have reached the top of the world though they are not climbing the Mt. Everest. The landing could be done any place normally in the terraced paddy fields. The best months programmed for a hot air balloon flight are October-November and March.

Paragliding is a comparatively new adventure based sport activity in Nepal. In this Himalayan kingdom, tourists can wonderfully enjoy paragliding. Basically, the adventure-seekers can experience unparalled scenic beauty of nature, village eagles, vultures and so on in the airspace. Besides this, a fantastic scenary of the majestic Himalayas can be enjoyed while floating over the villages, natural land, temples, hilllocks, lakes, rivers, forests, etc. Gliding conducted in Pokhara has been likened by adventure seeking tourists. It is a weather based sport activity commencing from November-February.

Ultralight aircraft established in Nepal is more adeventurious activity. The adventure seekers who would like to fly as birds can enjoy this flight in the sky. The spectacular views, scenic lakes and beautiful mountains can be watched by flying ultralight aircraft in the sky. Pokhara is the tourism destination whereby ultralight aircraft programme is organised. The ultra aircraft company operates flights from Pokhara airport starting from September-June. The flight exhibits the Annapurna range at the speed of 90-130 km per hour. The altitude attained at 12,000 ft high above the cloud is most adventurous to tourists.

Mountain Flight

Mountain flight is an appropriate means to view beautiful

mountains of Nepal. The one hour flight takes tourists at the highest peaks in the world. The first peak appeared on horizon is the majestic Gosaithan at the height of 8,013 m tall. At the right side, Dorje Lhakpa (6,966m) and Phurbi Chyachu appeared. After that the view of Mt. Gauri Shankar (7,134 m) appears. As the flight runs forward at the Eastern Himalaya, the majestic mountains follow as Melungtse (7023 m), Chugimago (6,297 m), Numbur (6,956 m). Likewise, Karyolung (6,511 m) and Cho-oyu (8,021 m) are also viewed.

The last and most exciting travel takes at Gyachungkang at 7,952 m height. To its right direction, Pumori (7,161 m) and Nuptse (7,855 m) can be viewed. Finally, Mt.Everest is viewed at 8,848 m height.

Bungy jumping can be experienced by tourists in Nepal as a new adeventure related tourism product. Located at 160 m over the wild Bote Koshi river closer to the Nepal-Tibet border, Bungy jumping can be organised. The jump designed by a New Zealand consultant at 160 m and operated by the experienced jump expert in the jumping business.

Jet scotter ride is next adeventure based sport. Tourists can experience it in Nepal with full entertainment. Located at 8 km from Narayanghat and 28 km from Mugling nearby a river side resort in Thimura, the 6 km jet scooter ride starts journey.

Relatively, Village tourism is a helping partner and best friend and common factor for means of production to ecotourism, ethinic tourism, cultural tourism, community tourism and sustainable tourism. Many more types of tourism can obtain advantages and assistance from village tourism at the larger extent. It is also merit to nature conservation, national parks, ecology, environment, ecosystem and so on.

Undoubtedly, village tourism is always merit to merit in terms of socio-economic benefit and village identity as a new tourism destination for everywhere and everyone, if carefully handled, operated and saved from its dark shaded picture. This can have a multiplier effect throughout the village economy. Some studies and experiences show that as much as 85 per cent of measured growth in the US per capita income is due to technical change-change driven by highly-educated, well trained people applying their talents and expertise in skills and scientific knowledge to solving the toughest challenges.[6] In the same way, Nepal's Village Tourism Concept can be applied in terms of new innovation, technique, skills and challenges for the developing countries like Nepal. The more village tourism we learn, the more our nation prospers.

To continue to prosper we need to invest more the wealth of ideas and think over rightly. That is why village tourism concept and its education have been an integral part of community enhancement for decades. We are also partnering with poverty alleviation, ecotourism, sustainable tourism and national economic development as a whole. Furthermore, we need to train new ones with specialised village skills and indigenous practices what we are forgetting in a necessary modified and new style of presentation in the greater villages of Nepal.

Over the long term, village tourism could also yield real progress in developing the new technologies required to address global challenges such as poverty, hunger, raise of civilian society life, living standard and economic development we can all support.

By thinking and investing more in village tourism and its education, we can strengthen Nepal's economic leadership, solve tomorrow's tough challenges and multiply our prosperity. We also renovate and restructure the national.

References

1. *The Daily News*, December, 15, 2006.
2. Da Gianni Ristorante, 21-50, 44 , Dr., Long Island City, Queens,USA
3. Café Salamanca, 79-05, Northern Blvd, Jackson Heights, Queens, USA.
4. Kathmandu Restaurant, *Nepali Food*, 2006.
5. Food Nepal,Kathmandu,Nepal, 2006
6. *The New York Times*, December 15, 2006.

Part IV : The Impact of Village Tourism and Regulations

Chapter 13

Role of Village Tourism in Village Economy

Village tourism is a village based and multifaceted industry that affects the village economy through different sectors, e.g. local product, skill, village craft, hut, food and so on. The village tourism industry creates multiplier effect. The multiplier effect measures the flow of effect of tourist expenditure on village products in terms of goods and services. This is the key role of village tourism. Tourist money comes to the hand of villagers, it will mobilise different economic activities in village and create multiplier effect in village economy.

Income, Employment and Revenue Generation

When the demand for international tourism in the developed countries increases, the tourist flow to the tourist receiving countries also increases. As a result, income will increase in the countries. The developing countries need foreign exchange earnings for economic development. Village tourism, in fact, is income elastic. The economic effect of village tourism is significant. Village tourism decreases the gap between the rich and poor. From the development of village tourism, the local tea-shop owners, yak herders, porters, local guides, villagers etc. will get benefit. The marginalised groups of people with low income will also get benefit. For example, thousands of village households from Sirubari, Ghandruk, Khumbu, Namche bazar etc. have economically benefited and raised their standard of living. Similarly, the Solukhumbu village developed by tourism is encouraging.

Before introducing village tourism concept, villagers were considered and used as commodities that satisfy tourists and tourism entrepreneurs. But now it has dramatically changed into tourism host and profession as villager's rights and duties. In the Everest region, the tourist flow in Sagarmatha National Park has amounted to 20,051 in 2004. Analytically, tourism, conservation and development cannot go on isolation. They have to join together in relation to village tourism as access corridor with local people.

Started in the early 1950, mountaineering tourism was developed in the Everest region of Nepal. Later on, trekking tourism was started in the late 1960. The number of village lodges increased from 7 in 1973 to 225 in 1997. Accommodation facility increased to 4,000 beds per night. Employment created by lodges are 759 persons and 8,000 porters. Namche Bazar has been tourist centre of the Khumbu village area. In Namche Bazar, the per capita income of villagers reached to US$ 1600. It is the wonderful and positive impact of village based tourism in the Khumbu village area. This has been a model capitalist village bazar locally driven village economy in the history of

Chorten (temple) at Khumjung Village

View of Khumjung Village in Solukhumbu

tourism economics of Nepal. Similarly, Sherpa ethnic group of people has been the model person benefiting from tourism. The Annapurna Conservation Area Project (ACAP) is the village based conservation area in Nepal. ACAP lies within the boundry of Annapurna region in Western Nepal, North of Pokhara. Annapurna started with mountaineering expeditions in the early 1950. After the conquest of Annapurna I (8,091 m) by a French team organised by Mourice Herzog, the Annapurna region has been very popular in the international tourism market. In 1970, trekking tourism developed in this region.

The first lodge in Ghandruk village opened in 1976 has been popular to trekkers and village lover tourists. Manang and Lower Mustang were also opened for tourists in the form of the Annapurna Circuit Trek. Jomsom/Muktinath, the pilgrimage site on the Manang/Mustang border was opened for tourism. Tourists were attracted from 14,332 in 1980 to 67,000 people in 1999 (Ministry of Culture, Tourism and Civil Aviation, 1999). Lodges were increased to 518 numbers exceeding 6,000 beds per night. Tourism provided job opportunities to 50,000 villagers during peak season. Hence, tourism has been the important economic activity in this region. Tourism benefit should be shared by villages and villagers of Nepal by developing village tourism concept. In fact, village tourism has promoted along with the trekking village. We have several trekking villages in trekking route that shoud be newly attracted by understanding the concept of tourism village. Consequently, village tourism and trekking tourism can be smoothly enhanced together side by side.

Tourists coming to Nepal budget normally to spend average US$ 100 per day, but they are not getting environment to spend that much of money in the Nepalese tourism market. In the rural areas of Nepal, they are spending only 15 per cent of their total expenditure in Nepal (KRC, 1999). Hence, to create tourism environment, village tourism should be highly enhanced for generating more income to village and villagers of Nepal.

The local government revenue from tourism was generally centralised by the government. The government collected revenue from various National Park areas. Later on, the government decided to spend from 30 per cent–50 per cent in the buffer zone as per the buffer zone regulation. In 2002/2003, the National Parks generated NRS 8,13,795 revenue in terms of national parks entrance fee as stated in the table. There is another table, revenue generated from mountaineering tourism in terms of royalty paid by mountaineers to the government.

The below Table 13 exhibits the revenue generated from mountaineers in terms of royalty paid to government and employees involved in mountaineering expedition. In 2004, royalty paid by mountaineers was NRS 127072000 and 9362 local people were employed.

TABLE 13: Revenue Generated From Village Based Mountaineering Tourism

Year	*Total No. of Team*	*Total No. of Mountaineers*	*No. of Person*	*Royalty Paid to Government Employed Nrs(000)*
1992	113	929	8,261	30,291
1993	95	730	5,423	39,102
1994	105	695	5,236	44,499
1995	91	624	5,123	37,257
1996	129	851	4,924	1,01,880

Year	*Total No. of Team*	*Total No. of Mountaineers*	*No. of Person*	*Royalty Paid to Government Employed Nrs(000)*
1997	120	861	7,003	1,08,237
1998	141	974	6,942	9,5479
1999	115	857	9,690	84,989
2000	132	773	1,15,587	1,19,893
2001	112	836	6,203	1,27,396
2002	134	913	10,599	1,28,030
2003	152	1,080	14,838	1,81,360
2004	140	1,042	9,362	1,27,072

Source : Nepal Tourism Statistics, 2004.

Besides, the local government,VDC started charging rafting fees and vehicle entrance fees to tourism entrepreneurs.

Trekking peak permit fee charged by government and Nepal Mountaineering Association (NMA) is the economic benefit from tourism.

Table 14: Growth of Lodges in Some Selected Villages

Village	*Until 1989/90*		*Until 1993/94*		*After 1995*	
	Lodge	*Per cent*	*Lodge*	*Per cent*	*Lodge*	*Per cent*
Everest Region	86	100	161	100	220	100
Lukla	12	14.0	19	11.8	23	10.5
Phakding	6	7.0	9	5.6	13	5.9
Monjo/Jorsale	5	5.8	7	4.3	8	3.6
Namche	16	18.6	26	16.1	32	14.5
Thame	3	3.5	5	3.1	9	4.1
Phortse	2	2.3	3	1.9	5	2.3
Gokyo	1	1.2	5	3.1	8	3.6
Pangboche	3	3.5	8	5.0	10	4.5
Pheriche	3	3.5	5	3.1	10	4.5

Source: Nepal, 2002

The Table 14 exhibits the growth of lodges in some selected villages of Everest Region. The Everest Region consists the villages such as Lukla (14.0%), Phakding (7%), Monjo/Jorsale (5.8%), Namche (18.6%), Thame (3.5%), Phortse (2.3%), Gokyo (1.2%), Pangboche (3.5%) and Pheriche (3.5%) in 1989/90. In 1995 lodges increased to 220.

Diagram Presentation

On the basis of Table 13 Revenue and Employment are exhibited in the above chart from village based mountaineering tourism:

Revenue and Employment Generation

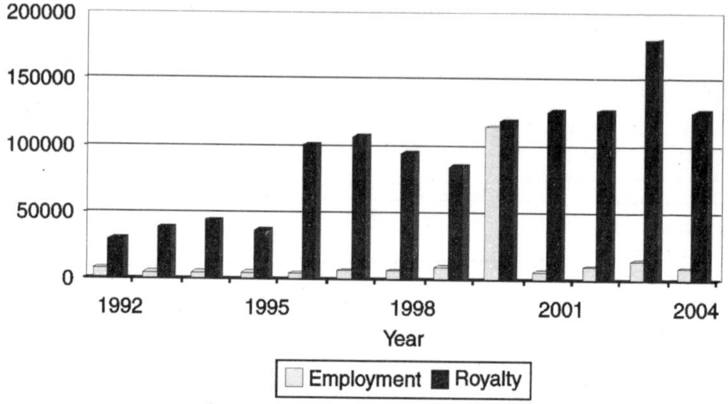

Source: Table 13

Growth of Lodges in Some Selected Villages of Nepal

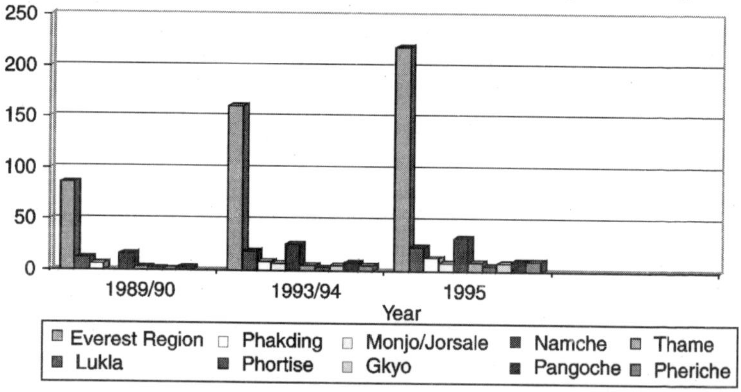

Source: Table 14

Table 15: Lodges Development in Villages

Village	*Until 1989/90*		*Until 1993/94*		*After 1995*	
	Lodge	*Per cent*	*Lodge*	*Per cent*	*Lodge*	*Per cent*
Annapurna region	191	100	311	100	489	100
Besisahar	4	2.1	5	1.6	10	2.0
Jagal	2	1.0	3	1.0	4	0.8
Tal	3	1.6	3	1.0	7	1.4
Dharapani	3	1.6	5	1.6	9	1.8
Chame	3	1.6	7	2.3	13	2.7
Manang and Braga	7	3.7	9	2.9	14	2.9
Muktinath	7	3.7	9	2.9	12	2.5
Jomsom	7	3.7	10	3.2	15	3.1
Kalapani-Lele	3	1.6	5	1.6	11	2.2
Ghara-Sikha	3	1.6	6	1.9	15	3.1
Ghorepani	13	6.8	19	6.1	22	4.5
Ghandruk	8	4.2	13	4.2	15	3.1
Chomrong	7	3.7	12	3.9	11	2.2
Landruk	4	2.1	8	2.6	11	2.7
Dhampus	6	3.1	7	2.3	13	2.7

Source: Nepal, 2002.

Lodges Development in Village

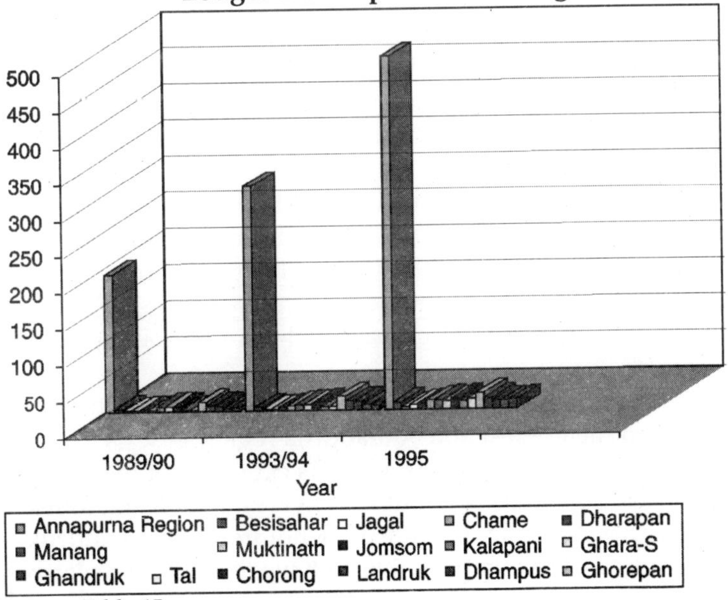

Source: Table 15

The Table 15 exhibits lodges grown in the villages of Annapurna region. Lodges developed in various villages like Besisahar (2.1%), Jagal (1%), Tal (1.6%), Dharapani (1.6%), Chame (1.6%), Manang and Braga (3.7%), Muktinath (3.7%), Jomsom (3.7%), Kalapani-Lele (1.6%),Ghara-Sikha (1.6%), Ghorepanai (6.8%), Ghandruk (4.2%), Chamrong (3.7%), Landruk (2.1%) and Dhampus (3.1%) show the enhancement of village based tourism.

TABLE 16: Growth in Number of Tourists and Lodges in Major Trekking Routes

Year	*Everest*			*Annapurna*		
	Number of Tourists	*Number of Lodges*	*Number of Settlements with Lodges*	*Number of Tourists*	*Number of Lodges*	*Number of Settlements with Lodges*
1980	5,836	17	12	14,300	45	29
1990	7,950	75	29	35,800	203	69
1998	22,826	225	38	65,587	518	84

Source: Nepal, 2002.

The above Table 16 shows tourist flows and lodges developed in the Everest and Annapurna regions. The major trekking routes of Nepal lie in these regions. The tourist flows (5,836), lodges (17) and settlements with lodges (12) developed are in the Everest region during the period of 1980. In 1998 the tourist arrivals (22,826), lodges (225) and settlements with lodges (38) were increased. Similarly in the Annapurna region the tourist flows (14,300), lodges (45) and settlements with lodges (29) were developed in 1980. The tourist arrivals, lodges and settlements with lodges were increased to 65,587, 518 and 84 respectively in 1998. Comparatively, in 1998 tourists were in full flow.

The following flow charts exhibit the growth of tourists and lodges in the Everest and Annapurna region:

Regarding lodge construction as exhibited in the Table 14, villages like Namche and Lukla in Everest region and Jomsom, Muktinath, Manang, Ghandruk, Chomrong and Landruk in Annapurna region in the Table 15 have topped. Speculatively,

Growth of Tourists and Lodges in Everest Region

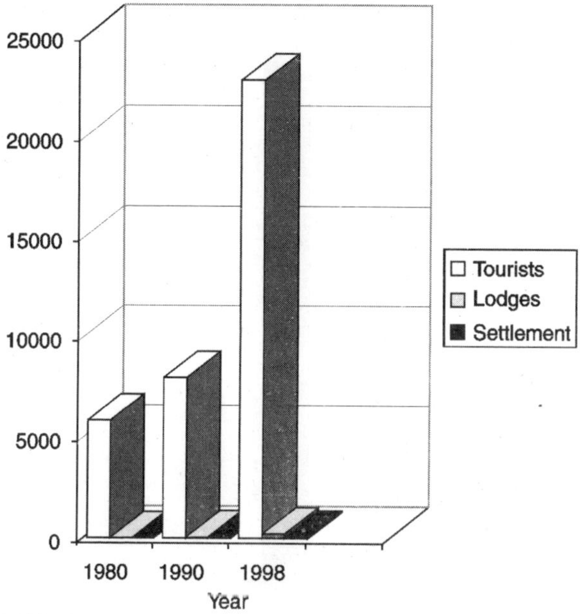

Source: Table 16

lodges were built in those areas without considering demand and supply function of tourism economics. On the speculative philosophy, lodges increased in construction result spill one effect. Tourists do not prefer to stay at the crowded lodges. Hence, we need the planned tourism village in these areas in relation to trekking village and trekking route.

In the Everest region, lodge accommodation was not started until the early 1970. In 1971, the first Sherpa lodge was established. Until 1978, 70 per cent of the trekkers to the Everest region stayed in tents under the organised tours. In 1990, more than 64 per cent of lodges in the Everest region were opened. During the period of 1980-89 more lodges developed in the Lukla-Namche route, the Kala Patthar route, the Gokyo route and nearby sites.

In the Annapurna region, lodge accommodation was developed in Ghorepani, Ghandruk, Jomsom and Ghara Sikha which represented 13 per cent in 518 lodges in 1999. In Everest

Growth of Tourists and Lodges in Annapurna Region

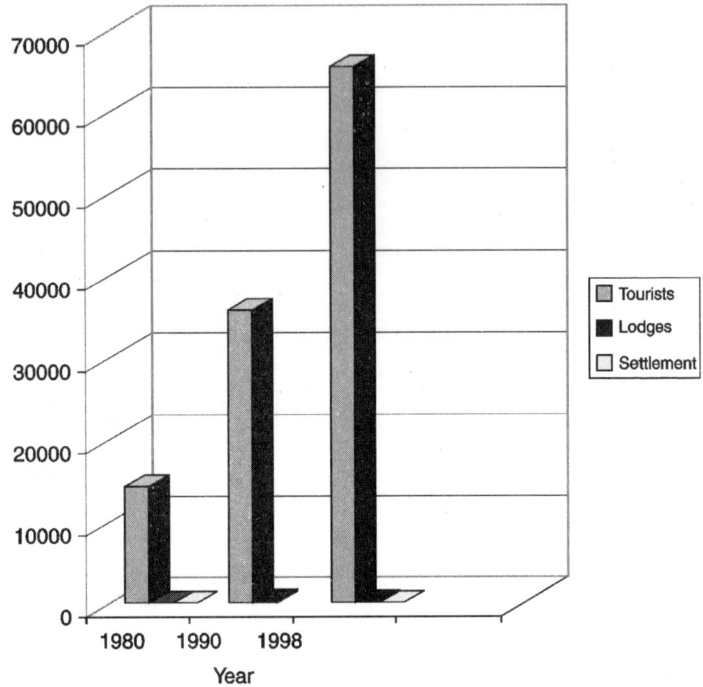

Source: Table 16

region, unlikely, Namche Bazar has had an unreasonable proportion of lodges (14 per cent) constructed while in the Annapurna region, Ghorepani has the highest share of contribution which is 4.2 per cent only out of the total number of lodges.

Economic Benefit from Surubari Village Tourism

Village tourism has all along been a main stay of the village economy of Nepal. Village people can get economic benefit from the implementation of village tourism. For instance, how Sirubari tourism village incurred benefit from its implementation is described below:

Nepal's Village Tourism is village golden goose that lays fresh double sized golden eggs. Designed to experience Nepal's villages, villagers and lifestyle, Sirubari Village Tourism at the core area of Panchamul Village Development Committee, Syangja district of Nepal has been presented as a tourism village model to the domestic and international tourism market. It has valued at the economic benefits generating income and employment.

The attraction of the Sirubari is the village itself and its cultivated land area. By selling the village product to tourists, Sirubari Tourism Village would generate jobs and revenue.

TABLE 17 (a): Economic Benefit from Sirubari Village Tourism During 1998-2003

S.No.	*Description*	*Benefit*
1.	Household Engaged	40
2.	Employment Generated	300 Persons
3.	Income Generated in Village	NRS 31,25,000
4.	Income Generated in District	NRS 70,00,000
5.	Average Length of Stay	2.5 Days
6.	Total Transaction	NRS 1,31,40,000

Source: Kathmandu Research Centre, 2004.
Notes: Sample Survey

The Table 17 (a) shows the income and employment generation in Sirubari.The Sirubari village having 40 households engaged in village tourism created 300 persons employed in the village and income generated in village was NRS 31, 25,000 and in district NRS 70,00,000. The average length of village tourists in the Sirubari village is 2.5 days. The total business transaction was amounted to NRS 1,31,40,000 from 1998-2003.

TABLE 17 (b): Village Tourist Arrivals in Sirubari During 1998-2003

Category of Tourists	*No. of Village Tourist Arrivals*
International Village Tourist in Total	1,000
Domestic Village Tourist in Total	35,000
Promotional Domestic Village Tourist in Total	15,000

Source: Kathmandu Research Centre, 2004
Notes: Included registered and unregistered village tourists.

In Sirubari village, several tourists from various countries visited to enjoy village and its attraction. The Table17 (b) shows village tourist arrivals during 1998-2003.The international village tourist 1,000, domestic village tourist 35,000 and promotional domestic village tourist 15,000 were recorded in Sirubari village.

Village Tourist Arrivals by Category

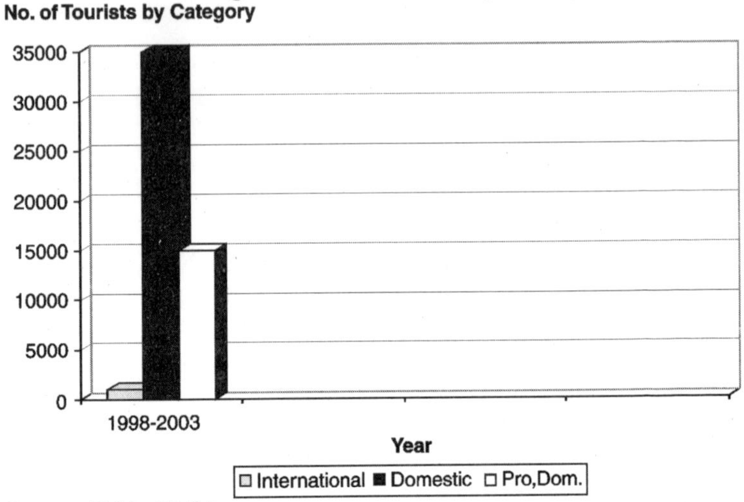

Source: Table 17 (b)

TABLE 17 (c): Village Tourist Arrivals in Sirubari by Nationality

Village Tourist Arrivals by Nationality	*No. of Village Tourist Arrivals*
Belgium	300
Japan	200
Germany	150
Others	350

Source: Kathmandu Research Centre, 2004.

Notes: Sample survey.

The Table 17 (c) exhibits tourist arrivals by nationality in Sirubari Tourism Village during 1998-2003. The tourist arrivals from Belgium, Japan, Germany and others were 300, 200, 150 and 350 respectively.

Village Tourist Arrivals by Nationality

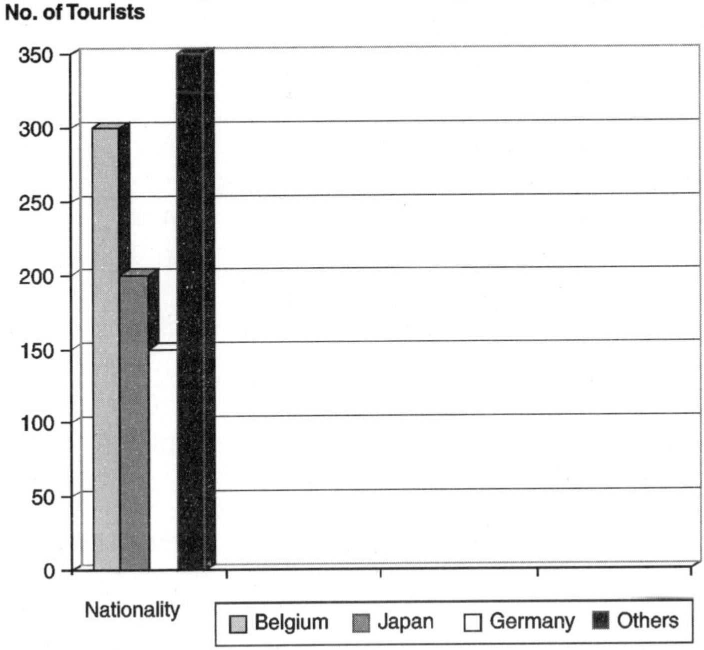

Source: Table 17 (c)

Increasing tourism activity is on the side of economic advantages of village tourism for a village. International village tourists introduce 'fresh money' into the village economy, thereby increases foreign exchange earnings. In this respect, village tourism can be said as an export industry along with the conceptualisation of service and hospitality industry. International tourists spent their money in buying local goods and services. For developing countries and villages, a huge amount of foreign exchange earnings is generated for their development effort whichever way it is looked at.

Poverty Alleviation

Based on the village philosophy, village people are rational decision makers, who create good opportunity for employment and free market environment, and try to earn more incomes through their business activities. The role of village tourism in its strategy is to build infrastructure and hold a favourable climate to stimulate the growth of village institutions and enterprises. The benefit increased from production is to trickle down to the poor.

Village tourism is anti-poverty plan recently launched. In Nepal village poverty is a great problem. It creates problems in both developing and developed countries of the world. It is estimated that more than one billion people in the world are living in poverty. The incidence of poverty is highly differentiated from country to country in the world. In South Asia alone, almost half of the world's poor exist that accounts 30 per cent of the world's population.

Considering the world statistics of poor, Nepal holds 31 per cent of people under poverty line (NPC, 2005). Poverty, being very vague in definitions and connotations, has no universally accepted definition. Poverty is normally characterised by poverty. The term, absolute poverty implies the lack of access to objectively necessited and determined goods and services to satisfy basic requirements for livelihoods.

Hence, village tourism plays a vital role in reducing poverty of village and villager in the country through the creation of job opportunities and income-oriented economic activities in the village society.

Microeconomic Growth

Village tourism is the microplanning approach. Each village promoting into tourist village, multiplies economic growth and development in the village. This is microscopic vision applied in action research on the principle of 'one to many' villages. The micro tourism economics concept is operated from an appraisal of natural and human resource development.

To develop village tourism, microplan creates interdisciplinary idea and chain approach connecting with various disciplines. This is village tourism concept operating to the framework of microeconomic growth model in the context of Nepal's village development.

NATIONAL ECONOMY

Village tourism affects the national economy as well as world economy which starts from microeconomics to macroeconomics and which extensively reaches to global economics. Village tourism, being a new concept, is in infancy and takes time to develop. By and large, it moves around the nation and world. Dr Pradhanang recently defined the concept of global tourism village as a common world travel and tourism agenda which can play the significant role in the upliftment of the world economy.

Started from village, village tourism attracts and multiplies more other villages. His, Majesty's Government of Nepal (Government of Nepal) has already included in its national plan and strategy. The effect of village tourism starts from village to village, village to district, from village to zone and from village to nation as a whole. Village tourism, if properly implemented in villages of Nepal, contributes 40 per cent to Gross Domestic Product (KRC). The labour force engaged in agriculture sector will be transfered to village tourism, if the agro-tourism development opportunity is given to people. Likewise, national productivity can be enhanced by increasing production in relation to consumption goods and services and capital investment. As a result, the national income also will be increased by improving productivity.

Village tourism represents the national tourism as a whole. The concept is that if the village is developed, the country is ultimately developed. On the principle of village as a nation and the world as a global village, the national economy through tourism development is discussed.

Today tourism is, no doubt, a big economic force in the world. Tourism business has been a major economic activity recognised by almost all the countries of the world.

Nationally, tourism is as a catalyst of national development pumping out more foreign exchange earnings to support national economy. Tourism earning for developing countries is highly significant than those for developed countries. For example, Caribbean depends upon tourist income, which contributes a major share to Gross Domestic Product (GDP). Even developed countries of the world, Canada contributed more than 11 per cent to its Gross Domestic Product (1989) from tourism development. For developing countries like Nepal, primary resources as well as products are main sources of income which are relatively concerned with tourism. There will be several items of income generated from visible and invisible sources that are highly significant and have very strong support and positive impact to the national economy.

The next important sector of national economy is concerned with balance of payments to foreign countries and its total receipts from them. It is, in fact, the statement of income and expenditure on international account. It is generally stated in major three aspects, e.g. (*i*) the visible balance of trade concerning with the import and export of goods (*ii*) invisible items concerning with services as shipping and insurance and (*iii*) capital transfers. The receipts from international tourism form an 'invisible export' equal to other 'invisibles' which are taken from transportation and shipping, banking and insurance income on investments, etc.

Tourism is the combination of various sectors and subsectors of various tourism and tourism related subjects. There are so many things to be linked with business in economic activities of tourism economics. For example, we have food, transportation, accommodation, travel, financial services, beverages, etc. Tourism development in Nepal relates to 20,000 businesses which derive more or partial revenue from tourism. Tourism in Nepalese economy is highly correlated in terms of income and employment generation. The businesses of Nepalese market is partially or wholly dependent on tourism (KRC, 1999). Really speaking, it is not possible to list jobs created in various segments and sub-segments of travel and tourism in the business world.

Tourism economic multiplier is larger than any other industry. A tourist dollar had multiplier effect of 3.2 estimated in 1999. Similarly, the employment multiplier effect in tourism is 2.4. That means direct employment of one person in tourism sector creates jobs for 1.4 persons in other sector of the economy

(KRC, 1999). Obviously, measuring income from tourism is not a easy task. It is more complicated in nature. The estimation of gross income contribution from tourism to Gross Domestic Product (GDP) is 17.17 per cent in Nepal. (KRC, 1999) while Nepal Rastra Bank stated that tourism contributed to GDP from 1.5 per cent (2003/2004) to 4.2 per cent (1999).

Village tourism associated with villages of Nepal contributes a lot to the national economy. Village, in fact, is the symbol of nation. Obviously, the development of village means the development of nation.

Chapter 14

Village Tourism Marketing

Gone are the days when tourism marketing was closely visualised at the maximum profit motive. Today tourism marketing concept is differentiated from old thought to modern thought for tourist satisfaciton.

Village tourism is marketed in accordance with the principle of 'business goes where it is invited but stays where it is well treated'. Tourism villages satisfying tourists expand market naturally. The services provided by host village/villager are to be well matched with the user's needs and expectations. Likewise, in this present day world, standard users urged to be convinced at the world class services. Similarly, the tourism environment ought to be created with the special attraction of village tourism. Here every tourist should feel 'I love Nepal's tourism village'. It tells us how marketing can tap the image of tourism village in the heart of tourists. This convincing message pulls up tourists in the villages of Nepal.

Village tourism popularised in tourism market is to attract tourists and stay in villages of Nepal. 'No tourist, no tourism' is the lead perception marketing to village and abroad. In fact, tourists are a determinant factor for tourism industry. However, we have to find out village tourist receiving source and also want and need of them. The marketing concept focuses 'the effort to determine and meet the needs and wants of current and potential customers'. Broadly, marketing is the art of buying from customers. The philosophy of salesmanship tells us how to buy customer's money in tourist village destinations.

For a successful village tourism venture, tourism villages have to get ready for welcoming village tourists. Villages should be managed for promoting tourism village destinations. Increasingly, the village tourism venture has to plan with the village based marketing philosophy in Nepal. Initially, village tourism marketing has to tap the tourist's desire and interest. For village tourist's attraction, tourism village destination has to be categorised into different sectors, e.g. Sirubari tourism village, trekking tourism village, mountain tourism village, trekking tourism village, Yarsagumba tourism village, Herb tourism village, Adventure tourism village, Sherpa tourism village, Yoga tourism village, Health tourism village and so on. Most recently, tourism marketing is being shifted from the vacation holiday hotels to pleasant tourism villages.

Animal Transporting Necessary Goods in Remote Village

The tourism market situation is determined by the theory of demand and supply that meets an equilibrium point. Thus consumer's interest has to match with the product supplied in the tourism market. Initially, village tourism has to be exposed in the international tourism market, so that tourists would get knowledge on the values of village tourism. By and large, village tourism market should be grown on demand-oriented nature. Regarding village tourism marketing, market research addresses two major questions: (*i*) what is the village tourism? and (*ii*) why does he or she buy the village tourism product? The search for answer to these questions should be undertaken as per the principles of marketing.

Obviously, a study of consumer behaviour in relation to village tourism is the best solution referring to the attitude of tourists. We analyse demand of international and domestic tourists for product development. There are several tourism activities preferred by tourists such as sight seeing, historic culture, leisure (sunbathing, bird watching), socialising (visiting family, relative and friends), recreation, adventure (skiing, rafting), business, entertainment (night life), religious reasons, service (meal and accommodation), conventions, festivals and exhibitions etc.

In selecting tourism village destinations, tourists look for the village areas that provide them the most in their favoured activities.

In order to select tourism village destination, tourists have been categorised into four:

(*a*) Seeking escape (freedom) into a dream of his own
(*b*) Seeking entertainment in tourism destination
(*c*) Desiring experience of other authentic cultures
(*d*) Desiring to involve as an active part of other cultures.

Analytically, a model of tourist decision making states that conscious tourists know themselves what activities and attractions they want from the selected destination. The model also states that the experienced tourists know about the values of destination to be selected. Tourists are perfect like a logical computer that weighs up the value of various destinations they visit.

For the selection of tourism destinations, the image of the destination has to be flavoured as that of the qualitative perfume in the international tourism market. Likewise, the tourism marketer has to think about the demographic values of tourists in terms of sex, age, youth, retired and so on. For promotional tourism village marketing, the study of potential US visitors carried out in 1974 can be important guidelines to Nepal's village tourism market development.

The study of US visitors in Canada was carried out in 1974, which showed the psychographic segmentation in market research. The US visitors in every country in the world are very important for tapping tourism market. Tourism without US visitors is not possible to market successfully.

The geographic and demographic bases of segmentation of the product or service buying or not buying in the market are related to the market development. The groups of tourists with similar personalities, interests or with similar lifestyles are studied and known for common market. This type of informative knowledge and inquiry produces 'psychographic' segmentation of the tourism market. The psychographic segmentation is subjective, which concerns with attitudes, perceptions, images, desires and values in the mind of the tourist or customer. It is the most effective way of looking in travel and tourism market in which necessary tourism product and attraction are developed and marketed. We ought to think of planning and management perfectly in this regard.

Today the recent study shows that more than 154 million American adults are categorised as 'traveler' having taken at least one trip 50 miles or more away from home. About 90 per cent of these travelers (139 million) have taken a leisure trip in the past year and over half have taken an air trip in the past.[1] This huge number of travelers has fueled for development of tourism including village tourism.The Geotourism Study of US states that Geo-savvys are more likely than any other cluster group to do the following activities:

* 83 per cent visit destinations with authentic historic and archeological sites
* 81 per cent prefer small-scale accommodations run by local people
* 81 per cent travel to experience people, lifestyles and cultures very different from their own
* 80 per cent visit small towns and rural areas
* 73 per cent feel it is important to learn about their destination's people, history and culture.

The results of The Geotourism Study: Phase I show that there are at least 55.1 million American who could be known as 'Geotourists' having travel habits of Geo-savvy, Urban Sophisticates and Good Citizens. For enhancement of Village Tourism marketing, the scope of Nepal's Village Tourism with the partnership of City Tourism can be boosted up in a revolutionary change and radical progress. The American travelers prefer small-scale accommodations, tourism villages run by local villagers/people by 81 per cent. Similarly they prefer small towns and village/rural areas by 80 per cent in the total Geotourists. Above all, the above statistics of US visitors is in favour of Nepal's Village Tourism as well as Nepal's Town Tourism.

Hence, it is suggested to catch up and promote village tourism management marketing model for developing village tourism in Nepal in the way (see Fig. 3):

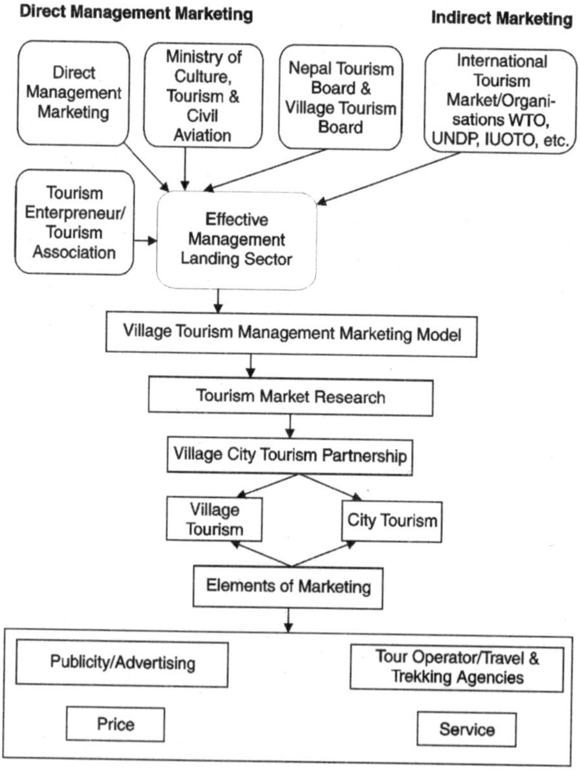

Figure 3: Village Tourism Marketing Model

The Figure 3 shows the Village Tourism Marketing Model in Nepal for the development of Nepal's Village Tourism with the village city tourism partnership. Marketing, in fact, is an essential element for successful tourism business, which is equally important to all level of tourism business management and promotion. At the operational marketing management, plans and strategies are needed to coordinate marketing activities according to a planned schedule and targeted goal and objectives. The plan also assists to watch and monitor the nature and trend of tourism market, evaluate business, tourism product and price fixed in the business. Today tourism has been the better source of income and provider of jobs and a means of investment.

Village Tourism Management Marketing Model is associated with corporate and institutional organisations related to tourism insusry.They accommodated in this respect are Village Tourism Committees, VDCs, Ministry of Culture, Tourism and Civil Aviation, Nepal Tourism Board, Village Tourism Board, Tourism Entrepreneurs and Tourism Associations. In short, these are regularly signified as Effective Management Sector having direct effect. There are some international organisations influenced for interest, attitude and demand through WTO, UNDP, IUOTO, etc. as indirect marketing influences to village tourism marketing. The organisations have their own objectives and goal.

Tourism market research is next important part of marketing management. Market research addresses who is tourist? and why do visitors purchase or prefer the tourism product? In addition to it, visitor's country of origin, age, occupation, attitudes to travel and destination, income, etc. should be known.

Marketing effort is directed at the most likely customers who prefer tourism village destination. The marketing effort in term of marketing mix such as product formulation, pricing, distribution and promotion is then tailored to fit. The organisation can think of product positioning and specific and target markets. Regarding market segmentation village city tourism partnership is taken into consideration, so that the target tourists for village tourism market and city tourism market can be promoted side by side.

Once this village tourism marketing model is set up, the corporate body and organizations can then successfully select specific and target markets in village city tourism partnership as a whole.

By using psychographic segmentation, possible visitors have been categorised into major six segments:

1. *Non-Active Visitors*

Non-active visitors seek familiar and interesting environment where they have already experienced and would take interest to visit with relatives and friends. They are basically known by activity visitor. Activity visitor consists of 29 per cent of potential visitors.

2. *Active City-Visitors*

Active city-visitors seek popular environment where they can visit friends and relatives. They are highly inclined to participate in several activities, e.g. city sight seeing, shopping, cultural and other entertainment. These types of visitors occupy 12 per cent of potential visitors.

3. *Family Sight Seers*

Family sight seers are known for looking for new vacation place as tourism village that would be preferred by children for enriching experience. These sight seers are led by 6 per cent of potential visitors.

4. *Outdoor Vacationers*

Outdoor vacationers would seek the beautiful environment like clean air, rest and quiet place and beautiful scenary. Most of them are campers and recreational seekers. Children also participate in such vacation. These types of vacationers constitute 19 per cent of potential visitors.

5. *Resort Vacationers*

Resort vacationers who are categorised as the lover of water sports are interested in rafting, swimming, kayaking and so on.

They would like the popular areas where big cities are located. These vacationers stand at 8 per cent of potential visitors.

6. Foreign Travel Vacationers

Foreign travel vacationers who prefer most the place with foreign atmosphere and magnificient scene and scenary are in search of new tourist destinations. Most likely, they can prefer Nepal's tourism village destinations, if they are perfectly convinced about it. They like exciting and enriching experiences of the places visited. Spending money is not a major subject in their views, but they seek good accommodation and excellent hospitality service. The vacationers having interest scored 26 per cent of potential visitors.

A market research study of the appeal of Australia to New Zealand holiday market was surveyed by the Heylen Research Centre in 1978 in New Zealand. Basically, six psychographic lifestyle market segments were analysed in view of tourist's past and future travel plans. With this reference the market for village tourism can be analysed.

TABLE 18: Six Psychographic Lifesyle Markets

S.No.		*Per cent of Population*	*Per cent of All Past Trips Taken*	*Per cent of All Future Planned Trips*
1.	New Experience Seekers	15	53	40
2.	Unadventurous Stay at Home	18	2	1
3.	Get Away From it Alls	20	6	16
4.	Organised Comfort Seekers	13	20	12
5.	Young Sun and Fun Seekers	13	4	12
6.	Bored Escapists	23	15	19
7.	Total	100	100	100

Source: Heylen Research Centre, New Zealand, 1978.

The above Table 18 indicates the characteristics of six psychographic lifestyle markets. They are depicted as follows:

1. New Experience Seekers

Regarding New Experience Seekers, there are no restraints on this group. But they are to be promoted; otherwise they would go elsewhere for travel.

2. Unadventurous Stay-at-Home

The name itself gives the meaning of this psychographic life-style market. The group of customers cannot be motivated to travel oversea countries.

3. Get Away from It Alls

Due to high income generated, these types of customers have the capacity to travel, but they need high commitments. The lack of commitment and management decrease their ability to travel even they have desire to travel.

4. Organised Comfort Seekers

These groups of customers are generally of older age persons who are wary of their lower income, but they are interested to travel oversea countries on low cost holidays.

5. Young Sun and Fun Seekers

These customers have a high desire to travel though they are categorised into low income earners. They are in need of commitments for travel.

6. Boared Escapists

These customers desire to travel oversea countries and represent a segment with good potentials.

These are important types of customers studied for tourism marketing.

Similarly, the Stanford Research Institute of USA conducted sustained research that demonstrates the classification of people into nine lifestyle types within four major categories such as need driven, outer directed, inner directed and integrated. Based on a combination of psychographics and demographic, the approach is popularised as VALS (Values, Attitude and Lifestyles).

1. Need-Driven

The need-driven visitor constitutes 11 per cent of the US population. This group makes decision on the basis of need rather than choice due to the limited financial resource.

Under this category there are two groups namely survivors and sustainers. Survivers having low income and lowest educational background account 7 per cent of the population. They are elderly people levelled at the VALS group.

2. Outer-Directed

The group of people who are within the cultural main stream constitutes 68 per cent of the population. There are basically three types of lifestyle grouped as Belongers, Emulators and Achievers.

Belongers, being the largest VALS group, occupy 38 per cent of the adult population, which take up the important market in any product or service. They are categorised as middle class people who give value to family, country and tradition.

Emulators

Emulators are known as ambitious, competitive and status conscious visitors who constitute 10 per cent of the population. They would enjoy 'beer budgets and champagne tastes' in their lifestyle.

Achievers and hard working visitors who comprise 20 per cent of the population. They are generally successful group of people and often affluent depicted as the 'American Dream'.

3. Inter-Directed

This group of visitors as Inter-directed category makes up 19 per cent of the population. They give more importance to their own desires and values than on traditional ones. Characterised by self-expression and individualism, they work out for themselves.

The group consists of three different lifestyle segments namely, I-Am-Mes, Experientials and Societally conscious.

I-AM-MES

'I-Am-Mes' are highly individualistic and impulsive people occupying 3 per cent of the population. They are young people seeking new things for their experience and ready to bear risk.

Experientials

Experientials accounting for 5 per cent of the population are artistic, intense, active, spirited and intellectual people who are interested in exotic and natural products and experiences. Generally, the young people are categorised in this group to which they are anxious to try new and differential things.

Societally Conscious

'Societally conscious' are accounted for a strong sense of social responsibility. This group is well educated and affluent. They are generally engaged in their professions and academia.

Integrated

This is the group categorised in a single lifestyle. Integrated occupy only 2 per cent of the population. They are interested to combine with the drive of outer-directed with the self-expression and social perspective of the inner-directed.

Considering the village tourism market potential, the European market for holidays in developing countries is overviewed here. The European countries consist of Germany, United Kingdom, France, Switzerland, The Netherlands, Denmark, Sweden and Norway. In the study conducted by Dr Peter Aderhold Institute for Tourism Research and Planning, tourism marketing for developing countries shows positive. As the study shows that 20 million Europeans are likely to visit a developing country in the next three years (1995-97). Of these 20 million visitors between 35 per cent and 45 per cent indicated Asia as one of the regions. The study of the preferences, motivations and characteristics of holiday-makers indicates the following segments:

1. Culturally-oriented
2. Nature-lovers

TABLE 19: Stanford Research Institute Lifestyle

S.No.	*Types*	*Per cent Over Population*
1.	Need-driven	
	– Survivors	4%
	– Sustainers	7%
2.	Outer-directed	
	– Belongers	38%
	– Emulators	10%
	– Achievers	20%
3.	Inner-directed	
	– I-Am-Me	3%
	– Experiential	5%
	– Societally concious	11%
4.	Integrated	2%

Source : Standford Research Institute, USA, 1980.

3. Adventure/experience-seekers
4. Beach-vacationers
5. Round-trip-tourists
6. Special interest groups as golfing, fishing, diving or surfing.

The developing countries involved in world tourism is generally increasing. The East Asia Pacific region is in front line. The international tourists grew from 21 million in 1980 to 74.7 million in 1994 in the East Asia Pacific. Similarly, the tourism receipt had grown from US$ 8 billion in 1980 to US$ 59 billion in 1994 in this region. In Europe, the demand for holidays in developing countries was growing in 1995. The German market grown by 20 per cent per annum is significant growth of all European markets.

The Table 19 exhibits the nature of European holiday market of 187.6 million holiday markets in 1994, 5.2 million were to visit developing countries. German contributed 3.6 million for developing countries between 1992-94.

The five major motives of holiday-makers are categorised below:

1. Experience/adventure	52%
2. Culture	33%

TABLE 19: European Market for Holidays in Developing Countries Market Dimensions: General Overview

Countries in Survey	*Germany*	*UK*	*France*	*Switzerland*	*Holland*	*Denmark*	*Sweden*	*Norway*	*Total*
Population in millions (over 13 years of age)	62,7	44,7	45	5	12,5	4,2	6,3	3,5	183,9
Sample size (n)	7780	3879	4001	2926	4045	4072	4000	3206	33909
Holiday intensity in %	78	60	63	72	58	66	68	66	68
Number of tourists in mil.	48,9	26,8	28,4	3,6	7,3	2,8	4,3	2,3	124,4
Travel frequency	1,4	1,6	1,6	1,5	1,4	1,5	1,7	1,6	1,5
Number of holidays in mil.	68,5	42,9	45,4	5,4	10,2	4,2	7,3	3,7	187,6
Actual tourists 1994 to developing countries in mil.	2,1	1	1,2	0,3	0,3	0,1	0,2	0,04	5,2
Actual tourists 1992-94 to developing countries in mil.	3,6	2,2	2,7	0,5	0,6	0,2	0,3	0,1	10,2
Potential tourists to develping countries 1995-97 in mil.	7	5	5	1	1	0,3	0,6	0,2	20,1

Source: Institute for Tourism Research and Planning, Copenhagen 1995.

TABLE 20: Potential Tourist Motivation for Travelling to Developing Countries, in Millions

Countries in Survey	*Germany*	*UK*	*France*	*Switzerland*	*Holland*	*Denmark*	*Sweden*	*Norway*	*Total*
Potential tourists 1995-97 to developing countries in mil.	7	5	5	1	1	0,3	0,6	0,2	20,1
Sample size (n)	452	188	244	337	177	121	187	90	1796
Beach/Relaxation	2,3	1,7	1,7	0,4	0,2	0,09	0,08	0,03	6,5
Experience/adventure	3,1	2,3	3,6	0,4	0,5	0,2	0,3	0,09	10,5
Culture	2,1	1,5	2,1	0,3	0,3	0,1	0,2	0,05	6,7
Nature	2,2	1,6	1,6	0,3	0,3	0,2	0,1	0,04	6,3
Sport/hobby activities	0,6	0,6	0,0	0,09	0,08	0,04	0,07	0,02	2,3

Source : Institute for Tourism Research and Planning, Copenhagen 1995.

3. Nature	32%
4. Beach/relaxation	31%
5. Sport/hobby	11%

Source: Institute for Tourism Research and Planning, Copenhagen, 1995.

The above data shows the potential European tourists (1995-97) motivations for travelling to developing countries. It shows that experience and adventure motive (52 per cent) is very strong in tourism market to developing countries. The tourist attracted by culture is 33 per cent. Similarly, Nature, Beach/relaxation and sport/hobby follow 32 per cent, 31 per cent and 11 per cent respectively to developing countries.

The Table 20 shows the market segment for the eight countries in the survey.

As shown in the Table 20, village tourism has greater scope followed by culture (6.7 million), Nature (6.3 million), Experience/adventure (10.5 million) and so on in eight European countries.

The study on selected attitudes of long haul tourists in German market (1988) shows that tourists are interested to come into contact with the local people and local family to learn about their conditions in the following motivations:

1. Interest in contact with locals
2. Interest in invitation
3. Interest in social aspects.

These tourists' motivations promote village tourism in Nepal. Obviously, Nepal can tap village tourism market in the world tourism market.

On the other side, the domestic market of village tourism is also variedly potential. Most of Nepalese are also environmentally conscious, they would like to enjoy non-polluted environment. Now-a-days, people have concience to organise different seminars and workshops in villages. The Nepalese people would go for trekking, mountaineering expedition, sightseeing and so on within the country. During 1998-2005 period, 35,000 domestic tourists visited Sirubari tourism village (KRC, 2005). The pay holiday travel proposed to the government is properly implemented, village tourism will dramatically boost up.

Considering the market structure of international and domestic tourism, Nepal's village tourism has a high potential for its development. It can be extensively developed as a new tourism product of Nepal and abroad. It can hold 25 per cent of American young and adventure tourists, who love natural tourism village and culture. Apart from this, tourists from Asia, Australia and Pacific and Western Europe can be drawn to village tourism in Nepal.

References

1. Travel Industry Association of America (TIA), *The Geotourism Study: Phase I,* Sponsored by National Geographic Traveler, Washinton, DC, 2002, USA.

Chapter 15

Tourism Model Village

Nepal is the best tourist destination in the world due to its wonderful natural beauty, cultural diversity and incomparable heritage. Nepal's village tourism concept leads to the development plan and strategy that creates village based employment and income generation and helps in poverty alleviation. Its wonderful hospitality service and friendly people attract tourists more. It has several beautiful villages, landscapes and mountains. In 1976, Dr. Pradhanang brainstormed the idea of village tourism from Dashrathpur village of Lekhpharsha Village Development Committee (VDC) in Surkhet district, while he stayed there for 10 months in connection with National Development Service (NDS). Later on, he conceptualised and propounded village tourism for the welfare of village people and country.

Now we have some tourism villages developed as tourism model villages in Nepal. They are described below:

Sirubari Tourism Model Village

Located on the lap of Thumre Hill at 700 meters above sea level, Sirubari is a beautiful village. It is an unexplored Gurung village at the core area of Panchamul Village Development Committee (VDC) in Syangja district. One can feel the village as a magnificent tourist destination. The lifestyle of Gurung community is indigeneous valued with culture and rites. The climatic condition of Sirubari village is very healthy with pleasing weather of warm days and cool nights. The village varies from 1,250 meters to 2,003 meters in its height. The total population having 2,000 is categorised into 45 per cent Gurungs, 40 per cent Chhetris, Brahmins and 15 per cent Dalit. This is a tourist village designed for international and domestic holiday makers for relaxation and entertainment.

The welcoming pattern for village tourists is wonderfully presented at the indigeneous Gurung style. The guests are honoured as God and Goddess. The honour that the tourists receive in the village cannot be imagined by them. The traditional musical instruments are played by the local musical instrument experts, and musicians. The rare instrument in the world, named, 'Panche Bajaj' of village is played to welcome visitors to village. The original Nepalese musical instrument is nowhere in the world, which has the special values treasured in Nepal's village tourism. The guests are garlanded with respect and also honoured with banquets.

Gurung Dance

The village looks very neat and clean with a good management system followed. The village environment is in a special order naturally developed and culturally preserved. The villagers are capable to speak broken English language for communication. The host villagers receive guests and march to village Gompa at 1 kilometer far distance. The Gompa is the Buddhist monastery managed as resting place for village tourists. The villagers provide the warm hospitality service with 'Tinpane raksi and boiled egg' to tourists. After relaxation for an hour, guests are grouped into different households for accommodation and food. They will be the family members of village households until their stay in the village. The tourists staying at the village household get family love and affection. In the evening the cultural programme is organised. The tourists enjoy a lot in the village. They taste Nepalese cuisine, for example, Daal-bhat, tarkari, achar, selroti, and so on.

The simple but hygienic type of toilets are managed by the villagers. Comfortably, tourists can use toilets and bathrooms prepared for tourists. The village tourism committee looks after tourists for their security and pleasure. Their stay at the village should be more pleasant and satisfactory.

'Home to home visit' programme is given by the villagers to those tourists who are more interested to know about family life and culture. The household host serves guests with sukuti (dry meat) and chhyang (local drink). The package tour programme is set for 2 nights 3 days or 3 nights 4 days as per tourist's demand and choice.

The first village tourists marketed from Austria liked the village tourism concept. By and large, Sirubari tourism village has been very popular tourist destination in the international and domestic market. For village tourism marketing, an agreement was made between Sirubari Village Tourism Committee and Nepal Village Resort Pvt Ltd for 10 years. Nepal Village Resort is a village tour operator that entered into a commercial contract to promote village tourism. It gains and shares the profits from the village tourism business in Sirubari. All households providing guest rooms for accommodation are members of village tourism committee. At the outset, 32 households of the total of 70 households involved in village tourism. The investment in this respect amounted to NRs. 25,000 to NRs. 50,000 for toilet and bathroom amenities. The income generated from village tourism is equally shared as per the service provided to tourists. Generally, the tourism village committee charges NRs. 150 per head for lunch and NRs. 150 per head for dinner and NRs. 100 per bed. In total a household receives NRs. 600 per tourist per night. A certain amount of tourist money goes to the VDC, Mother's group, youth's group, Gompa and Damai music group.

Income Generation to Sirubari

The tariff for the full package per tourist for a group of 3-6 is amounted to US$ 180

Sirubari Income	**Amount in NRs.**
3 night stay in household (3 × NRs 600 per night)	1800
Tourism Management Committee	300
Mother and Youth groups	150
Local porter	100
Lunch in Arjun Chaupariya (2 × 150)	300
Damai music group	150
Total income per tourist to the village	NRs. 2,800

The figure shows almost 25 per cent of the package price goes to the community. The marketing and handling costs charged by intermediate travel and trekking agencies are very high. Thus direct handling is preferred.

There are mother's group and youth's group involved in Sirubari tourism village. 'Ama Samuha' (Mother's group) is very active in village development work. Funds are collected through dancing and singing. Likewise, Nava Yuba Club (youth club) is also equally active in village development work. The club involved in different activities is described below:

1. Social functions
2. Trail development and maintenance
3. Drainage development
4. Guiding tourists
5. Security and prevention in village
6. Social service
7. Welcoming guests and bidding them see-off
8. Cultural programme for guests.

On the ground of the people's welfare, village tourism is being developed. Today it has been the world famous tourism

Welcoming Chief Guest in Village Tourism Festival

village of Nepal, which has tapped the international and domestic market.

Ghalegaun Tourism Model Village

One can see the next village recently developed as a tourism model village in Nepal. Ghalegaun is the name given as a magnificent village lying at the north west of Khudi which is the main entrance gate to the Annapurna trekking route. The people of Ghalegaun visited Sirubari tourism village and practically learnt the concept. The concept paper of village tourism developed by Dr Pradhanang has been followed by the people of Ghalegaun and started developing tourism village.

By nature, Ghalegaun is naturally surrounded by wonderful scene and scenary of the world famous Annapurna and Manaslu Himalayan ranges. It is a typical Gurung village endowed with rich culture.

Located at the southern side on the lap of Lamjung Himal at an altitude of 2,016 meters above sea level, Ghalegaun is an unspoiled Gurung village with a total of 105 households. Of them, 25 households consist of Chhetri and Biswakarma castes. Visitors can view splendid mountain peaks, green hill-locks, valleys and so on. The various tastes and experiences can be gained by travelling Ghalegaun. The village handicrafts, honey hunting adventures, religious rites and cultural heritages are major attractions of the village.

The welcoming pattern and hospitality service provided in Ghalegaun by the host villagers are more or less similar to Sirubari model. In fact, it is next to Sirubari tourism village led by the Gurung ethnic group of people in Lamjung district of Nepal, where Gurung dance, song, music and wonderful lifestyle of local villagers can be tasted. But Dr Pradhanang is in the opinion that each tourism village should be different from other showing its speciality and uniqueness.

Kadamandau Model Tourist Village

Kadamandau located at an altitude of 4,700 ft above sea level is a beautiful village which is 31 km away from Silgadi. The trekking route developed at the reach of Dhangadi-Santebagar Highway is accessible. Situated northwest to Chaukhuttee, it takes three hours gentle walk to reach the village of Kadamandau from there. The village is predominantly comprised of different groups of people such as Dhanuk (Chhetri) 25 per cent, Saut 25 per cent, Kathayat 10 per cent, Bogati 10 per cent, Chiral 5 per cent, Shrestha 5 per cent and others 20 per cent. Kadamandau has nearby villages surrounded by Batalagaun, Simpata Chirlagaun (Thapagaun) Dhanu Kanda, Barkataya, Bogatigaun, Nuwaghargaun etc.

Kadamandau having about 500 population is one of the villages of Kadamandau VDC which lies in Doti district. Kadamandau by name stands for both a village and a VDC. The name of village and VDC was suggested by Kadamandau Temple.

Historical Place

Kadamandau is a historical place where Amar Singh Thapa, the great warrior of Nepal had established a temple of

Kadamandau in 1717 BS. He prayed to Goddess Durga by establishing her image for a successful attack upon Kumau battle with English regiment in India. In 1754, he made a beautiful 15 dharni (80 kg) weighted bell and kept in front of the temple. There is an ever-burning lamp called as 'Akhanda Bati' inside the temple.

The temple served by a group of ethnic people and Guthi (committee) is an indigenous system. Birta Guthi having more than 365 ropani land is sufficient for a sustainable development. There are four wards included in the religious Guthi committee such as uper-Kanda (ward no. 1), Bukati Gada (ward no. 2), Nuwaghar (ward no. 3) and Patalagaun (ward no. 4), the production or income from land is entertained by Guthi and partially obliged to spend for worshipping Durga. At least, 47 goats and 2 buffaloes are slaughtered in the festival of Dasain as per the religious rites.

Long ago the Kazi (ruler) had fixed the price of commodities. Gone are the days, but still the price remains unchanged. Historically the price fixed for essential commodities has created an interesting story. Here is the price listed below:

Commodity	**Price Fixed**
1 buffalo	Re. 1
1 goat	75 paisa
1 mana ghee	4 paisa
1 mana rice	1 paisa

Guthi should provide the above mentioned commodities at the price fixed by Kaji. The committee should support the expenditure from the income derived from the land holding though the price of the commodities increased. The religious law and order maintained in the socio-religion Guthi is very practical and sustainable. The historical story could be interesting on preparing village tourism product. It will be good for village tourism marketing.

Similarly, the next important historical story is expenditure allocated for priest. There is a provision of chairmanship in Guthi. The chief or chairman of Guthi appointed by Kaji would receive NRs 5 remuneration per annum.

Furthermore, a priest would receive NRs 2.50 basic salary yearly along with 5 pathi dal, 7 pathi rice, 5 pathi ghee/oil and home yagya materials (worshipping materials). Annually, the priest should go for worshipping Goddess Bada Malika with religious materials and then send 'Prasad' (the blessing and good wishing of God/Goddess) to Kaji in Kathmandu by registered post. Still the custom is being practiced. Village tourism brings such culture forward. Kaji on his arrival would be honoured by warm hospitality providing all the expenditure on food, accommodation and transportation. The Birta Guthi land ought not pay any revenue tax to HMG of Nepal (the government of Nepal). But it is stricly prohibited to sell.

Besides, there is a temple of Shiva in Kadamandau which was supposed to have been established by the then king Kusal Shah before 1717 BS. The then king of Doti attacked Kusal Shah and defeated him.

Culture

Culture in Kadamandau is rich with popular tradition like Deura playing at the occasion of religious festival. Similarly, Bhuwa dance (Sword dance) is more interesting dance designed at its own traditional style. This dance was awarded first prize in the National Dance Competition organised in Kathmandu. It was preferred by thousand of audiences including international and domestic tourists and was telecast by Nepal Televison also. There is a traditional culture practicing as village tourism product in Kadamandau. The welcoming style with warm hospitality and delicious food is next cultural attraction to tourists. Specially, villagers provide pure honey and curd to guests.

Lifestyle

The different ethnic groups of people living in the village have traditional houses in which village lifestyle can be seen. The roofs are generally thatched and the wall painted with local white and red is pleasant.

The life of the villagers is very simple. They used to pay homage to God and Goddess by worshipping. They have religious mind and culture with obligations. The local people are engaged in their traditional occupation by farming and weaving bamboo baskets. Some food and food products are prepared at home such as Gundruk, dry fish, panchamol pickle, tale mada (a special delicious bread locally prepared) etc.

Bird Watching Programme

The bird watching programme in Kadamandau can be launched for tourist attraction. Especially parrot's gathering locally named 'Suga Dasne' can be exhibited as a village tourism product. It is a seasonal attraction preferably during the month of July, August and September.

Village Economy

The economy of Kadamandau village is predominantly agriculture. The major products are: rice, wheat, millet, and potato. The production of rice will be on an average estimated at 3.5 quintal per ropani. But villagers being very poor are not capable to meet their daily expenditure so they are compelled to be 'lahure' and go to India for their bread and butter. They generally earn NRs 1,000 per month. Women in village work in the field and look after children and home.

There is a potential of micro hydro electricity in Kadamandau. It was surveyed in Ekathare in 1981/82 by an INGO. Basically. Gandi Khola can generate micro electricity power. In 1987, a canal was constructed by the government for land irrigation. The traditional livestock are buffaloes, cows and calves. The average land holding ratio is 3 ropanis per family. There is health post facilitating with first aid health service in the village. Moreover, there are few water mills and kols (oil producing indigenous mill). Local people are very enthusiastic to develop village tourism but they do not know how to promote it. A special awareness programme for village tourism development should be launched. In fact, village tourism fulfils all its criteria can be started in Kadamandau after it.

Tahoon Tourism Village

Tahoon village located at the Palpa district of Lumbini zone is a beautiful spot where tourists can enjoy more with Magar culture and natural beauty. Tahoon is 30 km far from the east of Tansen. At 13 km distance, Tahoon has a mini-market known by Aryabhanjyang, which helps to market to the locales of Tahoon. Tahoon is the word derived from 'Tama-hook', which means edible bamboo shoots in Magar literature. Tahoon is the place of bamboo shoots known as Tama hook village. The Magar community would usually come to collect Tama-hook for their livelihood and income generation. Later on, people used to say Tahoon instead of 'Tama-hook'. Topographically, Tahoon stood at the height of 4,000 ft lies in the southern lap of hilly forest of Rambha Devi. The village market locally developed in Tahoon village is also found interesting. There are lots of natural boons and products are displayed and sold in the market. It has its own cultural and natural values with significant meaning. The Tahoon village is waiting for developing village tourism for a long time. Instead of full-fledged health facility, Red Cross building is conditionally providing accommodation to visitors, which is not the on line business of Red Cross. In Tahoon village there are many more panoramic views of the snow-capped Himalayas, which can be seen. Staying at Tahoon village, tourists can watch the majestic Himalayas like Dhaulagiri (8167m), Tukuche (6920 m), Nilgiri (7061 m), Tilicho (7132 m), Annapurna (18091 m), Himchuli (6441 m), Machhapuchhre (6997 m), Annapurna 11 (7555 m), Lamjung (6931 m), Manaslu (8156 m), Tkura (7835 m), Ganesh (7835 m) and so on. Besides this, Tahoon village has more other tourism attractions such as Rambha Devi hill station, Rimigha hill, Bakung Gadhi (fort), Elephant hill, Nachan Danda, Durbar area, Jalpa Devi temple, Purba khola valley, Angaha khola area, Bhimsen temple, Deurali, Sati Dhunga and so on. Tahoon, being the inhabitant of mixed ethnic group of people, the Newar community displays various beautiful folk songs and dances as illustrated in Lakhe dance (Demon dance), Gai Jatra (Cow festival), Dhan Ropai Pradarshan (Rice plantation exhibition), Bagh Parba (Tiger festival), and Bhimsen Jatra, etc. Likewise, Sorati Nach (Satoti dance) and Jhamne Nach (Jhamne dance) are popular cultural activities exhibited by the Magar community in Tahoon village. Tahoon village has several adjoining villages such as Deurali and so on.

There is a good scope of rafting tourism in Tahoon village and its adjoining spots. For river adventure seekers, Purbakhola can be an attractive tourism product in Tahoon village tourism. Similarly, Angaha Khola, which is 3 km far distance west from Tahoon village, can be a good attraction for village tourism development.

TABLE 21: Tahoon Village Household Structure

S.No.	*Ethnic Groups*	*Household in*	
		Number	*Percentage*
1.	Magar	413	60.8
2.	Chhetri	331	19.3
3.	Kami/Damai/Sarki	58	8.5
4.	Newar	52	7.7
5.	Brahamin	23	3.4
6.	Other	3	0.3

Source: Tahoon VDC, Palpa, 2060.

The Table 21 exhibits Tahoon village has 879 households belonging to different ethnic groups of people such as Magar, Chhetri, Kamai, Newar, Brahamin and so on.

TABLE 22: Tahoon Village Population Structure

S.No.	*Population*	*Household in*	
		Number	*Percentage*
1.	Male	1,671	44.85
2.	Female	2,055	55.15

Source: Tahoon VDC, Palpa, 2060.

The Table 22 exhibits Tahoon Village Population by sex. The male and female numbers of population by percentage are 44.85 and 55.15 respectively.

TABLE 23: Population Distribution by Ward in Tahoon VDC

S.No.	*Male*	*Female*	*Total*
1.	115	157	272
2.	73	84	15
3.	188	227	415
4.	210	256	466
5.	126	153	289
6.	237	292	529
7.	225	398	723
8.	226	243	469
9.	171	235	406
	Total		3726

Source: Tahoon VDC, 2058.

The Table 23 shows Tahoon Village has 3726 population followed by gender. The data shows female is greater than male in the village.

TABLE 24: Major Production of Tahoon VDC

S.No.	*Crop*	*Production in*	
		Metric	*Percentage*
1.	Rice	211.9	28.5
2.	Wheat	7.0	0.9
3.	Maize	478.2	64.3
4.	Millet	46.6	6.3

Source: Tahoon VDC, 2058.

The Table 24 shows the major production of Tahoon VDC followed by rice (28.5 per cent), wheat (0.9 per cent), maize (64.3 per cent) and millet (6.3 per cent) respectively.

TABLE 25: Literacy Rate in Tahoon VDC, 2058 by Gender

Literacy	*Percentage*
Male	53.2
Female	46.8

Source: Tahoon VDC, 2058.

The Table 25 shows literacy rate of Tahoon VDC on an average is recorded as 50 per cent. By sex the male and female literacy rates are 53.2 and 46.8 in the village respectively.

The tourism planners and developers of Nepal have to analyse the power of untapped potentials of village tourism, which can be explored as per the planning process. The principle and practice of village tourism in relation to public-private partnership is necessary to implement tourism of Nepal.

The villagers themselves can stand for economic development and sustainability at local or village level. They will be able to cope with poverty and underdevelopment when they will learn or achieve the technique of development from the grass root level. By the development of village tourism, village tourism market will be served from village to village, house to house and door to door. Consequently, village tourism market will be rooted and promoted from rural to rural and rural to urban and from domestic to international level. This is what we mean by the power point of village tourism industry for economic development in villages of Nepal.

Poverty in Nepal is basically a rural phenomenon. In 1995/96, 44 per cent of the rural population was living in poverty. Poverty was significantly lower only 23 per cent in urban areas. In Kathmandu valley, the poverty was only 4 per cent. Dalits in Nepal could be categorised as disadvantaged. Janajati groups like the Gurungs, Limbus and Rais traditionally joined the British army service and they have comparatively better income. Among the more disadvantaged Janjati groups with large populations are the Tharu, Tamang and Kham Magar. The Janajati groups have higher poverty (ranging from 45-49 per cent) than the national average while the Dalits have poverty level as high as 65-68 per cent. And the indigenous Limbus have the highest rate of poverty (71 per cent).

For good governance, social inclusion, social justice, social sector development, broad based economic growth, structural reform agenda and macro economic stability, village tourism development is essential. Poverty mapping and poverty monitoring will be initiated to provide a database for both mainstreaming by the line ministries and targeted programmes in order to better identify beneficiary groups and targeting modalities.

The development of village tourism in Tahoon will be an examplary model for Nepal. Village tourism, if we can develop in the planned way, will be a very successful story as well as good example for economic development and social change in impoverished village, district, region, developing country and, above all, the whole world. Village tourism is a new dimension of Nepal showing the new challenges and opportunities for economic development.

Its major beneficiaries are local villagers and communities such as poor, disadvantaged and underprivileged group of the community. Children and women will be given priority in the project as far as practicable. Tahoon village/community is targeted as beneficiaries in this project. Likewise, Dalit is also encouraged and the local indigenous knowledge and skill is also upgraded and strengthened. Most of the people are poor and have less access of facilities and opportunities to improve their livelihood.

Village Tourism Development Process

1. Developing and promoting trekking villages in relation to the village tourism development concept.
2. Developing village tourism package:

   Kathmandu-Sirubari-Tahoon-Tansen-Lumbini-Chitwan-Ghalegaun-Kathmandu.
3. Enhancing high quality products from village tourism to adventure tourism.
4. Strengthening the network and structure of village tourism.

Soft Trekking Development

Soft trekking can be developed in Tahoon village and the adjacent places such as Baugha Gumba, Chherlung-Ranighat, Begnas, Madan Pokhara, Madi and so on.

Trekking Season for Trekkers

1. To view scenic beauty of Rhododendron and alpine rose, blooming, the season for trekking is from February-May in high mountain regions of Palpa.
2. For low height trekking, September-Mid December (autumn season) is useful.
3. To enjoy Tansen, July-Mid September is enjoyed as Monsoon month.
4. To view the clear sky and the Himalayan range and beauty, November-January is the best season for tourists.

The trekking tourism along with village tourism is developed in Tahoon associated areas/villages of Palpa.

Income Generating Programme

The project initiates different local income generating programmes to villagers in support of Tahoon tourism village development. They are listed below:

Beekeeping Programme

Beekeeping program is initiated by local people for generating income. The necessary training and seminar/workshop have to be organized to meet the project objectives. Tahoon village has a good potential for bee keeping. Honey produced in Tahoon has commercial values. People who are keeping bees are not following modern techniques, but they are in very traditional ways. Today they need the modified system for promoting their income and being professional. They can harvest the honey at least thrice a year if the bee-keeping technique is improved. The production can be consumed in local market and to villager and tourists coming to Tahoon tourism village. The bee keeping can be a part of business in support of village tourism development. The proposed project can support to some persons at least 15 days training. The trainees will be supported with necessary things like gloves, queen gates, neck caps, plain sheets to make improved beehives etc.

Vegetable Production

The local people have initiated production of different vegetables. The organic vegetable production is standarised as per the demand of vegetable market. The vegetable market should be developed. Likewise, off-season vegetable is also produced in the village. Basically, local farmers are suggested to cultivate vegetable.

Horticulture

Fruit, being the nutritious food for human being, should be cultivated in the village. The local people are encouraged for cultivation of different fruits such as orange, apple, guava, and so on. The project encourages local farmers for fruit farming. It tries to distribute fruit saplings around 250 to 20 farmers to promote fruit farming dedicated and assisted to village tourism development. At least 'one fruit plant to each family' is encouraged as a strategic plan for development. For this purpose 3 days fruit farming training will be organised. A local resource person will be managed on hire from District Agriculture Office of Kathmandu Central Office. Fruit farms may either be established in individual capacity or by forming group/community as per villager's desire and convenience. Consequently, after some years the fruit farming will yield income to support to local farmers and they will understand farm as a model of integrated agriculture farm to their income and support to Tahoon tourism village.

Handicraft Development

The local handicraft production is initiated to promote as a basic income generation. For instance, doll making from the local maize-leaf, mat making by straw, basket making from bamboo. Souvenir goods making for decoration, etc. can be made as income and employment generation to the local people.

Toilet Construction Programme

Tahoon tourism village must have toilet and bathroom facility in each individual's household. Construction of toilet and bathroom is a must for maintaining health and sanitation in the village. The project will motivate the local people to use locally

Magnificent Himalaya

availbale materials for building toilets. This programme brings changes in the behavioural pattern of the local people.

Livestock Promotion Programme

Livestock is the best occupation of Tahoon villager inhabitants. Tahoon villager can adopt animal husbandry as a major occupation next to agriculture. To improve and promote livestock management, 3 days seminar / workshop is organised for 15 interested persons. The seminar aims to disseminate knowledge and information on livestock management system to all the locales, which will be supported by Tahoon tourism village expansion.

Institutional Development Programme

Institutional development is a key program for sustainable development as a whole. This programme incorporates major things like capacity building and programme support.

Institutionalising the village tourism development efforts is a must in the village community. Actually, the individual project cannot be sustained for a long time.

Entrepreneurship Skill Development

Entrepreneurship skill development is necessary for the promotion and development of tourism business. Due to lack of entrepreneurship skill, most people fail in their targeted objectives. To promote enterprises, entrepreneurship skill development training should be provided to local villagers. The proposed project in this respect initiates to disseminate knowleldge on business enterprise and possible benefits. The skill development helps people to understand how to calculate cost benefit ratio and how to be a real professional body in the business world. This conception assists in developing Tahoon tourism village also.

Linkage Programme Development

Tahoon tourism village develops linked tourism prgragmmes nearby its adjoining village and town. The village tourists coming to Tahoon village are motivated to visit different tourist spots for village-city tourism partnership development. The programme is listed as follows:

Shreenagar Hill

Shreenagar Hill is considered as a heavenly blessed spot located at the top of the hill. It consists of 1,650 m height from the sea level. The beauty of this hill station is wonderfully gifted by the nature. There are various attractions such as pine forest capped hill, parks, gardens, playground (for golf course), picnic spots, meditation spots, and camping facilities. Tourists can enjoy the longest magnificent Himalayan range consisting of Dhaulagiri, Manaslu and twin peaks of Machhapuchhre to the northernside. Similarly, the view of sunrise and sunset can be enjoyed.

Besides this, the top of the hill has been beautifully decorated with tourist cottages, camping and tripping. The unique model of 'Twadewa' an oil lamp decorated in the Shreenagar Park area is an additional attraction.

Amar Narayan Temple

Amar Narayan Temple is next attraction to tourists. The Narayan temple built by Amar Singh Thapa has historical and architectural values. Built in 1807 A.D. (in pagoda style), the temple shows the wonderful art picturised in the woodcarvings. The temple is protected by the Great Wall of Palpa with one-meter stonewall. In addition, there are other attractions like Mahadev temple, ponds, parks, rest houses and natural water spring in the temple area.

Bhagwati Temple

Built in 1951 A.D. by General Ujir Singh Thapa, Bhagwati Temple is the glorious sign of victory over the British troops from India. The brave Nepali defeated the powerful British troops as the divine power enlightened them in the battlefield. The Goddess's chariot is celebrated with military honour in every August as the glory of Nepal.

Shreenagar Ganesh

It is next important temple known as Shreenagar Ganesh or Siddi Binayak symbolising the God of success. This temple, which was built by Amar Singh Thapa, has wonderful artistic values.

Parileyak Ban

Located at the eastern side of Shreenagar, Parileyak Ban (forest) is famous for meditation done by Lord Buddha. This spot or forest related to Lord Buddha's life story concerns with a monkey and an elephant served Him to make meditation most successful. The spot, being very peaceful, is suitable for meditators and tourists.

Rose Garden

The Rose Garden known, as Birendra Phulbari is an interesting spot for visitors, where more than 150 kinds of roses are beautifully blowing. Interested researchers and rose specialists can enjoy and study this Rose Garden as the specific and unique product of Tansen, Palpa in connection with Tahoon tourism village.

Parvas Lake

There is a small pond with Lotus flowers located at 8 km south of Tansen. It is an interesting place for tourists.

Tansen Durbar

Tansen Durbar was built by Pratap Shamsher Jung Bahadur Rana in 1927 A.D. It is the then Rana palace located at the heart of the Tansen city. Once it was the administrative office of Rana Government and secretariat of Palpa district.

Shitalpati (Round House)

Shitalpati, which was built by Khadga Shamsher, is an octagonal shape. It is the round house where tourists can enjoy the 'Baggi Dhoka', the biggest gate in Nepal in the Shitalpati Square by tourists.

Ridibazar or Ruruchhetra

Ridibazar is an interesting place for trekking. Located at the bank of the Kali Gandaki river, the Ridibazar is 30 km north west of Tansen. Tourists can enjoy Ridibazar by walking 4 hours after an hour bus ride from Tansen. It is said as 'Banaras of Nepal' to the Hindu. One can go to Muktinath or Jomsom through the Kali Gandaki at Ridi to Narayani via Ranighat and Mugling.

Ranighat

Ranighat is a beautiful place for tourists. It is a popular spot for love. One can reach there by two hours trekking to the north of Tansen. Ranighat, the Taj Mahal of Nepal built by Khadga Shamsher in memory of his dearest wife Tej Kumari is an enchanting palace. It is 7 km far distance from Tansen to Ranighat.

Rishikeshav Temple

Rishikeshav is the lotus shaped temple, which is 30 km far away from Tansen. It was built by Mani Mukunda Sen. In Ridi, a black stone was found as the idol of God. The temple is the showpiece of wood carving of Nepal, which can be enjoyed by tourists.

Village Tourism Model Development in Tahoon Village

Tahoon village is selected as a tourism village in Palpa district. It will be focused and developed on the basis of community participation and community's welfare. The villagers themselves will be initiated by forming Tahoon Tourism Village. At least, 15 to 30 village households will be chosen as village tourism accommodation centre. The local resources and skills will be utilised to a large extent, so that the leakage in tourism will be checked and balanced. The villagers of Tahoon will be able to generate more income and employment through village tourism development and Village Tourism Development Committee.

The village tourism development criteria developed by Dr Surendra Bhakta Pradhanang will be major guidelines in the project formation and implementation.

Tahoon Tourism Village Development Works

Some consturction works related to Tahoon tourism village development will be done as follows:

1. Tourism Meeting/Conference/Training House
2. Exhibition Centre
3. Tourism Information Centre
4. Culture Centre
5. Village Tourism Committee
6. Toilet and Bathroom Construction in Selected Village Tourism Households
7. Cleanliness and Environment Awareness
8. View Tower Construction
9. Cable Car in and around Palpa Hills
10. Road Renovation.

Conclusion

Nepal, being the country of villages and home of Himalayas has to develop village tourism as a new dimension for economic development. Today it is the crying need of Nepal to meet the sustainable development. Tahoon VDC proposed for action research on the prospect and development of available tourist heritage is necessary. To meet the mission of developing Tahoon tourism village, infrastructure development related to tourism sector such as tourism road, communication, drinking water, health care centre, village tourism information centre, meeting hall, exhibition centre, etc. in coordination and help of ministry and related implementing agencies should be undertaken. Besides this, village tourism seed money and funding investment has to be managed.

Chaughare Tourism Village

Chaughare is a beautiful village of Lalitpur district selected for action research study. Lalitpur is one of the famous three cities of Kathmandu valley. Chaughare village lies at the southern Lalitpur, the hilly area of Lalitpur. Lalitpur, renowned for its social and pilgrimage harmony, historic temples and monasteries, magnificent arts and crafts and ethnic culture, is known as the city of Fine Arts. Chaughare, passing through Sainbu VDC, Sunakothi VDC, Dhapakhel VDC and Lele VDC is reached at the distance of 35 kilometers from Kathmandu. Though Chaughare is under the umbrella of Lalitpur district is purely a virgin and unexplored land of hill and mountain predominantly inhabited by the Tamang ethnic group of people. The population of this district is about 5,000. The literacy rate is only 5 per cent. The young people who passed SLC examination are not more than 20 in number. Out of the total population only 30 per cent people of total people are economically sound, who can live their lives with their limited income. 70 per cent of total people are below poverty line. The fifty per cent of people of this area work as a daily worker in the local areas while the remaining 50 per cent people involve in labour work force by migrating to urban area for work. The compact settlement of the Tamang ethnic group of people lies at Dhomba tole, ward no. 2 of Chaughare VDC where 25-30 houses are in ring settlement and altogether there are 70 households in the ward.

The micro hydro-electricity power generated from Thosne Khola at the cost of 95,000 by VDC, is a good example of local initiation and love towards development of this Chaughare VDC. Similarly, 2.50 kilowatt hydroelectricity power was generated from Mokta Dol. The hydroelectricity power distributed at the ratio of 96 watt each to 25 households in the village is the sign of development process modelled by villagers. Chaughare stands at 2500 ft above the sea level. It has a prestigious culture predominantly dominated by the Tamang culture. There is a temple of Gupteshwor Mahadev in Chaughare where a grand Mela is annualy organised at Baisakh purnima (fullmoon in April).

The major occupation of the villagers is agriculture and the major production is potato, maize, rice, wheat and so on. The vegetation like cauliflower, onion, cabbage, pumpkin, radish, etc. produced more in this area is a good source of income. The livestock is next important occupation of the Tamang. There is more prospect of developing handicrafts like Nepali paper making industry in Chaughare where a sufficient amount of raw material is available. Furthermore, a diverse flora and fauna invites tourists for amusement. Vegetation that ranges from tropical to alpine provides more bird species and endangered animals. The scenic beauty of Himalaya can be viewed and enjoyed from Kamlechaur. Tourists frequently come and go for trekking. Village tourism development in Chaughare village provides benefit directly and indirectly to village and villager and nearby neighbouring villages such as Katub VDC, Gotikhel VDC, Sankhu VDC, Bhardeu VDC, and Nallu VDC. The poverty of Chaughare will be reduced by village tourism development. Similarly, the health and sanitation will be upgraded by changing villagers' habit and nature of maintaining of cleanliness with the consensus of tourism development. The several income generating activities linked with village tourism will be developed through local job opportunities and income. Besides, horticulture and agriculture will be flourished. Village tourism based economy will be cultivated in Chaughare when model tourism village will be developed.

The villagers themselves can stand for economic development as sustainability is guaranteed in local or village level. They will be able to cope with poverty and underdevelopment when they will learn or achieve the technique of development from the grass root level. By the development of village tourism, village tourism market will be served from village to village, hut to hut and door to door. Consequently, village tourism market will be rooted and promoted from rural to rural and rural to urban and from domestic to international level. This is what we call the power mechanism of village tourism industry for economic development in villages of Nepal.

Nepal, being the country of villages and home of Himalayas, has to develop village tourism as a new dimension for development. Today it is the prime need to meet to local and sustainable development. Chaughare VDC proposed for action research on the prospect and development of available tourist heritage. To meet the mission of developing Chaughare tourism village, infrastructure development related to tourism sector such as tourism road, communication, drinking water, health care centre, village tourism information centre, meeting hall, exhibition centre, etc. in coordination and help of ministry and related implementing agencies should be accounted. In addition, village tourism primordial investment capital has to be accumulated.

Bhadgaun Tourism Village

Tourism development in Bhaktapur is not a new subject. It is favoured by all local government and people. But it has certainly been ignored, and the issue of developing Bhadgaun as tourism village destination has often been forgotten. Indeed, the concept of village tourism institutionally introduced and pioneered by Kathmandu Research Centre is a new thought-provoking dilemma that concerns Bhaktapur and its villages. In fact, this author is the brain behind village tourism development in Nepal.

Popularised by nickname Bhadgaun at an altitude of 1,401 m above the sea level, Bhaktapur is a home for ancient art and architecture especially with focus on the medieval art of Nepal. Bhaktapur has spread in an area of 119 sq. km; is a beautiful destination where the city area covers an area of 4 square miles. Bhaktapur having 2,25,461 population is densely populated area, followed by 1,72,455 male and 1,65,330 female. The percentage lead by this area is 0.97 in total population. The number of households is 41,253 consisting 5.47 average household size. The density of population is 1,895 persons per sq. km. Topographically, Bhaktapur which is shaped as a cronch-shell, means much to devotees while the term, Bhadgaun gives a separate meaning as sporting familiarity of rice-village where plenty of rice is grown, stored and played. Today Bhaktapur has been a popular tourist destination for a half day visit to the international tourists. Among the three famous cities of Nepal, Bhaktapur is one such unique city brightening as the possible village tourism centre. Bhaktapur having two municipalities and 16 VDCs is the hidden treasure of ancient art and architecture.

Bhaktapur, we understand, has plenty of tourism attractions in terms of natural and man-made heritage culture. Bhaktapur, by nature, is a wonderful land for pleasure tourists where heart touching scene and scenary is gifted. Similarly, man built architectural showpieces illustrated in the Durbar Square, the lion gate, statue of king Bhupendra Malla, the picture gallery, the golden gate, the palace of 55 windows, the Batsala temple, the bell of Barking dogs, the replica of Pashupatinath, the five-storied pagoda, Nyatpola temple, the Bhairavnath temple, the Dattatraya temple, the Pujari Math, the Suryavinayak temple, the Changu Narayan temple and so on are openly exhibited as Bhaktapur's uniqueness for tourists.

The lifestyle of 'Jyapu and Jyapuni' is the next type of charming tourism product for international visitors. The Jyapu standing on Daurasurwal (Nepali dress) and the Jyapuni wearing Haku Patasi (the typical dress) of Jyapu community of Bhaktapur is a symbol of uniqueness and originality for Bhadgaun tourism village. The Jyapu dance and Jyapu song composed in different lyrics are merits to village tourism development. Village tourism deploies the hidden culture and practices of people into the tourism world. The indigenous households of Bhadgaun built in Lichhavi and Malla periods are good assets for developing village tourism. Tourists would prefer those ancestor's skill and technology led houses, which are Bhaktapur speciality. It is helpful in enhancing village tourism.

Village tourism carrier benefits to all especially proletarian class of people. It is the new economic development model for the developing countries like Nepal. Village tourism is likened by the people. It is good for all. Some tourism entrepreneurs of Nepal, who are holding big power of Nepal's tourism industry, have lambasted the village tourism concept. They are more selfish and they block development of tourism in village tourism roads remained crowed with people having a field a respite from the daily hustle and bustle of city life. Tourism village provides a peaceful atmosphere for holiday and relaxation tourists, which shows the road map for tourism and economic development of the nation.

Gone are the days of greasing our palms by government and concerned high authority for programming development plan. This is high time to conduct and implement the plan and programme for village tourism concept in each village. On this principle, Bhaktapur can start developing village tourism. Bhaktapur, as a rising and powerful municipality/district has greater responsibility to help the smaller villages like Tamang village, Karki village, Khadka village of Dadhikot VDC, Hala village of Tathali VDC, Madigaun, Rautgaun, Bistagaun, Pilagaun, Thapagaun, Bahungaun, Dhanasargaun, Basnetgaun and Suyalabgaun of Sirutar VDC, Dadagaun and Shantigaun of Nankhel VDC, Sudan village, Changu village, Gundu village, Gamcha village, etc., where village tourism industry can be operated. Those villages and villagers selected for developing village tourism should be rightly encouraged to go forward for modality.

Analytically I say, 'Bhaktapur can be announced and transmitted into ancient Nepal and the best village tourism destination that can be picturised, civilised and symbolised through Nepal's village tourism concept. Bhaktapur destination is Nepal's Nepal where indigenous Nepalese culture, art and living pattern are highlighted from sixth century to seventeenth century. The masterpeice endangered types of culture, art and architecture and Bhaktapurian civilisation can be merged and displayed in terms of living museum in the world tourism history. Consequently, Bhaktapur and its locals get a lot of economic benefits in return.'

Bhadgaun tourism village should be extensively developed by balancing tourism development in the district. Herein, the proposed ring road in Bhaktapur should be constructed as soon as possible. The tourism environment should be tactfully created as such that those tourists who visit Kathmandu must visit Bhaktapur and Lalitpur and their adjoining tourist villages. It is said, in other words a fantastic package tour programme to be developed as 100 per cent tourist arrivals coming to Nepal must visit three cities of Kathmandu valley. The time is coming very soon to sketch Bhaktapur developed as Bhadgaun tourism village destination.

Besides this, several Nepal based tourism villages are in the process of development, for example, Khokna village, Illam village, Kartike Deurali village, Thuloparsel village, Briddim village, Chepang hill village and so on.

Prospective Village Tourism

Nepal has had an immense potential of developing village tourism destinations. Recognised as the country of villages brightening silver and golden mountains and Sagarmatha–the top of the world, Nepal has prospective village tourism places. Some of them are discussed below:

Kathmạndu Research Centre conducted a research study on Kermigaun of Humla which has more potential to develop it as a tourism model village in Nepal. The village has a lot of attractions like lifestyle of village, culture, natural beauty, pollution free environment, typical dress and ornament and so on.

The most special, unique and wonderful lifestyle and village social practice identified and highlighted by KRC is walking through roof to roof from one household to other household and from one short village destination to other village destination at the alarming style, which is nowhere in the world. Instead of road, roof is used as village road in practice. It is most amazing super practice and adventure to the domestic and international tourists of the world. This is the country of villages treasured many more uniqueness and adventurous products which can be displayed to village tourists. The local villagers put on 'Bakhu' dress in their on speciality and used to insert needles in the dress as their fashion. There is no need of refrigerator for storage of goods in Kermi village, but they used to dig a big pit for storage and would keep Bhojpatra leafs and barks around the storage place. That traditional technology protects fruits, vegetables, etc.[1]

KRC associated with village tourism study stated that more than 900 tourists visited Tashigaun of Khadbari district. In Tashigaun the tree of Dinosaur's period is found as said as 'Tedasenton Sinens Oliver'. This type of tree has been spread out from the boundary of Nepal to Tibet China.

An American trekker claimed that he saw the footprints of Yeti–the snowman in the Tashigaun.The tourists coming to Tashigaun would generally make enquires and search for yeti. The area of Tashigaun located at the altitude between 435 m and 8,463 m is spread at the Makalu Himal. There is a unique biodiversity followed by six different diversities in the Makalu area, which is very interesting to enjoy nature.

Regarding the prospective of Village Tourism in Nepal, Manaegaun, which is 9 km far distance from Dhulikhel, can be a model Tamang Tourism Village in Nepal. There are 600 persons living in 45 families of the locality. Lodgegaun (Phulbari) developed by private entrepreneurs in 200 ropanies can be taken as a village tourism model. As per the local village picture, tourism village having 36 rooms at the capacity of 100 visitors is planned to develop as a tourism village with the financial support of foreign investors.

Khunde Hospital

Flowers Accommodating Around Stone in Nature

In addition, Tansen-Palpa and its adjoining villages are next destinations for the prospective of Village Tourism development in Nepal. In 1972, Tansen-Palpa was included as an important centre among the five major tourism centres of Nepal. It is still beautiful and pleasant to tourists. In Tansen the village tourism product as ' Hans Ko Chhoyla-Ayala-Bajee'- Duck burnt meat-liquor-flattered rice is very popular and delicious cuisine as speciality of the Tansen tourism spot in Nepal. The tourists are honoured in a typical welcoming pattern on the ground of traditional culture. There are various villages attracted for developing village tourism in Nepal. The Magar village, for example, can be a model for village tourism development in Nepal. Now-a-days, we have more than 5,000 tourists who came to visit Tansen for enjoying natural and cultural beauties. The pleasure tourists and honeymoon makers and adventure tourists can enjoy a lot in this spot.

Tansen is nearer to Lumbini, which is the popular birthplace of Lord Buddha. Here Tansen can be promoted as a three- phase attraction focused tourism spot such as Lord Buddha and His parents. The message given as 'Travel Lumbini and stay Tansen' is a favourable to tourists. This spot can be promoted as a hilly village tourism destination in Nepal.

Besides, Lomanthang village of Mustang district has become an attractive place for tourists. The village lying 105 kilometer north of Jomsom at an altitude of 12,000 ft is one of the remote Himalayan villages. After arriving at Jomsom by air, foreigners trek for five days to reach Lomathang and enjoy the natural beauty, pollution free and peaceful environment and delighting scenery there. But more tourists could have been attracted to Lomathang, if more attention is given this aspect. According to KRC, Lomanthang, at present only 700 foreign tourists visit annually. Lomanthang, which has a population of 900 and 400 houses, can be an ideal place for village tourism.[2]

The 700 years old historical wall located at this village is an attraction for the tourists. Inside this wall, there are two 700 years old monasteries Thicheng monastery and Namghyal monastery beautiful golden pattern are engraved in this ancient wall.

KRC has identified and recommended Chitwan based villages which are magnificent and suitable for village tourism development in Nepal. The selected villages are spelled out such as Bachhouli, Bhagaha, Janakauli, Meghauli, Telauli, Jagatpur, Sauraha, Madi Kalyanpur, Kumrose, Bhandara,

Transporting Goods in Village

Andrauli and Baghmara.[3] Besides, Simranghadh of Bara district, Panauti, Sunthan, Namobuddha, Thuloparsel and Kartike Deurali of Kavre district, Gundu village and Magar village of Bhaktapur district, Pyang village, Kailash Kuti and Sanugaun of Lalitpur district, Maithali village of Janakpur and so on have potential for developing Village Tourism in Nepal.

Located in Lamjung, Siurung village is also the destination of mountain to support village tourism development in Nepal. Tourists can enjoy the spectacle view of high peaks of the Annapurna and Manaslu ranges. This beautiful village can be developed as tourist village. It can be reached after a trek of six hours from Khudi Bazar.

Biddim is another village located at Rasuwa district. It is a beautiful village inhabited by the Tamang ethnic group of people. Its culture is like that of Tibet and exhibited as a small Tibet and its tradition. Tourists can enjoy it after a three hours walk from Syabrubasi.

Simrangadh situated at Bara district is next important historical village of Terai Nepal. It can be developed as tourism village. There are several historical and natural values in the Simrangadh village. The history of the village can attract village tourists more.

Owing to awareness created on village tourism development; there are more other villages like Ilam village, Bandipur village, Gorkha village, Manakamana village, Dhading village, Magar village, etc. are on the pipelines of developing village tourism in Nepal.

References

1. *The Himalayan Times,* March 20, 1996.
2. *The Kathmandu Post,* May 25, 1996.
3. Surendra Bhakta Pradhanang, *Village Tourism in Chitwan,* Adroit Publishers, Delhi, 2002.

Chapter 16

Village Tourism Policy and National Policy

Village tourism is a newly developed plan and policy in the overall national policy of Nepal. The importance of village tourism to the national economy is great. Its development and growth are to fit with the plans for national, regional and village (local) level. It also assigns to public and private sectors for development. The Nepalese tourism policy has beautifully focused the village tourism policy to be developed on a continuous long-term basis for the first time in 1995. The planning on village tourism is the gradual development based on the outcome of its scientific research conducted by KRC. The use of microeconomics and macroeconomics modelled in village tourism is relatively new attempt in national policy. The significance of village tourism policy is to boost grass root level of tourism and economy and at the same time to increase the income and employment generation, regional development and balance of payments in the country. The government of Nepal has brought out Tourism Policy 1995 to specifically code the respective roles of the government and the private sector. Similarly, Nepalese Tourism Policy placed the high priority to village tourism.

Considering the good perspective of tourism in the national policy and programme, the government has adopted the long term tourism policy as follows:

Long Term Objective

1. To develop tourism sector as an important part of the overall economic development.

2. To establish Nepal as a premium destination on the world tourism map.
3. To expand the benefits of tourism down to village level.

Long-Term Strategy

1. Necessary understanding and negotiation will be established with neighbouring countries to achieve growth in overland tourist transport.
2. Physical development in tourist cities and rural areas will be carried out on the basis of zoning.
3. Indigenous, value-based and endemic tourism activities will be promoted with a view to diversifying tourism products and establishing Nepal as a premium destination.
4. Local communities will be mobilised in the conservation and management of tourist resources. Village tourism (rural tourism) will be established as a viable alternative to the local economy by seeking active participation of the local people.
5. Tourist services will be standardised by amalgamating them with traditional hospitality.
6. Natural, cultural and historical resources will be conserved and consolidated through coordinated efforts of local government bodies tourism entrepreneurs and bodies responsible for cultural promotion.

Nepalese Tourism Policy 1995 (2052)

1. Expansion of investment in the tourism sector shall gradually be made and mobilisation of investments shall be made in construction and development of infrastructures of new tourism spots.
2. Private sector shall be encouraged to provide sightseeing of the places of the religious and cultural importance of the country, high Himalayan peaks and enchanting natural beauties to the tourists having utilised existing physical infrastructures in a systematic and effective manner.

3. Private sector shall be encouraged to operate various recreational and adventurous tourism activities based on water, land and air in the various parts of the kingdom without prejudice to the original culture and traditions of the country.
4. Facilities and incentives shall be expanded to the trusts, temples, monasteries, etc. Of religious and cultural importance and to the existing pilgrimages in a way to attract the internal tourists and such places shall also be developed as international spiritual centre.
5. Wildlife observation tourism shall be developed and promoted by utilising existing biodiversity in the country.
6. In order to expand mountain tourism as a sectoral basis, new trekking routes and new Himalalyan peaks for mountaineering shall gradually be opened.
7. Inter-countries tourism activities based on mutual benefits shall be increased by coordinating with neighbouring friendly nations.
8. Meeting, conferences, trade fairs, cultural and youth festivals, international sports competitions including other creative and promotional tourism products shall specifically be encouraged.
9. Rural communities shall be encouraged to operate various programmes of rural tourism (village tourism) development having specifically encouraged the rural tourism.
10. Programme for tourism-public awareness in various level shall be framed and executed.
11. In order to prevent adverse effects in environment from tourism, a Tourism Environment Guideline shall be framed in national level and the same shall be introduced.
12. A local code of conduct concerning environment shall be framed in accordance with the prevailing international norms and customs as well as National Guidelines and shall be brought into execution.
13. Land under the ownership of the government seemed appropriate from the tourism development point of view shall be made available to the private tourism

entrepreneurs to develop as tourism resorts on long-term lease or joint-venture on the basis of their working efficiency and working plan having made it environmental compatibility.

14. If any private sector desires to provide services to the tourists by expanding any infrastructure services and facilities, permission to that effect shall be given having prescribed certain criteria.
15. Tourism entrepreneurs shall be encouraged to introduce through their professional organisations a code of conduct to increase quality and standard of the tourism service and facilities.
16. Trekking areas shall be classified into three areas namely General, Guided and Restricted trekking areas.
17. General Trekking Areas: Areas where outlines of routes and ways are already clear and where minimum tourism services and facilities are available shall be classified as general trekking areas.
18. Guided Trekking Areas: Area opened for tourism trekking, but where tourism infrastructures like routes and ways and tourism services like hotels, lodges are not available in a basis level shall be classified as guided trekking areas. Arrangements shall be made to permit for trekking in such areas only to the tourists who travel in-group with a definite number through the Trekking Agencies in a year.
19. Restricted Trekking Areas: Areas deprived from the effects of modernity, located in the high mountain areas where extremely sensitive natural structure and ancient as well as original culture are found, shall be classified as restricted trekking area. Arrangements shall be made to permit for trekking in such areas only to the tourists who travel in-group through the Trekking Agencies along with a liaison officers as designated on behalf of His Majesty's Government.
20. Certain portion of the income raised from the tourism spots prescribed, as economically backward and remote areas shall be spent for the protection, promotion and

development of the same area.

21. Special Programmes shall be operated in order to maintain the pride of the Mount Everest, the supreme peak of the world.
22. Special emphasis shall be given to promote tourism industry in the markets of the Asian nations. At the lean season of tourists from overseas countries, attraction shall be given to the tourists of neighbouring nations.
23. A Tourism Study and Research Unit within the Ministry of Tourism shall be established in order to direct the trends of the tourism development of the country timely and objectively.
24. His Majesty's Government shall appoint a mission abroad or a national or foreign representative involved or interested in the tourism industry as representative for the sake of tourism promotion in Nepal and mobilise them accordingly.
25. Nepal shall be promoted as a primary destination in the international markets where there is a direct air link and tourism promotion shall be made jointly having included Nepal in other tourists originated markets where there is no direct air link and shall be publicised accordingly.
26. Special attention shall be paid for the security of the tourists coming to Nepal. Particularly, necessary practices shall be started in order to maintain rescue groups for the mountaineering tourism.
27. A separate 'Tourism promotion Fund' shall be established for the promotion of tourism and special programme shall be operated for the same.

Follow up, evaluation and or review the Tourism Policy shall be carried out regularly.(NPC, HMG, 1995).

Ninth Plan (1997-2002)

The Ninth Plan has realised tourism as a lead industry for the economic development of the country. The plan stresses that tourism can be developed as an important factor in the prosperity of a nation. It has greater comparative advantage.

The Ninth Plan has set the following objectives and strategies:

1. To establish backward and forward linkages of the tourism sector with the national economy so as to develop it as an important sector for the overall economic development.
2. To establish Nepal as a premium destination in the world tourism market through effective publicity and promotion.
3. To enhance employment opportunities income generation and foreign currency earning from the tourism sector and external these benefits down to the *village level.*

Policy and Implementation Strategy

1. Additional destinations will be developed and diversified on the basis of feasibility study.
2. Historical, religious and cultural sites, temples and monasteries scattered throughout the country will be registered in the form of national heritage sites, they will be conserved and used for tourism purpose.
3. An inventory of lakes, caves, waterfalls and historical facts will be prepared so as to develop them into tourist destinations.
4. Indigeneous culture, traditional hospitality and tribal traditions will be preserved and promoted to enhance tourist attractions.
5. New trekking routes and climbing peaks will be opened up in a methodical manner.
6. Local bodies in each development region will be encouraged to develop *a model tourist village.*
7. Quality of the tourism products and services available in the central region will be upgraded. Special interest tourism spots will be expanded in the eastern and mid far-western regions.
8. A survey will be carried out into Kathmandu valley's cultural heritage, festivals, cultural and religious traditions. Festival tourism will be promoted in the valley.

9. Periodic studies and evaluation will be carried out into the inputs, outputs and effects of the tourism investments.
10. Rafting will be opened on the major river systems wherever it is feasible.

Programme

Model Tourism Village

Village based tourism will be promoted so as to expand tourism down to the village level. Village tourism (rural tourism) destinations will be developed in all appropriate representative geographical areas of Nepal, targeting domestic and foreign tourists.

Civil Aviation

The 44 operating airports in the kingdom of Nepal will be upgraded and Biratnagar, Bhairahawa and Nepalgunj airports will be promoted into hub airports for operation of short haul services.

Helipads will be built in remote areas deprived of roads and airports. Surveys of potential sites for Second International Airport will be carried out during the Ninth Plan.

TENTH PLAN (2002-2007)

The introduction of village tourism concept and its development have widened the tourism development consciousness to village/villager at the larger extent. This village tourism is specially developed for villagers of Nepal to strengthen the village economy and to make progress in livelihood.

Considering the significance of tourism industry, the long term vision on tourism has been reviewed and set up as follows:

Long Term Vision

1. Developing tourism factor as an important part of the national economy and re-establishing the country globally as a prime destination.

2. Expansion of earning from the tourism sector to rural areas through qualitative improvement of tourism related services.
3. Emphasis on cultural tourism by conservation and proper management of living heritage sites and movements of national importance.
4. Making international and domestic air services simple, efficient, safe and reliable and develping convenient road network in tourism areas.

Objective:

The effective and prioritised implementation of the programmes in the tourism sector that has already emerged as an important organ of the national economy, will not only contribute to national economy but will also provide benefits to foreign tourists as well as increase the income generating and employment opportunities. In view to this, following objectives have been set forth in the Tenth Plan:

1. Sustainable development and qualitative promotion of the tourism sector.
2. Conservation and preservation of historical, cultural, religious and archaeological heritages and enhancing their practical utilisation.
3. To render air transportation services easily accessible, secure, standard, and reliable.

Strategy

Development of the tourism sector assists the overall development of the national economy and generates foreign currency; it also helps in the economic development of the hilly region that has low agricultural productivity and creates employment in the region.

The hilly and backward regions are highlighted with unemployment and poverty; at the same time, they are bestowed with astonishing natural beauty and enormous potential for mountaineering and white-water rafting that calls for greater emphasis in the development of tourism in this area. This will also promote social justice in development. The quality of civil aviation is equally important when considering the development of the tourism sector. Similarly, culture is the treasure of the country and its development and conservation will promote the fame and identity of the country; at the same time, it also helps in the overall social development of the country and the development of the tourism sector.

1. Besides the established tourism markets, less risky tourist destinations will be promoted. Likewise, Nepali tourism will be promoted in the neighbouring countries.
2. By increasing the use of locally produced goods and services, local retention of the money spent by the tourist will be encouraged. Women and backward communities will be encouraged with special priority in such activities.
3. Tourism activities in the recently opened (previously banned) and other potential areas will be encouraged through infrastructure development and domestic tourism will be established as an economic alternative.
4. Eco-tourism will be promoted and Nepal will be developed as one of the major destinations for eco-tourism.
5. Competitive and collaborative capacity of non-governmental and private sectors associated with the tourism sector will be enchanced.
6. To encourage involvement of non-governmental sectors in management, preservation and utilisation of cultural, religious, archaeological and natural heritage in accordance to decentralisation policy.
7. Study, conservation and preservation of literature, art and culture will be done.
8. The airport and airlines service with necessary infrastructure will be developed to ensure domestic and international travel.
9. Private sector will be involved in airport construction, operation and long-distance airlines service.

Policy and Action Plan

- Implementation of sub-regional plan and programme in co-operation with the South Asian countries.
- Priority to neighbouring countries in promotion activities.

- Foreign diplomatic services, any agency representing His Majesty's Government of Nepal abroad and individual or organisation with business relationship will be mobilised in promotion and publicity activities.
- Increasing employment opportunities through protection of local skills and its commercial use.
- Emphasis on the use of locally produced goods and services.
- Offer clean environment, qualitative service and courteous behaviour.
- Preparation and implementation of the code of conduct and improvement in the quality of residence, travel, entertainment, etc.
- Implementation of a strong and reliable security system for the safety of domestic as well as international tourists.
- Development of the infrastructure related to tourism sector such as road, communication, drinking water, health, etc. in coordination and help of the ministry, and related implementing agencies.
- Execution of various acitvities in an integrated manner through the establishment of regional tourism centres (hub).
- Expansion of mountaineering, trekking, and other adventure tourism in new areas through participation of the local bodies and non-governmental ogranisations.
- Mountaineering tourism will be made more attractive by allowing to summit new or less used mountains and adoption policies for mountaineering through promotional subsidy, low price or free of cost.
- Exploration of new areas including incentive, convention, sports, *village tourism* and practical development of available tourists heritage.
- To implement priority programmes such as environmental protection, garbage management, alternative energy, employment generation and awareness raising activities, coordination among the governmental, non-governmental and private sector will be enhanced.

- Special monitoring will be done to check pollution in protected areas like trekking, mountaineering and other environment-sensitive areas.
- Implement Destination Nepal Campaign 2002-03 with priority.
- Carryout institutional reforms of Nepal Tourism Board and Civil Aviation Authority of Nepal.
- Operationalise and or fully privatise Royal Nepal Airlines Corporation with joint investment of government and or domestic/foreign agencies.
- Play a role of a facilitator in promoting positve attitude of people towards cultured tourism to support tourism service.
- Archaeological survey, exploration, protection, and excavation of the areas of national importance will be carried out.
- Protection and conservation of cultural uniqueness and religious tradition that supports tourism sector.
- Mandatory implementation of guidelines for the protection of the areas under world heritage and of archaeological importance.
- Participation of the local, non-governmental and private sector in the protection and promotion of the heritages to make such activities self-reliant and income generating.
- Legal protection and recognition of works of various literatures, writers, musicians, artists etc and encouragement to new talents.
- To render air travel less risky and secure, a satellite-based communication system will be established, developed and expanded.
- Construction and expansion of existing facilities in the international and domestic airports such as hangers, communication facilities and other necessary technical equipments and coordination of skilled technical manpower to provide a secure environment for landing and take off.
- To make air service regular and reliable the quality of

existing airports in remote areas will be upgraded and new airports will be constructed.
- Renewal of international air agreements and encouragement to new agreements.
- Creation of necessary infrastructure and service in the domestic airports to start flights to neighbouring countries.
- Beginning of a construction work of a well-facilitated international airport in the Terai area.
- Encouragement Promotion of regular of chartered international flights.
- Maximum use and enforcement of air routes in the Nepali sky.

Programme Log Frame

Development of Touristic Areas

Tourism model village : Shree Antu, Dhanushadham, Tanahu, Khaptad, Jumla.

Tourism Activities Expansion

Trekking routes expansion
Cable car
Funicular rail
Rafting, etc.

Village Tourism (Rural Tourism) Development

Tourism programmes for poverty alleviation:

Kanchenjanga, Solukhumbu, Lamtang, Chitwan, Lumbini, Dolpa.

Village tourism development:

Terathum, Kavre, Nuwakot, Tanahu, Sakhu, Khokana, Lakuri, Kakani, Ghalegaun, Junbesi.

Nepal Tourism Board

Established in 1997 as per the Nepal Tourism Policy 1995, Nepal Tourism Board (NTB) is an autonomous body functioning as a partnership between His Majesty's Government of Nepal and the private sector. Later on, it was empowered to work as a National Tourism Organisation (NTO).

The role of NTB is to act on the ground of statutory responsibilities assigned by the Nepal Tourism Board Act 2053. The major role played by NTB is to develop and introduce Nepal as an attractive tourist destination in the international marketplace. It tries to increase the Gross Domestic Product (GDP) and foreign exchange income by means of promoting the tourism industry. By and large, NTB realised the concept of village tourism propounded by Dr Pradhanang. Now its major role and responsibility have been shifted to promote the concept of village tourism in Nepal and to follow the promotion of tourism market international. According to National Policy, directed to promotion of village tourism, NTB and its partner organisation Tourism for Rural Poverty Alleviation Programme (TRPAP) have recently embarked on a joint programme of village tourism development and poverty alleviation. After the promotion of brand, Everest and more. It has explored Nepalese new tourism brand, 'Naturally Nepal-once is not enough' for the promotion of Nepalese tourism in the international tourism market. 'Naturally Nepal' will be followed by travel agencies, trekking agencies, hotels and tourism related organisation of Nepal.

Future of Village Tourism

The future of village tourism is very bright in Nepal and abroad. Since no tourism is better than village tourism for the country of village Nepal. It can bring the revolutionary changes in the national economy. Historically, travel and tourism has been a fascination for mankind. Exploring new areas to taste and experience is not a new thing. But the subject we talk about is a relatively new tourism village travel agenda.

Obviously, tourism is an international force linking one to many in terms of fellow citizens of the world. There are special days devoted to 'Global Tourism Village' for making merry and peace in the earth. Nepal's village tourism concept gradually develops and invites the global tourists for tasting and experiencing Nepali natural villages where the citizens of the world can enjoy real nature, culture and unexpected village uniqueness and unseen love and affection they rarely feel. Very soon Nepal's village tourism concept will boost up village tourist destinations into the 'Centre for International Village Tourism'. Village tourism, being the peace establishing concept, upgrades human life and environment into the prosperous state of the world. Obviously, Nepal's village tourism takes over the 'tension free world' where rest and relaxation with nature and natural life will be created. The present day people are not living a relaxed life.

The medical science states that a combination of negative factors such as pollutants, imbalanced diet and lifestyle and high aspirations have turned the human mind restless, thereby making the body perpetually ill. We can analyse our own body that constitutes of about 20,000 million cells. The brain alone constitutes of 12,000 million cells of which about 5,00,000 cells maintain inter-cellular relationships. All these cells may not be able to function their designated obligations if there is an imbalance due to physical and mental unrest. However, meditation expands the volume of breath intake and develops the blood circulation, but we need better relaxation centre for rest and peace. In this circumstance, tourism village drives away the affected central nervous system-tension from mind and body. Hence, village tourism gives the message as 'goodbye to tension' and 'welcome to global village tourists and global tourism village' to the world.

Dark Side of Village Tourism

Village tourism, although a very positive, fruit-bearing concept, cannot escape its darkness and overwhelming danger to the village society and ultimately the nation. The amazing village world exhibits some possible funny moments to the village host and tourists. One may be amazed when the funny things would happen. Warning on the village tourism development could be sensed through the saying, 'the water can make the boat float, but it can sink it too'. This doctrine is more applied in the context of tourism village and village community as a whole.

Village tourism can, no doubt, uplift villages and villagers, if the village community can understandingly esteem the village tourism philosophy particularly its code of conduct and disciplinary measures.

Village tourism has pros and cons regarding the socio-cultural structure of the country. Talking about the cons of village tourism, we spell out decline in the traditional norms and values, increase in crime, social conflicts, wave of materialism, over dependence on money, heavy traffic of tourists, loss of calm and quiet environment, degradation of natural environment, and dependency on industrialised and developed countries. The traditional values of host countries may be gradually weakened owing to the impact of tourism in the village. The other important thing is the loss of indigenous village identity deprived of wonderful rites and lifestyles. The similar type of culture will be undesirably copied out in other regions too. There is danger that the unidentified and untouched zone will also be exposed badly. The loss of identity bears risk on the speciality of village tourism by fading the village tourism product. The charm of villages and villagers will gradually go down. The personal and family value and relationship will be unnaturally calculated in terms of the sum of money. The system of 'paying guest' is indigestive to rigid villagers and also against the social laws and religious practices. Guests are honoured as God by providing delicious food and accommodation on free of cost. Village tourism unlikely breaks the traditional practice, which is the demerit and risk to the downfall of traditional culture. Breaking human relation and love in terms of sum of money towards the guests are the threats. Religiously, commercialisation in human relationship is a danger for village tourism. The money matter looses and cuts intimacy in human relation. The traditional cultural values are badly marked by money in the unique culture of the village and village economy.

Below are spelled out as demerits of village tourism that show dangers to the village community and nation:

1. Migration

Village tourism, being the means of income and employment generation, boosts up village economy. The rich villagers will go away from the village to city. They may have 'body in the village and soul in the city'. The villagers transferring their income and money would migrate from village to city. They just exploit village resources and transfer the benefit and accumulated wealth from village to city. It is very bad and dark side of village tourism development left to the shadow of village tourism. The shadow comes with the mass and body through the light of village tourism.

2. Lack of Capital Investment in the Village

Transformation of capital and income from village to city is a danger for capital gap in village. The income from village is transferred to city in the purchase of land, building construction, departmental store, supermarket and business. The rich villagers would take advantages from the village as exploitation of villagers, labour, skill and resources. This will leave out villages and villagers poor and backward instead of development. As a result, the risk of capital investment can be appeared in the village and village administration/government. The village income multiplier effect may be shortened or paralysed in such a circumstance.

3. Cultural Shock

The indigenous socio-culture may be loosely affected by developing village tourism. Tourism village, if excessively dominated by the foreign tourists and their cultures, may be polluted the village culture and tradition. Some teens of village can badly fall into the trap of western culture. The originality and charm of tourism village may be depreciated and lost as malpractice of tourism village. The western culture can be easily transmitted into behavioural pattern of life. The lifestyle of villagers in habit of lodging, fooding and speaking may be affected. Similarly, possible danger of western club can be entered to the village. Despite the Nepalese dances, rock and roll and twist can be launched and exhibited. In spite of 'Jhayaure' song the western song and music may be played and marked as bad influences of the foreign tourists.

4. Spread of Prostitution

Village tourism is a family attached principle which should be wisely practiced. The family love and affection liberalised into the family values creates a super family benevolence in the village community and environment. The family love, sometimes, may be badly turned into illicit connection or sexual relation with village tourists and villagers, particularly teens. Accidentally, village tourism may be a possible way of

Nepali Farmer

prostitution and prostitutes would automatically grow to take advantage from the situation.

The growing malpractice of gay marriages and homosexual habitants in the world can attack and pollute village tourism. In the western world, gay marriage has been legalised as an unnatural sexing in USA and Europe. Besides, sex beast should not be allowed to enter into the tourist villages. These unnatural gay practice and sex beast are growing day by day. Those gays may be possibly come as village tourists. This may create terrible constraints and issues about village tourism development in near future, if we are not timely conscious on the way of developing village tourism in Nepal. The tourism village should not be the gay's recreation or prostitution destination in the long run.

5. Change in Lifestyle

Village lifestyle is a major attraction of village tourism. We find a long ago indigenous lifestyle of villages so real and friendly that gives a very sweet smile and love. Tourists passby the adventure walk and even a dirt road compromising to experience ancient villages.

In tourism village the lifestyle of local villagers can be affected by the heavy flow of tourists in the village, which will be very bad and negative impact. Negatism in village tourism may be spread at that time, which is the danger of developing village tourism.

6. Change in Religion

The increase of foreign people in tourism village will affect religion. It may spoil the indigenous beliefs and practices.

The development of village tourism may loose village secrecy. Everything will be opened. The hidden things may not be maintained and restricted to foreign tourists. The precious things of village can be disappeared or lost from villages.

7. Effect of Modernisation

Time is not on our side. It is the ugly truth that time cannot be controlled in our favour. Every change in walk of new and modern thought is natural. But the wave of modernisation and ultra-modernisation seriously affects the village society and disappears the beauty and significance of village. On tourism business, the foreign tourists directly or indirectly affect the village culture and community through their behaviour and modern culture. Modernisation to the village tourism concept kills its charm and values. Hence, it is necessary to save from the ultra-violet ray of modernisation in the tourism villages.

8. Risk to Village Socio-Economic Structure

The village society is wonderfully composed of its own indigenous system and practices. Those which may have a high risk in village society are damaged by tourism village development. Local villager's attitude can be changed by money making business and behaviour. The people's attitude will be monetised by money power. The social structure of the village is affected by the monetary economics, so that the charm and bright side of indigenous village structure may be gradually perished.

9. Risk to Ecology

Village tourism may be a contributor to environmental damage to some extent. It can be regarded as an unqualified panacea for economic ills. The position of developing countries like Nepal is bad in economic aspect, so that village tourism has been today's concern to its economic development. But village tourism, if mishandled, may be prone to damage in ecology.

Due to the infrastructure development for village tourism, village beauty and nature may be destroyed. Digging and increased extraction of village building materials may result a loss to the natural landscape and vegetation. Village vegetation will be damaged by walking or crushing by tourist's buses or jeeps. Hikers, trekkers and mountaineers damage and pollute the natural environment. This causes deforestation, soil erosion and disturbance to the habitant of wildlife.

The effect of village tourism activity on ecology can be spelled out as follows:

(*a*) Negative effect due to tourism infrastructure development

(*b*) Negative effect due to flow of tourists
(*c*) Negative effect due to linkages

Linkage development of village tourism invites more problems. Owing to the project development many construction works will be accelerated such as construction of roads, buildings and business houses, which disturb the eco-system in nature.

10. Reaction of Tourists

The increase in popularity of a tourism village destination results more tourists would visit the area developing much larger infrastructure and related amenities. At the outset, tourists react positively to its development and facilities provided. Later on, regarding the economies of scale flow, the price of the tourist facilities goes down due to the high competition overreached the capacity thresholds of the destination. Then the negative effects start flowing and the satisfaction level of tourists falls down.

11. Economic Pain

The village economic development is painful to each village and village administration. 'No pain, no gain' is denied in economic activity. 'Yes pain, yes gain' is the symptom of village tourism, where a large number of villagers are involved in their village economic activities. They are in search of better income and employment generation. Hence, village tourism and its relevant villagers have economic pain.

Village tourism eliminates problems but also introduces risks.

Measures:

The possible dangers of village tourism have to be controlled and measured from the very beginning. In management of village tourism none of the loopholes should be left out.

The suggested measures are given below:

1. Understanding Village Importance

The importance of village has to be known by the village community. Village is the beginning of the development in the history of human civilisation. Village having the scenic beauty and storehouse of natural resources can attract village tourists on the other side. As a matter of fact, village is a paradise for nature lovers. A real rich and conscious rational being stays village rather than city.

Hence, the golden message 'love to village and its nature' ought to be given to all, especially village community. This consciousness discourages migration. The village government also encourages villagers to develop and promote village. Opportunities should be given to the local villagers to generate income through various jobs.

Villagers leave village because of lack of job opportunity and career growth. A major straightforward reason is the gap of income and income substitution. Locally, the annual rate at which villagers quit their villages is high. Hence this trend should mainly be controlled in time.

2. Setting of the Traditional and Religious Framework

Setting the traditional and religious framework of the country is necessary for best practices. This is the right time to consider and plan on the social and religious agenda. This time we have to follow the principle of 'less word and more deeds'. The public who cherish this socio-cultural heritage awaits useful guidance to promote this joyful manifestation of our religious folklore and to control any malpractices.

3. Ruling of Village Tourism

Village tourism needs a new breed of watch dog for a positively evergreen development in village. Self-ruling mechanism-self-starter has to be introduced as an engine of village tourism growth. Basically, a system ought to be commonly introduced to all as measures and controls the basic laid foundation for best practices. The village local administration and state has to regulate law and rule and regulation for proper function of village tourism industry.[1]

An automatic traffic light box giving signal is to go on green light and to stop on red light, which measures and controls the possible road accidents. In the same way, Village tourism also has to operate as per the tourism traffic rules. Anybody who voids the rule and regulation is punished by the village tourism regulation and local and state administrative law. The watch dog–village traffic police or local administrator can take action against the violators.

Ruling village tourism relates to the following aspects:

(*i*) Village tourism code of conduct
(*ii*) Village tourist code of conduct
(*iii*) Village tourism entrepreneur's code of conduct
(*iv*) Village local administrative law
(*v*) State law

4. Opening of Prevention Link.com

For the safety or preventive measure of tourism and tourists, prevention link.com or safety link.com is a new and innovative tourism service that has to be designed to save village tourism, village tourists, village tour operators, village tourism guides, village tourism entrepreneurs and time and money in the quest of finding right tourist destination at the right time as per tourist's interest and demand.

Prevention link.com or safety link.com offers answer of tourist's query to find out the perfect village destination.

One has to just fill out the search questionnaire with the criteria that closely matches one's requirements. Visitors can choose from a listing of results that provide a detailed description of the facilities that match visitor's search and security. Visitors are kept in control having a specific provision of facility. It is cost-effective because it is free. This system assists planner's job obligation and duty.

5. Protection of Typical Village Policy

The protection measures of typical villages of Nepal have to be mentioned in the national plan so that the wave of urbanisation and modernisation will be timely checked up. The direct and indirect barriers and seen and unseen dangers to developing village tourism ought to be monitored and controlled beforehand. The directives measure 'Look before you leap' is a brilliant idea for operational management and policy for village tourism. The strong and committed plan and strategy is needed in developing village tourism. The government has to prioritize village tourism as 'Nepal's own original concept' at which every Nepali individual can be accommodated for social and economic development and progress. The people and government should think of its glory and obligations too.

6. Formation of Village Tourism Board

A separate Village Tourism Board has to be formed in order to specifically develop and promote tourism village in Nepal. To strongly support village tourism development and monitor village tourism activities, this sort of Village Tourism Board episode has to begin for accelerating its development speed and controlling mechanism at any time. This Board will follow up as an autonomous body and a separate organisation taking pros and cons into consideration of tourism village development, so that the dark side of village tourism will be consciously monitored and controlled as an appropriate function for sustainability of village tourism in Nepal.

Several precautionary measures are taken beforehand for epidemic disease like cholera. In the same way, for the development of village tourism, people and government should be highly conscious. For example, vaccination is given as a preventive measure before suffering from diseases. Thus for eliminating or minimising the possible dangers of village tourism in future, we must be rightly ready to cope with the dangers of village tourism from every angle of vision.

7. Establishment of Tourism Village Particularly in the Cold Place

Establishing tourism village particularly in the cold place is suited for longevity of life of visitors. Village tourism is conversely associated with health tourism too. By studying mice, scientists believe cooler body temperatures could increase the lifespan of human beings. The cool mice are living longer at the Scripps Research Institute in La Jolla, Calif. In the study published in the Journal Science, Core body temperature was a lowered a mere 0.5 of a degree in mice and males, on average, lived 12 per cent longer.

The International Longevity Centre and Mount Sinai School of Medicine located at Manhattan stressed on not just about living longer but living better while alive. The conscious people exercise and avoid trans fats, sugar and salt.[2]

Hence, tourism village has to better develop and build in the cold temperate climate or cold places for its longevity and sustainability.

8. Village Gallery

The concept of village gallery has to be displayed in the country of villages. The different types of villages of Nepal encompassing beauty, nature, culture, lifestyle, villager, mountain and village Nepal have to be exhibited in the village gallery. The picturesque and master art of villages models are necessary to display to international village tourists. The wonderful villages having their significance and speciality have to be introduced in the international tourism market. To support village gallery, village fair including village 'Haat Bazar' also can be occasionally organised in the micro level in villages of Nepal. This type of activity encourages the promotion of village tourism and analyses the negative side of villages and village practices for village tourism development.

9. Villagemoon

Young couple go on the honeymoon after marriage. Villagemoon travel could be developed to attract just married couple. Villgemoon is good for tourism village where the young couple can enjoy more in the unique environment of village. The couple would repeatedly enjoy honeymoons in different tastes of village culture and natural environment.

Then the familymoon starts with kids and family members creating a high family values. Childmoon displays with amusement and recreation with kids. It is tied and marketed by the travel industry in the special honeymoon and other moons in the village. Villages that provide villagemoon are a naturally demographic attraction and beauty of nature. It makes more enjoyable to newly weds and kids. Wedmoon is delightfully celebrated in traditional village culture style in the village, which is more enjoyable and pleasant to couples. There is a start of giftmoon to tourists in the village. Locally made products can be gifted such as toys, purses, hand bags, sewing baskets, village hut/house bags and so on. Lovemoon is produced in village to village tourists with natural love and invaluable hospitality. Then homemoon is lightened as own home or better than home tourists feel .This tourism village can create a new experience and high entertainment. 'Living small, but living well' is the message to make village tourism more enjoyable and sustainable.

10. Village Economic Development

Village economic development through the concept of village tourism is a must. The proper implication of village tourism must show the proof and confidence of economic development to the village and village community as a whole. Village tourism having some dark side has to eliminate its negative effects through economic revolution by the means of village tourism.

11. Peace and Prosperity

Peace and prosperity is a common factor for national development and progress. Neither industry nor business can be accommodated unless peace is established. Tourists would like to travel when the tourist destination is totally saved and peaceful. Hence, tourism village has to be totally safety having secured peace and security.

Owing to the Maoist people's war, Nepalese tourism and economy were badly disturbed and affected for more than a decade. The negative message has gone to the international tourism market. As a result, tourism has gone down for a long time. Hence, peace and security has always to maintain throughout the kingdom of Nepal and abroad for the development tourism.

12. Evergreen Speciality

Village tourism has to be categorised into an evergreen speciality, which should not be touched upon the Mass tourism. Mass tourism creates the environment boring and cheap destination. Village tourism could be developed in a more specific and meaningful manner from the viewpoint of culture, nature, environment and adventure as per demand and interest of the village tourists. From time to time psychological test, demand analysis and research have to be conducted in order to cope with the negative and dark side of village tourism in the Nepalese tourism market and abroad.

Village tourism has both pros and cons. Deprived from modern facilities and township tastes, the rare and new taste of village tourism has to be formed as its significance and values. Village tourism developing is a victory, by any definition. After all, it is the formula for economic development for village Nepal that brings peace, prosperity and progress through domestic resource mobilisation, income and employment generation in the country. In sum, the danger and dark side of village tourism should be eliminated by supplying preventive measures of tourism vaccination and antidote.

References

1. Surendra Bhakta Pradhanang, *Village Tourism in Chitwan*, New Delhi: Adroit Publishers, pp. 102-114, 2002.
2. Newsday, *Longevity Theory: Chill Out* (Health & Science), p. A41, Friday, November 3, 2006, New York, USA.

Bibliography

Aderhlod, Peter. *The European Holiday for Development Countries 1995.* Copnehagen: Institute of Tourism Research Planning, August 1995

Annual Operational Plan 2003/04, Nepal Tourism Board 2004.

Allan, Charles M. *The Theory of Taxation,* Penguin Books Ltd, England, First Edition, 1971.

Agenda, *Mineral Pani Barseni Saya Arab Dollar Khapat,* Falgun 17, 2062.

Beun, Monique and Laamichaane, Anupa, *Feasibility Study on Village Tourism* (in Nawalparasi Hills), Action Aid Nepal, Kathmandu, May 1999.

Bien, Amos. *A Simple User's Guide to Certification for Sustainable Tourism and Ecotourism,* The Intenational Ecotourism Society (TIES) 73315 the St. NW, Washington, DC 2005, USA, September 2003.

Bhaktapur Vikash Sahyog Sangh, *Khopring 2005-2006,* BVSS, Bhaktapur, 2006.

Batta, R.N. Tourism and The Environment A Quest for Sustainability, MIGadwani Indus Publishing Company, New Delhi, 2000.

Bajracharya, Dhanabajra and Shrestha, Tek Bahadur *Dolkhako Aaitihasik, Ruprekha,* Jilla Bikash Samiti, Dolkha, Second Edition, 2059.

Batra, G.S. and Chawla, A.S. *Tourism Management A Global Perpective,* Deep and Deep Publications F-159, Rajouri Garden, New Delhi, 110027, 1995.

Cooper, Chris, Fletcher and Gilbert, David. *Tourism Principles and Practice,* Pitman Pulishing 128 Long Acre, London, First Edition, 1993.

Critchfield, Howard J. *General Climatology* Prentice Hall of India Private Limited, New Delhi, Third Edition, 1975.

DNPWC, *Biodiversity Conservation Efforts in Nepal,* Department of National Parks & Wildlife Conservation, HMG of Nepal, April 2004.

DNPWC, *Annual Report 2002-2003*, Department of National Parks & Wildlife Conservation, HMG of Nepal, April 2004.

Doshi, S.L. and Jain, P.C. *Rural Society*, Prem Rawal for Rawal Publication, Jaipur, India, 1999.

Dewett, K.K. and Varma, J.D. *Elementry Economic Theory*, S. Chand & Company Ltd, Ram Nagar, New Delhi 110085, 1995.

Daily News, Habitat Adaptations, May 17, 2007.

EUROSTEP and ICVA, *The Reality of Aid 1998/1999*, Earthscan Publication Ltd, London, First Publication, 1998.

French, Christine N., Smith, Stephen J. Craig and Collier, Alan. *Principles of Tourism*, Addison Wesley Longman Australia Ptv Limited, 95 Coventry Street, South Melbourne 3205 Australia, First Publication, 1995.

Gittinger, J. Price. *Economic Analysis of Agricultural Project*, The Economic Development Institute, International Bank for Reconstruction, 1972.

Harbison, Frederick and Myers, Charles A. Education, Manpower and Economics Growth *Strategic of Human Resource Development*, Oxford & IBH Publishing Co. New Delhi, Third Edition, Indian Edition, 1968.

Handicraft Association of Nepal, *Handicrafts of Nepal*, HAN, Kathmandu, Nepal, 1972.

Higson, Phil, Ward, John and Campbell. *Leisure and Tourism*, Stanley Thornes, First Edition, 1994.

HMG of Nepal, Ministry of Local Development, *Nationalities of Nepal*, National Committee for Development of Nationalities, Chaitra, 2057.

HMG of Nepal, NPC, *An Assessment of the Implementation of the Tenth Plan (PRSP)*, National Planning Commission, Singh Durbar, Kathmandu, Nepal, June 2005.

HMG of Nepal, Ministry of Tourism & Civil Aviation, *Some Provisions Relating to Mountain Tourism in Nepal*, HMG, 1994.

HMG of Nepal, Department of Tourism, *Nepal Tourism Plan*, December, 1972.

HMG of Nepal, *National Planning Commission, The Tenth Plan*, (Poverty Reduction Strategy Paper 2002-2007) Summary. NPC, Kathmandu, July 2003.

HMG of Nepal, Ministry of Forests and Soil Conservation, *Terai Arc Landscape – Nepal Stretegic Plan*, MNFSC, 2004.

HMG of Nepal, NPC, *Ninth Plan (1997-2002)*, National Planning Commission, 1997.

HMG of Nepal, NPC, *Tenth Plan (2002-2007)*, National Planning Commission, 2002.

International Council for Local Environment Initiatives, *Tourism and Local Agenda 21*, United Nations Environment Programme, France, First Edition, 2003.

Inskeep, Edward. *National and Regional Tourism Planning: Methodologies and Case Studies*, Rouledgo, New Petter Lane, London, First Publication, 1994.

Inkeles, Alex. *What is Sociology? An Introduction to the Discipline and Profession*, Prentice Hall of India Private Limited, New Delhi-110001, 2001.

Jackson, *An introduction to Tourism*, Hospitality Press Pvt. Ltd., Melbourne, First Publication, 1983.

JNTO, *Your Guide To Japan*, Japan National Tourism Organization, 2002.

Jha, S.M. *Tourism Marketing*, Himalaya Publishing House, Bombay 400004, First Edition, 1995.

Koutsoyiannis, A. *Modern Microeconomics*, Macmillan Press Ltd, Houndmills, Basingstoke, Hampshire RG 216 XS and London, Second Edition, 1979.

Kathmandu Metropolitan City, *Hanuman Dhoka. Durbar Square*, World Heritage Site Monument Zone, KMC, 2003.

Kathmandu Research Centre, *Bandha Affects Economic Growth*, The Rising Nepal, Kathmandu, Nepal, June 3, 2004.

Kathmandu Research Centre, *Newar Feast*, The Rising Nepal, Kathmandu, Nepal Baisak 29, 2046.

Kathmandu Research Centre, *Nepalma Gaun Paryatan Ko Sambhabana Ramro*, The Gorkhapatra, Poush 11, 2061.

Livelihoods and Forestry Programme in Collaboration with TANGO International, Inc. USA and Development Vision Nepal, *Hill Livelihoods Baseline Study, A Report of Livelihoods and Forestry Programme*, Kathmandu, Nepal, September, 2003.

Lindberg, Kreg and Hawkins, Donald E. Ecotourism *A Guide for Planners and Managers*, The Ecotourism Society, North Bennington, Vermont, First Edition, 1993.

Mowfarth, Martin and Munt, Ian, *Tourism and Sustainability*, Routledge, 11 New Feather Lane, London, First Publication, 1998.

MC Eacherm J and et. al *Prospects For Tourism in Manaslu A Recannaissance Survey*. IUCN, 1995.

Makalu-Barun Naional Park and Conservation Area, *Trekking Tha Salpa Pass/Arun River Route*, MBCP, 1998.

Middleton, Victor T.C: *A Marketing Perspective*, Butterworth Heinemann, 1998.

Madnani, G.M.K. *Introduction to Econometrics Principles and Applications*, Oxford & IBH Publishing Co. Pvt. Ltd, New Delhi, 1998.

Nepal, Sanjay K. *Tourism and Environment Perspectives from the Nepal Himalaya*, Himal Book and STUDIEN, Verlag Innsbruck-Wien Munchen, First Edition, 2003.

Nepal Travel Trade Reporter, *Village Tourism Observed* March, 2005.

Nepal Tourism Board, *The Ultimate Adventure Destination*, NRB, Bhrikuti Mandap, Kathmandu, Nepal, 2001.

NTB, *Cultural Attractions in Nepal*, Nepal Tourism Board, Kathmandu, 2002.

Nepal Mountaineering Association, *Parbat*, NMA, February, 1997.

Nepal Rastra Bank, *Aarthik Barsa 2060/61 ko Pratibedan*, NRB, Aarthik Bibhag, 2061.

NTB, *Calender of Events Festivals & Events*, 2005.

Nepal Travel Trade Report, *Tourism in Nepal*, July 12-18, 2004.

Nepal Tourism Board, *National Ecotourism Strategy and Marketing Programme of Nepal*, NTB, Kathmandu, 2004.

Nepal Tourism Statistics 2004, HMG, Ministry of Culture, Tourism and Civil Aviation, 2004.

Nepal Tourism Board in Focus 2004, NTB, 2004.

Nepal Samacharpatra, *Pani ra Samskritiko Antarsambandh*, March 22, 2006.

New York Post, Glamming Holiday Inn to Become, April 10, 2007.

Prakash, Nirupama and Dash Motilal. *Conflict Resolution: Peace and Development*. Shri Sunil Kumar Jain, First Publication, 2004.

Poudyal, Radha Krishna, *Hamro Desh-Darshan*, Ranju Poudyal, First Edition, Kathmandu, 2059.

Prabhupada, A.C. Bhaktidevdanta Swami, *Bhagvad-Gita AS It Is*, Narmoda Goswami For The Bhaktidevdanta Book Trust, Mumbai, India, 1986.

Pradhanang, Surendra Bhakta. *Villages Tourism in Chitwan*, Adroit Publishers, New Delhi, 2002.

Pradhanang, Surendra Bhakta, *Tourist Consumption Pattern and Its Economic Impact in Nepal*, Adroit Publication, New Delhi, First Edition, 2000.

Pradhanang, Surendra Bhakta. A Traditional Scientific Nepali Balanced Feast, Quarterly Development Review, VOL XI, NO 15, Jan-June, 1995.

Pradhanang, Surendra Bhakta. *Goodbye To Pro Poor Tourism*, Nepal Travel Trade Reporter, August 24-Sept 4, 2005.

Pradhanang, Surendra Bhakta. *Gaun Paryatan Ko Bikashma Shree Panch Gyanendra*, Raj Parishad Smarika Bishesank, Kathmandu, Nepal, 2061.

Pradhanang, Surendra Bhakta. 'Productivity in Tourism Sector', *Current Issue of Productivity*, ISC, Kathmandu, Nepal, 1999.

Rogers, Paul and Aitchison, John. *Towards Sustainable Tourism in the Everest Region of Nepal*, IUCN–the World Conservation Union and ICPL, 1998.

Sen, Amartya. *Growth Economics*, Penguin Books Ltd. Harmonds-worth, Middlesex, England, First Publication, 1976.

Sachdeva, T.N. and Sachdeva, S.K. *Economics of Development*, Subha Publication Pvt. Ltd, New Delhi-8, Fourth Edition, 1968.

Shrestha, Amrit Man. *Nepalese Economy*, Gayetri Shrestha, Fourth Edition, 2058.

Tribe, John. *The Economics of Leisure and Tourism*, Butterworth Heinemann, 1999.

Trekking in Nepal, Nepal Tourism Board, Kathmandu, Nepal, 2004.

TAAN, *Silver Jubilee Ceremony 1979-2004.*

The Prakash Weekly, *Gaun Paryatan Darilo Arthik Srot*, Dec. 1, 1997.

The Rising Nepal, Village Tourism is Self-Sustaining Concept, February 3, 2004.

The Rising Nepal, *Nepal Yet To Cash Is On Village Tourism*, September 12, 1996.

The Explore Nepal Weekly, *Sirubari, Model For Village Tourism*, December 2, 1997.

The New York Times, Losing Homes and Neighborhoods, April 10, 2007.

The Wall Street Journal, The Jobs Expansion, April 9, 2007.